Frank Lake

Frank Lake

The Man and his Work

JOHN PETERS

Foreword by
Sylvia M. Lake

Darton, Longman and Todd
London

First published in 1989 by
Darton, Longman and Todd Ltd
89 Lillie Road, London SW6 1UD

British Library Cataloguing in Publication Data
Peters, John *1944–*
Frank Lake: the man and his work.
1. Great Britain. Counselling. Lake, Frank 1914–1982
I. Title
361.3′23′0924

ISBN 0–232–51842–4

Phototypeset by Input Typesetting Ltd, London SW19 8DR
Printed and bound in Great Britain by
Courier International Ltd, Tiptree, Essex

Contents

Foreword *by Sylvia M. Lake* vii

Preface xi

Acknowledgements xiii

Author's Note xv

1 Introduction 1

2 The History of the Clinical Theology Association (1962–82) 10

3 A Sketch of Frank Lake's Life 35

4 Some Personal Viewpoints 79

5 Listening and Helping – a Guide to Frank Lake's Seminal Ideas 104

6 In Retrospect 161

7 The History of CTA: the Post-Frank Lake Era 187

8 Conclusions 199

Notes 214

Appendices

A Frank Lake's 'The Work of Christ in the Healing of Primal Pain' 223

B A Bibliography of Frank Lake's Writings 242

C Select Bibliography 246

Index 249

Contents

Foreword by [illegible] Lake [illegible]

Preface

Acknowledgements

[illegible]

1 Introduction

2 [illegible] History of the [illegible] [illegible]

3 [illegible] Frank Lake's Life

4 [illegible]

5 [illegible] and Theology – a [illegible] Frank Lake [illegible] 101

6 [illegible]

7 The [illegible] Frank Lake [illegible]

8 Conclusions

Notes

Appendices

A Frank Lake – The Work of [illegible] the Training [illegible]

B A Bibliography of Frank Lake's Writings

C Select Bibliography

Index

Foreword

When Darton, Longman and Todd asked me to write a short introduction to this history of the Clinical Theology Association, I sat down and began to let the memories flow over me, and I think perhaps to share some of these may be a way into a subject that otherwise would seem too overwhelming.

I remember the loneliness for me of the early years, and how separate our three children and I seemed to be from the mainstream of Frank's life. Later on, when the family were safely launched, it was a privilege for me to go round with Frank, to meet so many wonderful people at this deeper level. I am not a teacher, but I found there was also a place for me in all that was going on.

Once it was not so.

The first Nottingham seminar was held in our home, and I asked if I might sit in to hear what it was all about. 'Oh no,' came the answer, 'these groups are for clergy alone', and so it was at first.

In the seminars we had representatives of every kind of human possibility, which enriched our chances to learn and our experiences of encounter. Of course, there were clergy, some tough, seasoned and set in their ways, and some fresh-faced young curates, aware of their abysmal lack of experience and already plunged into the deep water of suffering with their parishioners, like the curate from Flixborough at the time of the disaster there. We had nurses, midwives, marriage guidance counsellors, a policeman, an artist, nuns and a Cistercian monk, Church Army, Salvation Army, social workers, prison chaplains, some doctors, RAF chaplains, and many wives of men in vocations which called for skills from them also. I suppose we had an age range from about eighteen to eighty. I remember a very bright, retired headmistress from somewhere in the north, in her eighties, who was as eager to learn and experience as any of the young.

I remember many different meeting places too, some cold church halls with hard upright chairs, and some warm, comfortable homes, where the chairs became temptation to any who were overtired!

I recollect looking round sometimes at a somewhat unpromising group of faces, and then Frank would begin, and to him every seminar was a fresh chance, a new experience and he would come alive with his subject and inspire those listening with understanding and knowledge; and then we would take part in our role-plays, and the sharing groups of four afterwards, where many hearts began to share perhaps for the first time what had been a hurt, or a sorrow hidden and suppressed. Many tears were shared in this way, and the hand of comfort reached out to be either received or turned away, which taught us that the way of helping is different in each case. The relationships forged in these conditions were deep and real, and many of the groups went on meeting of their own accord, long after the second- or third-year seminar syllabus had come to an end.

Then there were the tutors' conferences, the first-year, second-year and third-year tutors meeting regularly before they went out to teach, and friendship and trust built up during these ongoing experiences.

In the organization itself there were many difficulties, as Frank's real interest lay not in maintenance and routine duties, but in new ideas, and new fields and new encounters, and he often leapt ahead leaving others to carry the burdens and sort out the unforeseen complications, and this made for resentments and stress. He did seem unable to be what he saw with such depth of insight and taught with such enthusiasm and brilliance. Here was where there was gain for others, for perhaps they could use and integrate what they heard so that it became the inner truth for them, lived and shared.

Who of us is without blemish in this matter? Yet I believe it becomes a most important work in our lives, to unite the opposites in our nature, to will wholeness wholeheartedly, and to have our loves transformed into an unfeigned love. So that one day it may be said of us as was said of St Benedict, who, St Gregory the Great says: 'could not have taught otherwise than he lived'. The amazing thing is that God's great gifts come to us in spite of our humanity and poverty, and through our broken and inadequate vessels, and nothing in the end can stop his glory and grace breaking through into the midst of us if we are open to receive him.

I struggled to love Frank; sometimes it was very difficult to love him, yet for me it was an unbreakable bond of love. Sometimes it seemed as though he deliberately tried to destroy love, as though to prove once and for all that love was a fallacy. Of course I failed over and over again. But I believed in love, knew from whence came the love that does not fail us, and held on firmly to God even when it seemed that all the ground had been kicked from beneath my feet. Archimandrite Sophrony speaks of the experience of the hell of love. These words have meaning for me.

I do not think anyone would have called our house a peaceful place to be in those days. Yet I see now that the great battles of humanity were being lived out there in our tiny environment; the battles of the heart, the battle of love versus selfishness and self-centredness; the battle between light and darkness; the battle between life and death.

And that is exactly how it is for every one of us here – now – in this paltry little back street, with these sordid emotions, and tears of self-pity and of glory.

Blessings emblazoned that day;
Everything glowed with a gleam;
Yet, we were looking away . . .*

People have referred to the cost to his family of all that Frank did and all that he was, both before and after his death in 1982, and cost there was. Yet, in God's plan it became a means of grace, a crucible without which I would not have been where I am today.

It is as we go *through* the little deaths that resurrection follows. 'Be ye faithful unto death, and I will give you a Crown of Life.'

* Thomas Hardy, 'The Self Unseeing', *Collected Poems*. (London, Macmillan, 1928)

I have looked back, but what the Association needs now is to look ahead, to look into what has stayed with them and grown ever more real for them, and is of this day, and this hour.

SYLVIA M. LAKE

Preface

This book came about in a slightly unusual way. Towards the end of 1986 I received a letter from the Revd Peter van de Kasteele, then Administrative Secretary of the Clinical Theology Association, asking if I would be interested in writing a study of the association's history. I knew very little at that time about the Clinical Theology Association or about Dr Lake apart from the fact that his conception of psychiatry had been influenced by the psychoanalytical writings of such people as Freud, Melanie Klein, Pavlov and Arthur Janov. So I embarked on a course of reading, including Dr Lake's massive own work, *Clinical Theology* (DLT 1966; revised and abridged 1986). In addition, I was able to talk to a number of people who had worked with him and also – and this was vital – with his immediate family: Sylvia Lake (his wife), David Lake (their son), Monica and Margi (their daughters). I quickly became fascinated by Frank Lake's personality, driving motivation, and by the association he founded in order to front his work. Here, I soon realized, was a story well worth telling and I agreed to accept Peter van de Kasteele's invitation with a feeling of excitement.

JOHN PETERS

Acknowledgements

In completing the task of writing this book I have been helped by many people. Some of them wished to remain anonymous, but I have permission to thank publicly the following people who either saw me personally for interviews, or who put me in touch with others who could help in a direct way, or who sent me relevant material for use in this book: the Revd Derek Atkinson; Mrs Joyce Banbury; the Venerable Paul Barber; Mr Michael Barker; Mrs Joan Bashford; the Revd David Bick; the Revd Michael Bordeaux; the Revd and Mrs Michael Brown; Dr Brenda Buck; Dr Alastair Campbell; the Revd Ernest H. Chitty; Miss Edna Clarke; the Revd James Cotter; Mr Peter Cousins; the Revd David Crowther; Miss Joan Dick; Mr Fred Elgar; the Revd Ronald File; the Revd Oliver Forshaw; Mr Hugh Freeman; Dr R. F. R. and Dr E. S. Gardner; the Revd David Goodacre; the Revd Tony Gough; Miss Jean T. Graham; the Revd Peter Graham; the Revd John Gravelle; Mr David Guyett; Mr D. M. Hancock; the Right Revd Michael Hare-Duke (Bishop of St Andrews); Canon Derek Head; Mrs Evelyn Holliday; Mr John Hughes; Miss Alison Hunter; the Revd Michael Jacobs; Mrs Pauline Keeley; Mr Ted Kettell; Mrs Janet Lake; the Revd Ronnie Lawson; Dr Arthur Laxton; the Revd Professor A. R. C. Leaney; Mrs S. R. Lilley; the Revd Anne Long; Dr David Lyall; the Revd Duncan McClements; the Revd Louis Marteau; Mrs Mary Maslen; Mr Hamish Montgomery; Rachel Moore; Dr Roger C. Moss; the Revd Christopher O'Neill; Elisabeth Paine; Mr John Patterson; Miss Catherine Pither; the Revd John Potter; Mr Robert W. Rentoul; Mr William Rook; the Revd Marc Seccombe; Lady Meredith Sinclair; the Revd Tom Smail; Canon J. E. Swaby; the Revd E. G. Symonds; the Revd Kenneth Tibbo; the Revd Robert W.

Turnbull; the Revd Bertie Vokes; the Revd Tony Waite; Captain Roy Ward; Miss Shirley Ward; David Wasdell; Mr and Mrs John Wattis; the Very Revd Alan Webster; the Revd John Weir-Cooke; Judith Weston; Mrs Doreen Whitaker; the Revd W. L. White; the Revd Geoffrey Whitehead; Sister Hilda Wood; the Revd Martin H. Yeomans.

I am grateful to the Council of the Clinical Theology Association for their permission to have unrestricted access to the Lingdale Archive, which contains invaluable information both about Frank Lake himself and the work he founded.

I am also grateful to the Editor of *Renewal* (Mr Edward England) for permission to reprint, as Appendix A, Frank Lake's crucially important article, 'The Work of Christ in the Healing of Primal Pain'. Too lengthy to publish as a quotation in the body of the book itself, its publication will enable readers to sense Frank Lake's heartbeat: emotionally, psychologically and theologically. Without this article my study would be devoid of the careful qualification and insight it provides.

This book would not have been possible without the active support and participation, at every stage, of the Lake family. Sylvia, David, Monica and Margi not only agreed to see me personally, but also provided me with written submissions which shed light, in extensive detail, on the 'Lake family'. Sylvia was a mine of information about the early days of the Clinical Theology Association and, with enormous courage, was prepared to speak, in a forthright and unvarnished way, about the rigours of life with Frank. I was particularly delighted when she undertook to write the Foreword to this work. Frank's brothers, Ralph and Brian, also gave wise and tactful advice on a number of occasions.

Lesley Riddle, Editorial Director at Darton, Longman and Todd until the end of 1988, gave unstinting support, timely advice and great encouragement. I am indebted to all these people; all remaining imperfections are, of course, mine.

I also wish to thank my wife Elisabeth, and our children Daniel, Kathy and Joanna for their love and unflagging support at all times. This book is, quite properly, dedicated to them.

Author's Note

This is an explanatory note on the structure of this volume. The introductory chapter deals briefly with the psychiatric, medical and theological background to Dr Lake's work. Chapter 2 charts the history of the Clinical Theology Association from 1958 (when Clinical Theology was taught in eleven dioceses) through October 1962 (the year CTA was set up as a charity organization) and on to May 1982 when Frank Lake died. Chapter 3 chronicles the main events in Frank Lake's life – this account is based on documentary evidence, together with written submissions provided by the Lake family and CTA colleagues. Chapter 4 is a 'warts an' all' portrait of Dr Lake through the eyes of people whose lives were influenced, in varying ways and to different extent, by his dynamic personality. Chapter 5 is a lengthy analysis of his controlling ideas as enshrined in three works in particular: *Clinical Theology* (1966), *Tight Corners in Pastoral Counselling* (1981) and *With Respect* (1982). Chapter 6 sharpens the perspective by critically appraising key aspects of Frank Lake's life and work: a life of considerable achievements. Chapter 7 brings the history of CTA up to date by considering the developments since May 1982. Chapter 8 continues the process begun in Chapter 6 by looking carefully at the *extent* of Frank Lake's achievements; it also includes suggestions for CTA's future growth and development.

Throughout these eight chapters readers will notice that the focus switches interchangeably between Frank Lake the man and Clinical Theology, the movement he founded. This is precisely because from 1958 to 1982 Frank Lake embodied both the successes and failures of Clinical Theology.

1

Introduction

> Clinical Theology's aim is the re-integration of the person through the healing and reconciling resources of God in Christ, through the Holy Spirit.'[1]

Dr Frank Lake, the inspiration behind, founder and first director of the Clinical Theology Association, died on 10 May 1982. He was sixty-seven. This date, as with his life and career in general, is worth recalling at the outset of this study because of the unique position he occupied in the field of pastoral care and counselling.

Dr John Roberts, an academic otherwise highly critical of Lake's *magnum opus, Clinical Theology* (1966) and the association itself, perceived of his influence in the following terms:

> It is quite clear that Frank Lake and Clinical Theology have responded to a very real need within the Church and society. They have drawn our attention to the scandalous deficiencies in the training of our ministers. They have attempted to face and meet the need of those in our community who are psychiatrically ill. In so doing they have written another chapter in the history of the Church's caring ministry – as far as impact is concerned it is the first determinedly Christian effort in this direction since the Quakers opened The Retreat in York in September 1777.[2]

One implication of this evaluative comment is perfectly obvious: that Lake and CTA helped individual ministers to evolve a meaningful role for themselves by offering them a frame of reference which, despite its shortcomings, gave them the confidence to approach problems which previously they would have considered insurmountable. This is also the considered opinion of a high-ranking Anglican like Bishop Hugh

Montefiore: 'I am one of those who believe that the Clinical Theology Movement has done a very great deal to raise the level of self-awareness among the clergy and to make us more conscious of the need for psychiatric medicine. But the danger could be that we clergy come too easily and too quickly to clinical and even theological conclusions about mental and affective illness; and here again we need to meet and listen to our professional colleagues.'[3]

To this valuable work Frank Lake brought considerable intellectual gifts, a background in scientific research, many years as a doctor, and a deeply committed faith. It is important, however, to give the evaluative opinions quoted above a slightly sharper focus, by placing them in their critical and historical framework.

There are four specific points to be made in this context. The first is that theological colleges in the 1950s and 1960s were doing little by way of pastoral training. Such training was considered to be the task of the vicar in charge of the parish, supplemented by whatever was offered by post-ordination training. But the fact is that many vicars and those in charge of post-ordination training did not possess the requisite skill and ability to relate psychological insights and perceptions to the traditional patterns of pastoralia. Frank Lake took up precisely this point in a short article for *The Times* headed 'Counselling and the Ministry': 'Judged by the failure to give time to educate theological students in the principles of counselling, or to provide supervised training in pastoral counselling during the post-ordination period, the Church today does not regard pastoral counselling as a necessary subject requiring serious study. This applies also to education and training for spiritual direction and evangelical counselling. At best it is haphazard, dependent on an individual's image of what it means for him to be in "holy orders", not one which is shared by the whole profession.'[4] Hardly surprisingly, many priests at this time became painfully aware of a serious deficiency in their vocational training. Frank Lake summed the whole matter up, in a highly descriptive and delightfully quaint way, in *Clinical Theology*:

> Another major difficulty which the professional man encounters when he attempts to begin the practice of clini-

> cal pastoral counselling is the necessity to divest himself of the superior role of the one who knows, of the one to whom others come begging for advice. Popular expectation, both of general practitioners and clergy, sees them in an active role either in *taking something away*, whether it be an appendix or a donation, or by *giving something*, as a tonic or a word of comfort is given, or, thirdly, by *doing something* to the person by manipulation or the laying on of hands. All these things can be done without a personal relationship being made at all. None of them require us to 'step forth out of the role of professional superiority'. While every pastor should have rich experience of receiving donations and speaking a word in season, and finding that the laying on of hands is followed by the grace of God given according to His promise, the difficulty about clinical theological dialogue is that the parishioner is going to be disappointed if at first we decline to do any of these three things to him. We disappoint his expectations. He came for treatment and we wanted to talk with him. He wanted us to adopt at once a fatherly – motherly role. He wished to place himself with absolute confidence in our hands to receive 'the treatment'. But we declined that role. We treated him as an adult. We resisted his temptation to regress into dependency.[5]

Clinical Theology therefore arrived at a period of, at best, uncertainty and, at worst, disillusionment.

It would be inappropriate to cite example after example to illustrate this disillusionment, but one instance is worth alluding to. Here is an Anglican clergyman reflecting on the early days of his ministry and the various problems he encountered:

> When I was a young priest, I was asked to visit a young woman in hospital who had attempted to commit suicide. I found her in great distress, with a great burden of guilt, and feeling that she could never be forgiven for the dreadful thing she had done. I spoke to her of the forgiveness of God. I gave her all sorts of good advice, and persuaded her to make a Confession and to receive Absolution. I urged her to turn to God in prayer and make use of the sacraments, but I had no training whatsoever in trying to help her understand why she had felt this urge to take such desperate measures. I don't suppose she had any idea

herself. I gave her advice, as though she hadn't been giving herself any advice probably for years, but I was quite unable to give her insight. You might say, 'well, this is a case for the doctors, a case for hospital'. But she was in the hands of the doctors, and she was hospitalized. Evidently they were not very much better equipped than I was, for very soon after she made a second attempt and this time succeeded. Now the tragedy is that I did not know that I had failed her; I thought I had done all that could be expected of me.

A young man came to see me some years ago. Let's call him Albert. He was in the depths of depression, tears running down his face as he spoke. He cried; he was utterly miserable. Sometimes in the place where he worked, he could not bear anyone to speak to him. Well, I tried to give him good advice; I urged him to make the effort to overcome this sin of melancholia; and I spoke to him about the love of God. Again, as with the young lady referred to earlier, I persuaded him to make his Confession. I gave him the Laying-on-of-Hands. And after all that I'm afraid I sent him out into the night.

You might say, 'well, this is a case for hospital'. He did go to hospital. He had a course of drugs and electric shock treatment. But I had lost touch with him. Not very long ago I met somebody who knew where he was, and I asked how he was getting on. They replied, 'well, he is carrying on'. His treatment in hospital enabled him to carry on, maybe it had saved his life – I don't know. But this person then said, 'Though he is still carrying on, he is not at all happy'.

The significance of all this is that I had had no training in helping such a person like him in how to apply the medicine of the Gospel. I was not able to share and lighten his burden, and I have a feeling that what he received medically was the ability to push his burden out of sight, and to be able to 'carry on', as my friend quite rightly expressed it.

One day when I was in church, I saw a man sitting in a pew looking very worried, and I thought that I would go up to him. I said, 'Is there anything I can do for you?', and he replied, 'No, no, I just came in. I just want to sit here'. But after I had walked away, he called me back and said, 'Perhaps you can help me. The trouble is that I am so jealous. I love my girl-friend so dearly, and yet I am so insanely jealous of her. I can't bear her to look at anyone else. I am making her life miserable, and my own, and one of these days I shall have to end my life altogether.'

Well, I tried again to talk to him. I urged him to realize how utterly unreasonable his attitude was, and I encouraged him to try harder, and so on and so on. But I had no training in helping him to understand how or what could be the cause of such an uncontrollable and irrational jealousy, nor how to apply the medicine of the Gospel to his wounded spirit. God knows what happened to him.[6]

This disillusionment in the Church was also reflected in Canon Eric James's preface to *Spirituality for Today* (SCM Press 1968) in which he said: 'The traditional forms of spirituality have gone dead on many of the most conscientious clergy.' Thus Clinical Theology[7] met a very real need within the Church of England, but soon its techniques were made available to other – equally needy – branches of the Christian Church in this country.

The second point is that the 1960s were a time of theological uncertainty too, with much questioning and reassessment going on within the Churches. In 1959, the Bishop of Woolwich, John Robinson, confidently asserted at a confirmation service, 'You are coming into active membership of the Church at a time when great things are afoot. I believe that in England we may be at a turning of the tide.' Then he added: 'Indeed, in Cambridge, where I have recently come from, I am convinced that the tide has already turned.' It is interesting to take up the Bishop's point about Cambridge, because it is exactly the location dealt with by Canon Alan Wilkinson (Chaplain at St Catherine's College, Cambridge, 1961–7) in the March 1983 issue of *Theology*.[8] The picture he paints does not accord with John Robinson's. This is what Canon Wilkinson says:

In 1961 I became a Cambridge college chaplain. Theologically it was like living on an erupting mountain side: *Soundings* (1962), *Honest to God* (1963), *Objections to Christian Belief* (1963). The Second Vatican Council (1962–5) showed that

> even Roman Catholicism was changing. At first, the radical movement seemed to me an absurd throw-back to the modernism of the 1920s which (I had assumed) was totally discredited. But as I queued up with 1,500 others to hear lectures on 'Objections to Christian Belief', I knew that a chord had been struck. I began to see what Dr Vidler meant: 'We've got a very big leeway to make up, because there's been so much suppression of real, deep thought and intellectual alertness and integrity in the Church.' I agreed with Nicholas Mosley: 'Should we not now just be glad that we are at least giving reverence to the God that we have enshrined for so long but have ignored – the God of movement, of change, of the world's liveliness?'

In addition to this internal soul-searching, radical magazines like *Prism* (1957–65) and *New Christian* (1968–70), showed how uncertain clergy were of their role as they became aware of the chasm between the Church and the world outside.

The third point concerns the state of psychiatry in relation to the Gospel in the 1950s. Again Dr John Roberts's opinion is appropriate in this context:

> At the time when Dr Lake was beginning to formulate his ideas and to interest others in them there were few psychiatrists in Great Britain who would have admitted that the Gospel had any relevance for the patients under their care. The 1950s saw a psychiatry which was optimistic and successful. It was inundated with well-qualified applicants who wished to be associated with this promisingly powerful branch of medicine. This image of psychiatry was derived from some real achievements in the field of social policy within hospitals with the use of 'open doors' and therapeutic community ideas. Also there was now available for the first time a number of drugs which seemed to be able to control, in a specific way, symptoms and signs which had previously been resistant to treatment.[9]

The fourth point relates to medical training, another issue dealt with by Lake in 'Counselling and the Ministry':

> . . . of the doctors, all of whom are educated and trained to give standard treatment for an acute abdominal crisis, but only a few of whom have taken the trouble to be

> educated and trained to care competently for people in an acute emotional crisis.[10]

Thus Frank Lake became convinced that the work of pastoral counselling had to be assumed by the theologian and the pastor in co-operation with the medical profession:

> The pastor works with and towards strengths that are made perfect in weakness. Negativities become assets. The situation cannot be too paradoxical for the man of God. Christian theology is focused upon the active, willed passion of the Son of God, as the beginning of wisdom and the climax of a revelation of the truth about God and man shot through with paradox. Pastoral counselling is the activity that relates all these resources of paradox in theology to all that is going on in the individual, in every aspect of his life and in all that threatens it, in society now, at all levels of being, and from the unhealed memories of the past. Counselling cannot be left to the doctors or the caseworkers. Human existence is paradoxical and the clues to the paradoxical that derive from theology are crucial. To be trained to mediate these facts within dialogue should be a primary task of a Christian pastorate. It calls for life-long as well as for initial training.[11]

So he evolved a technique for integrating religious values with clinical practice, thus 'Clinical Theology'.

Clinical Theology and the Clinical Theology Association invoked strong reactions, and because they were for many people synonymous with Frank Lake, so did he. Slightingly referred to by some as the 'guru' of CTA, more approvingly and respectfully by others as its 'apostle', what is indisputable is that he was a pioneer in attempting, in the way he did, a creative fusion between theology and psychiatry; it is equally indisputable that he took pastoral counselling out of the 'doing good' syndrome, placing it thereby on a sound professional footing. All pioneers are open to criticism and even vilification, to misunderstanding and misrepresentation, but what is again indisputable is that the attempt he made was worth making.

How all this came about is the purpose of this study to unravel and illustrate. It is not written for experts – be they medical, theological, psychiatric – for they are more than capable of looking after themselves, nor will it be concerned with a highly technical assessment of what Lake achieved. It is written out of the conviction, however, that his work was of significance, and that CTA had, and still has, a positive and valuable contribution to make to the life and pastoral care of the Church.

In this study then, three major themes will become apparent. First the history of CTA, from its inception in 1962. Second, Frank Lake's experience and understanding which led to the rise and development of the association. Third, an attempt to indicate both the positive and negative aspects of CTA, with an eye to its possible future developments. As these themes unfold, four images of Frank Lake will emerge,[12] giving not only substance to the man that he was, but also cohesion to the work of the association he founded.

The parasitologist

He was engaged in a life-long search for the single and purely malignant invader. His original study of physical parasites was superseded only by his concentration on psychological parasites. The Revd John Gravelle thought Frank was seeking an 'ambiguous security' in his desire to isolate one single cause for neurosis, but insisted that this very ambiguity made for his creativity too.

The prophet

Frank Lake attempted to link Pauline teaching on grace and works with reactive depression. The resultant mix was not always comfortable, perhaps because in all of this lay an eschatological tension, the true fulfilment of which lies beyond us.

The psychiatrist

In this too he was a pioneer, constantly searching for new ways of understanding stress in others, for ever pushing the frontiers of knowledge outward. To this task he gave himself unreservedly and sacrificially.

The priest

This image of him, in my opinion, binds the others together. His faith was a deeply committed one. He was a man of prayer. He took seriously the life of Jesus as an example and as an inspiration. He was prepared to serve other people, and two illustrations of this are pertinent at this point. The first was sent to me by a former member of the Lee Abbey Community, North Devon, who encountered Frank Lake just twice, way back in 1963:

> The first time was when he was conducting a three-day seminar introducing us all to Clinical Theology; the second when he made a fleeting visit some months later.
>
> On both occasions I had the privilege of chatting with him very briefly – possibly no more than 4–5 minutes. Today, 1988, I recall Frank himself, though not our text, as if it were a meeting of yesterday. He seemed to me almost transparent – just a medium for clear light, positive thought – and ME. Yes, it was like that, and on both occasions he made me feel special to him, able and wanted.[13]

The second illustration is provided by the Revd Ronald Lawson, Dumbarton, Scotland:

> I once arrived from Scotland for a conference – the car had broken down on the way. When I reached Lingdale after midnight, it was Frank who was sitting up waiting for me – and who fed me – although the following day was going to be a most demanding one for him and he was up and about around 5 a.m. That was typical.[14]

This chapter has indicated the main lines of inquiry as far as this book is concerned, and it is to the first of the major themes indicated above that we shall turn in the next chapter: the history of CTA.

2

The History of the Clinical Theology Association (1962–82)

The Clinical Theology Association (CTA) was formally instituted on 25 October 1962. It was incorporated under the provisions of the 1948 Companies Act as 'The Association of Clinical Theological Training and Care Limited', and registered as an educational charity. The history of its work, however, goes back to the 1950s, in particular to the year 1958.

Early days

In that year, and with the personal recommendation of Dr Donald Coggan, then Bishop of Bradford (and subsequently Archbishop of Canterbury), the Bishop of Knaresborough, the Revd Geoffrey Rogers, the Warden of Lee Abbey, and Canon Ernest Southcott, the teaching of 'Clinical Theology' (the term was adopted in the same year) was started in eleven diocesan centres: Liverpool, Manchester, Chester, Derby, Southwell, Coventry, Birmingham, Leicester, Lincoln, Ripon and Bradford. Eleven seminars in pastoral counselling and care began in direct response to Frank Lake's offer to the bishops of each of these dioceses.

Each seminar lasted for three hours, and occurred every three weeks, twelve times a year. They were intended in the main for Anglican clergymen wanting help to deal with the pastoral care of those with spiritual and emotional illnesses, psychoneurotic and psychotic illness, and personality disorders. Free Churchmen were included in the next and subsequent years.

The title, 'Clinical Theology', was perhaps a little unfortunate, since neither 'clinical' nor 'theological' evoked a favourable popular image at that time. The two words taken together, however, accurately described the essential aims of the seminars. They were clinical in the general sense of the word: 'a class, session or group meeting devoted to the solution of actual cases'. That is, the focal task of the seminars was to relate as *helpers* to people with a wide spectrum of needs. They were theological in that Frank Lake and his staff felt it appropriate from the beginning to have a christological model as the backbone of their psychodynamic and sociological formulations, though respect for religious or non-religious heritages other than the Christian one was implicit in their attitude. This joint search, of the helper and the person seeking help, for firmer and deeper resources of meaning within the framework of the counsellor's own beliefs, was perceived, quite properly, as one of the important functions of counselling.

The basic pattern of the early seminars was that of training in pastoral care and counselling, while personal therapy was also offered to clients. The educational method and procedure adopted in those days was one with which clergymen were familiar and could thus tolerate without feeling threatened: a talk by the tutor, taking up some aspect of Clinical Theology, followed by role-play which both illustrated the subject and gave counselling practice to the bolder and more adventurous ones in the seminar.

The staff required to service these seminars expanded both pastorally and medically, and by the fourth year seminars were being regularly held in approximately sixty centres throughout the United Kingdom, for Anglican, Free Church and Catholic priests and ministers.

Important developments

What was needed now was an organizational backing for this work and that of Frank Lake in particular. So, on 5 October 1961, a group of men met at Scargill House, Yorkshire, to form a Council as a preliminary measure to the official setting-up of CTA. Those present, in addition to Frank Lake, included Dr Brian Lake (his brother), Tony Bashford, Chad Varah, Basil Higginson, Jack Smith of the Church Army, Dr Kenneth Soddy, Harry Walker and Richard Dupius.

Five months before this, a brochure had been issued (together with an appeal) describing the intended work of CTA, while the Councils of Lee Abbey and Scargill House had agreed to circulate their friends and prayer-partners in order to discover those Christians who would support the proposed work of CTA. Approximately 700 people responded to the appeal and this brought in £9,000 in donations and £3,000 in loans. In addition, 120 people agreed to covenant their subscriptions with the association.

Other important developments quickly followed, one being the purchase (on 11 October 1962) of Lingdale, Weston Avenue, Nottingham, as the centre for the association. Soon too (on 5 November 1962), the first Pastoral Director was appointed. He was the Revd Michael Hare-Duke, formerly Vicar of St Mark's in Bury, Lancashire, and now Bishop of St Andrews, Scotland. Ninety seminars were started in October 1962, fifty of them continuing from previous years, but by the New Year over 100 were operating.

CTA's founding objects

The Clinical Theology Association was thus, in essence, a *training programme*, and was specifically formed to continue the interdisciplinary seminars involving applied social science, social and dynamic psychiatry, and the theology of pastoral care. Its official description was 'a course in Human Relations, Pastoral Care and Counselling'. In more detail, the founding objectives for which the association was established were set out as follows:

> The furtherance of training within the Church of England and other member churches of the World Council of Churches in pastoral care in general, and especially the training of those whose concern is with persons suffering from spiritual and emotional distress, from psychoneurotic and psychotic illness, from personality disorders and the like (this special concern being referred to as clinical theology) and the provision of facilities for . . . care and counselling.[1]

The title of the course and its stipulated objectives given above are both highly significant. CTA *did not exist to train counsellors*; rather, it offered professional 'carers', lay pastoral people and voluntary bodies, a fundamental training in *coun-*

selling that would supplement any training and experience they might already have.

The mood among Frank Lake and his staff, as expressed in their first prayer-letter, was buoyant but realistic:

> On this first occasion we felt you would want to share with us especially in praise and thanksgiving for the Glory of God revealed in our Lord Jesus Christ, whose ceaseless activity through the Holy Spirit is the source of all our work. Even if you can only use the whole of this prayer-paper once over the next four months we would be grateful. To some of you there has been committed a ministry of intercession, because your circumstances, or your illness, may confine you at home or away from much activity outside it. You know that at all times there are people coming to us as doctors or clergy from all over the country. Among them are operating many forces which destroy faith and hope and love. What we suppose in the New Testament are spoken of as 'evil spirits', spirits of fear and the destructive emotions of hate and envy and jealousy have taken deep root in them. We wrestle, therefore, not against flesh and blood but against forces much greater than ourselves. In this constant battle of love against hate, light against darkness, 'being' against 'non-being', fullness against emptiness, purpose against meaninglessness, we need the intercessory prayers of all Christian people to whom God has committed an intercessory ministry.
>
> There is bound to be opposition arising from many quarters to work of this kind. Some of it will be justified and we will be, in gratitude, ready to change our ways of working. We are convinced that Christ is the Healer; we are by no means convinced that we know how to express this on many occasions. Other criticism will be the hostility of entrenched positions. This we must meet with gentleness and firmness, merely desiring freedom to express the Love of Christ towards those who wish to come to Him and to His pastors in their need.[2]

An important keynote here is that the work of intercession (and of intercessory prayers) belongs to all Christians, who can all express love to those in need. Or, in the words of the association's early brochures, we can all 'care for troubled people'.

On 15 March 1963, the Clinical Theology Centre was officially opened, blessed and dedicated by the Bishops of Edinburgh and Southwell. Frank Lake suggested that the chapel might have been called 'The Chapel of the Agony', for, as he rightly said, 'it must be a place where the starkness of reality is faced'. In the same newsletter from which the last sentence comes, he went on to ask:

> Was this even what the Cup meant for our Lord, that He should abandon for good the notion that there was a way out; that He should say a final 'no' to the 'legion of angels'?[3]

and he comments:

> There He was coming to terms with the only possibility that was open – the way of the Cross. But to reach the sure note of decision which was in his voice as He woke the disciples, had cost the struggle when the sweat ran down like blood. There was nothing to cushion His decision to obey. There was nobody to approve His choice and support Him in it. He chose utterly alone.
>
> Now this is one side of the Christian life which all of us must reckon with. That sooner or later we have to stand alone and choose. When all has been said of our involvement with each other, when we have laid deep emphasis on the importance of the Church's common life, yet we are also utterly individuals. Our faith must be our own, even if it is only based on the cry 'Help thou mine unbelief'.[4]

In the first completed year of CTA, seminars (that is, each one with twelve clergymen plus twelve doctors and caseworkers meeting twelve times a year) were being conducted in thirty-seven dioceses. An interesting fact is that Frank Lake had driven 100,000 miles in the five years between 1958 and 1963, indicating not only his enormous energy and enthusiasm but also his commitment to the work.

In one of the association's early newsletters too, Michael Hare-Duke directly posed the question: 'What is the CTA?', and a little later on he shared his insights with the members, in the following way:

(a) *Counselling.* As a Parish Priest I have found that my two years as Pastoral Director at the Centre have not encouraged me into any deep counselling relationships with my present parishioners. While I continue to see people at the Centre and also have had a number of people referred to me from neighbouring parishes, I have felt it right to keep my practice with them quite separate from those whom I see in a great number of roles as their Parish Priest. In one case, with someone whom I had been seeing at the Centre for a considerable period, when she came to live in the Parish, it proved right to ask one of the staff Psychiatrists to see her for therapy and for myself to remain more in the role of friend and Vicar.

(b) *Establishing local liaison.* I have felt very strongly that the insights given one by Clinical Theology made it possible to establish a fairly easy rapport with the caseworkers in the neighbourhood and I was lucky enough to be brought in on the early planning of a Council of Social Service for the urban district. This is a body which endeavours to bring together both voluntary organizations and statutory workers to consult about the things which they are already doing and also to look at the neighbourhood to see where new work needs to be promoted. Through becoming secretary of this Council, and therefore having considerable contact with the National Council and also having attended their bi-annual conference this year, I am convinced that this is a most valuable means for any Parish Priest to bring together all the clergy of a neighbourhood together with statutory workers and people from voluntary societies into an understanding and sense of co-operation which it might be hard otherwise to achieve.

(c) *Liturgical practice.* It is always difficult to know where one ends one's Clinical Theology and begins with any other sort, and hence I have some diffidence in introducing this topic, but at the same time I am convinced that it is out of an understanding of human relationships that I have come to think as I do about present liturgical practice. In the first place I am becoming increasingly aware that though we use 'family' or 'primary group' language about the Eucharist, this is largely inappropriate if we are thinking of a congregation of one or two hundred at Parish

Communion. The level of personal interaction on these occasions can only be minimal and one needs to think of it more often as an inter-group exercise. Yet since meeting at depth would seem on reflection to be an integral part of the Eucharistic action one is led to the thought that perhaps the house meeting which begins with some considerable discussion and then ends with the Breaking of the Bread should be far more nearly the normal pattern.[5]

New initiatives

In 1964, there was a growing interest in Clinical Theology among doctors, so much so that a conference was convened at Lingdale for medical people. In the same year the Archbishop of Canterbury's Working Party on clergy–doctor co-operation concluded that the 'co-ordination of our work with that of the Clinical Theology Association to be a matter of the highest priority': a most welcome official boost. One of the consequences of this working party was the setting-up of the Institute of Religion and Medicine, its Chairman being Dr Kenneth Soddy, a member of CTA's Council.

The question of money

By its seventh year CTA had provided 3,240 three-hour seminars in thirty-eight dioceses, while about two-thirds of the twelve to sixteen clergymen who began the two-year course (of twenty-four three-hour seminars) had completed it. All of this went on against a background of financial need. At the same time the numbers of those wishing to take the two-year course were increasing, and Frank Lake, in *Newsletter 6*, felt it necessary to reiterate and define the scope of the training being offered:

> The aim of the Council is to provide a standard of training which will give, to anyone taking the course seriously, a reasonable assurance that he:
> 1 Has been trained to understand the problems of the human spirit and its basic relationships.
> 2 Is able to deal more creatively with his own anxieties in accepting pastoral responsibility for distressed people.

3 Is able to elicit the factors in the personal history of the parishioner which are relevant to coming to a meaningful understanding of his personal condition.
4 Is able to accept any category of distressed person without evasion or revulsion, establishing a rapport of interpersonal commitment in which the parishioner may sense a new and secure relatedness, at least to one human being.
5 Has a clear sense of direction in counselling the distressed person to look towards those aspects of Christ's resources which are relevant to his need, with confidence in the power of the living Christ to effect this help through the Word and Sacraments and Fellowship of the living Church.
6 Will experience the value of working together with colleagues in pastoral consultation, subjecting himself to the disciplines of a learning process by which he can become a more effective personal instrument of pastoral help, and gain familiarity with the wider body of experience available to those who work together systematically.
7 Will have a clear understanding of the primary areas of concern appropriate to the other helping professions, general practitioners, physicians and psychiatrists particularly, and to the welfare services, with a knowledge of the proper indications for, and methods of referral to them.

To this, we have added, in recent years, a second-year syllabus which covers in some detail all kinds of group situations and group dynamics from the family to the larger units of society.[6]

By 1965 too the association was beginning to forge increasingly meaningful links with Europe and America, while Frank Lake travelled abroad and also received visitors at Lingdale.

A crucial year

1966 was a very important year for CTA, for a number of different reasons. There was, for example, the increasing involvement of the laity in its work. In *Newsletter 7* (February

1966), Frank Lake reported that forty-two per cent of those enrolling for the first-year course were lay people. Many of these forty-two per cent were caseworkers, medical and psychiatric, in 'moral welfare' or the probation service, and in this sense were professional helpers; but at least fifty were Samaritan counsellors, while the rest were, in Lake's words, 'dependable people on whom the leadership in community care depends'.

There was, too, the expansion in psychiatric help offered at the centre in Nottingham. During 1966 also Frank Lake took the message of Clinical Theology to South Africa, a visit which included a time in Kampala.

But, towering above all these admittedly significant developments was the appearance of Frank Lake's massive volume, *Clinical Theology*. It was only published after a series of frustrating delays, not the least of which was the disappearance of the proofs from his car. His secretary, Mrs Mary Maslen explained: 'There was a bad time when his briefcase was stolen from his car in Harrogate, but it was subsequently found intact in a hedge bottom, obviously cast away by the thief as of no particular value.'[7] The last laconic comment could only have been made by someone who had typed the whole mammoth undertaking.

The appearance of *Clinical Theology* gave the opportunity for those *within* the movement to take a serious and penetrating look at the whole meaning and methodology of Clinical Theology, as well as assessing what tangible results had accrued since the seminars were first started. This is how Michael Hare-Duke saw it:

> One of the fundamental problems that theology faces at the moment is the right understanding of God's work in the field of the secular as well as the sacred, so that we are not afraid of the increasing advances of the scientific understanding of man and his place in the world. Clinical Theology has helped us to see the growth of the individual, linking the work of grace with the insights of dynamic psychiatry. The emphasis has largely been on the distorted patterns of development for in practice pastoral care necessarily begins with meeting need as it is presented to one. Yet once one has begun this sort of inquiry one must go

> on and perhaps we can learn more of the meaning of the Image of God in man by looking at his development in community. Here the bridge must be between the secular understandings of sociology and the experience of the Church as the Body of Christ. Of course we shall still be led back to the growth of the individual person, yet there is the added question of how far individual psychology influences a culture or how far the cultural patterns govern the norms and the deviations of individuals. Once one begins to follow the trail that Clinical Theology opens up, the field is vast.

But he warned:

> The pastor may be greatly reassured by having some theoretical formulation at the back of his mind which will help him to relate cause and effect more satisfactorily. But this need not involve him in the highly technical discussions which are going on between various schools of psychiatry. This is a field for the specialist and the specialists are undoubtedly disagreed about the meaning of the evidence. It would be a thousand pities if the pastoral concern of the clergy and the immense value which they can draw from the authentic bridge-building which has been done in the name of Clinical Theology were to become suspect because it were linked with one particular theoretical construct. This would seem to be especially true if it does not seem necessary to emphasize it for practical purposes.[8]

Its publication also allowed those *outside* the movement to formulate their opinions, and while this is not the place to consider at length the verdict of the reviewers, reference must be made to Francis Huxley's perceptive review, in which he pinpointed the limitations of Lake's ontological approach to the dialogue between theology and dynamic psychiatry in the following way:

> The self always has a body, no matter whether it is defined psychologically or theologically, and its faculties correspond to its organs of perception, knowledge and action. The ontological self, however, tends to limit itself to a small number of those faculties: language and verbal experiences are made to define its centre of activity, while visual images

and non-verbal perceptions are stripped of their power. It looks as though one of the elements in ontological anxiety exists here: the Protestant refusal to understand things in terms other than language breeds its own anxiety, and the schizoid position comes about when sensory expression loses its meaning and speech tries to fill the gaps. Protestants have always suspected the worst of man's physical body, but have clamped down on the images it spontaneously produced in its efforts to give life a shape: one might thus call demythologizers the great schizoids of our time.

Dread, as Dr Lake shows, comes before words are learnt, at the moment when the outer world is sensed and found wanting: it thus can never be talked out and can only be exorcized by a proper re-establishment of sensory experience. I take this to be the central process in conversion, which underlines Dr Lake's main thought. Characteristically, however, the ontological approach focuses on this crisis with instruments which seem to obscure the very process it is looking at.

So, though grateful for Dr Lake's book and favouring many of his expositions and much of his approach, I cannot feel that psychiatry and theology have been finally married in the ontological sacrament. The Self has a body, and the body has faculties by which one may see images of the Self: and until psychiatry and theology agree on the value to be placed on these images and in this body, the work is not over.[9]

Huxley's evaluative and fair response was that of an expert, but how did non-experts respond to *Clinical Theology*? Two responses – by their very nature gentler, less developed and perhaps less deliberately analytical – are worth quoting. The first is by Rachel Moore, of Seaford, Sussex, who wrote to me as follows:

Clinical Theology influenced me greatly in understanding myself and Christianity. When I read it it seemed as if a great light had been switched on and illumined dark places.

Soon after reading it, I encountered great problems, and it was by remembering what was written in it that I man-

> aged to break through the barrier of pain and find the power of the peace of God.[10]

The second is by Miss Joan Dick, of Wimbledon, Surrey:

> Some eighteen to twenty years ago I found myself the 'victim' of what those responsible later realized was in fact an injustice, and I felt utterly crushed. I was considering giving up a way of life that had been very dear to me, even, fleetingly, giving up my faith in God. But one day in the local library I came across a copy of Frank Lake's book, *Clinical Theology*, and moved I think by the Holy Spirit, I borrowed it, and it caused quite a revolution. I realized that in point of fact a great deal of my mental agony was a replay of something that had happened in my very early childhood. My next sister was born about fifteen months after me, and in those days, early in the century, a confinement in a comfortable 'professional' home meant several weeks isolation for the mother, with a consequence of a period of isolation for me. I in no way blame my Mother – 'child psychology' was in its infancy then.
>
> And having seen this, I was able to come to terms with my current situation, and even to understand recurrent emotions, fits of depression, a compulsive need to be needed, a deep sense of insecurity.[11]

Yet another interesting development in 1966 was the commencement of short courses for missionaries on furlough, an initiative that shows how Frank Lake was constantly searching for ways and stratagems for spreading the message of Clinical Theology across as broad a spectrum as possible.

Problems for CTA

Not all was plain sailing, however. One particularly thorny problem had to do with the *image* of Clinical Theology, notably its use of the drug lysergic acid, or LSD-25. A report in the national press, giving an inaccurate account of the association's work, led to wave of unwelcome publicity. Frank Lake took up several aspects of this contentious issue in *Newsletter 9*. The central core of his argument was this paragraph:

> My use of LSD-25 has, from the beginning, been intended

rather to evoke the painful memories, for it is these that distort the face of 'god' in the ground of personality, creating difficulties in the conduct of daily life, distorting relationships, and making trust of God difficult in the here and now, because 'god', small 'g', then, was so devastatingly unreliable. So severe are these memories of evil days, passively endured in the uncomprehending innocence of babyhood, that they cannot be recalled to mind, even with the aid of an abreactive agent, unless the spirit be fortified to meet them. The nature of this fortification is partly personal, in that the patient must have a high level of trust in the therapist, who must be present during the full four or five hours of the abreaction, and partly theological, that is to say, christological. For it is the Holy Spirit who sustained Christ in Gethsemane who makes the ultimates of commitment anxiety tolerable, and on Golgotha who makes the ultimates of dereliction anxiety also bearable. That God suffers with us, and in us, in our worst stretches of mental pain, of whatever sort, whether acute and agonizing, or long-drawn-out and exhausting, is the central theme of Clinical Theology. (It is also the theme of a remarkable book by a Japanese theologian, Kitamori, *The Theology of the Pain of God* (SCM Press 1966. 22/6). I do recommend it highly.) This therapeutic resource from the Word of God, first taken into account in the exigencies of the abreactive session, has since proved equally valid quite outside this special psychiatric therapeutic setting. The correlation is equally valid in the ordinary run of our psychiatric care, most of which is conducted under the ordinary conditions of conversation without any use of this agent, and also, which is most important, of pastoral care as clergy and laity go about their work to help the afflicted.[12]

Another recurring problem was the financial burden of running CTA.[13] The whole problem was compounded by the fact that some dioceses regarded CTA seminars as an integral part of the in-service training offered their clergy (for example, the diocese of Chelmsford had, since 1960, paid the fees of their clergy and also assisted them with their travelling expenses), while other dioceses were not so accommodating.

But in spite of these difficulties, the work of the association went steadily on, meeting a real need within the corporate life of the Church (admittedly with a heavy Anglican bias) in Britain, and was greatly valued as such.

What did all this mean for those working on the inside? Dr Brian Lake clarified his feelings about Clinical Theology in an article in *Newsletter 11* (June 1968):

> In the first place, I do not see that it can be divorced from other theological disciplines, provided that they are concerned with revealing and not obscuring reality. It seems to be an important section of pastoral theology, when pastoral theology derives its categories from the active, present and observable relationship between God and man. It is grounded in dogmatic theology, and ultimately the thing which brings it alive. It borrows from moral and ascetic theology when practised in a form which is in keeping with modern human relations and conditions. It derives insights from the science of liturgy – especially in its study of a patient's use of and capacity for symbols – which as Goldbrunner points out are 'human pre-requisites for the celebration of liturgy'.
>
> In the second place, the task of Clinical Theology as I understand it is to inform and train us in the many ways in which man becomes ill, and the many ways in which God seeks to heal him. It is in other words concerned with giving contemporary reality to the Gospel of Salvation and Redemption. The material for diagnosis comes from the wide variety of sciences and humanities, each with their own perspective, questions, instruments and methodology. The particular Association in which I work exists to promote an understanding of the disciplines of psychiatry as it relates to theology.
>
> Clinical Theology is the discipline which provides a truly diagnostic and therapeutic Body of Christ in the world. The Body is active wherever a searching and healing love is practised. Within it biochemists and geneticists, psychoanalysts and psychologists, sociologists and anthropologists refine their diagnoses; parents and priests, nurses and doctors, social workers and Samaritans, improve their healing techniques. The boundaries of this Body are the boundaries between those who do the will of God in loving their

neighbour, and those who do not. And the Church is where the Body of Christ is at work in the expectancy of faith – a faith which can remove the mountains of anxiety, pessimism and despair.

The Clinical Theology I am talking about involves us all whether we like it or not. The parable of the Good Samaritan expresses the priority which Christ gives to it. It is tested out in the crucible of everyday living, and to practise it means accepting some of the perils and dangers which are undeniably present. There are plenty of hazards to overcome on the modern road to Jericho. We may end up being robbed of health ourselves. I only hope we don't end up by passing by on the other side.

There was indeed no passing by on the other side, and the largely unwavering pattern of courses, seminars, therapy, counselling, travelling, administration, wrestling with finances, receiving visitors from abroad, staff coming and going, all went on from year to year, with Frank Lake the overwhelmingly dominant figure at the head of CTA.

The nerve centre of CTA

It is worth stopping at this stage in the history of CTA to emphasize one fundamental fact: its nerve centre was not Frank Lake himself, dazzling and wide-ranging though his gifts were. It was to be found essentially in the work of the tutors and the seminar experience over which they presided.

The tutors

Without them the work of CTA – either in Frank's day or today – would not be possible. In the formative years especially of the association many of the tutors worked sacrificially, in terms of the time they gave to it, the travelling, and the expenditure, in order to ensure the success of the work. They were as deeply committed to the vision as Frank Lake was himself; and no one realized the enormous debt the association owed to them more than he did. In *Clinical Theology News* (December 1978), for example, he reviewed twenty years of clinical theology seminars with this genuinely warm appreciative notice:

In October 1958 the first Clinical Theology Seminars were set up in eleven Midland dioceses. Two Bishops gave their support to the project, Donald Coggan, who was then in Bradford, and Henry de Candole of Knaresborough. Ernest Southcott of Halton, Leeds and Geoffrey Rogers of Lee Abbey added their weight to my letter to the diocesan Bishops asking to be put on offer to their clergy for some in-service training. Twenty years later we take stock of what has happened and look forward. In connection with appeals we are making for support from trusts and others who might help if they grasped the scale and significance of this work, we have prepared a map which shows the geographical coverage of the seminars, and the number of year-long seminars held in each place.

In recent years what is known as 'Theological Education by Extension' has been introduced, to take the teachers to the students. The achievement of CTA in doing just this for twenty years shows that it is possible, if the teachers care enough to travel. I am deeply grateful that the many-more-than-a-million miles of motoring that I and my colleagues, pastoral consultants and the volunteer tutors have done, most of it in the winter months, have been without personal injury. It is fitting here that I should express to them all a deep appreciation for their keenness through the years, a gratitude which I am sure is echoed by many seminar members.

In some towns and cities we have had a continuous presence for these twenty years. In eighteen major towns we have held more than twenty seminars (in London 87, Nottingham 52, Liverpool 41, Manchester and Guildford 38). In another 23 towns we have held ten or more years of seminars. The total number of year-long seminars, each of twelve three-hour meetings, is 1,427. What began for Anglican clergymen spread to all the churches and then to other professionals who worked with people; teachers, social workers, youth workers and doctors. In many cases, wives have followed their husbands on the courses, or husbands followed wives. Whenever one spouse enters into pastoral caring or counselling, the marriage relationship is affected. In a poor marriage it adds stress, while it adds a creative element to a good one. Many married people have been helped in the seminars to understand and deal creatively with the tensions of professional life. Single men and women have found a supportive group in which very perceptive burden-sharing has been reliably available. About 18,700 people have taken a year's course, which was all we offered at first. About 7,000 people have completed the two-year course.

The achievement outlined by Frank Lake in the article quoted above would not have been possible apart from the dedication, discipline and sheer enthusiasm of the tutors. Some tutors, like the Revd Tony Waite, have been conducting seminars right through from the early days until now: a remarkable example of loyalty and perseverance. The statistics and information given by Frank eloquently disprove the perception that the tutors and other members of the staff were merely appendages, in the organization, to the Chief Engineer. It was without doubt a team effort, in which as much adaptability and energy were required of the administrative staff as of Frank, his immediate advisers, and the tutors. Here is Edna Clarke (who had first met Frank at Lee Abbey in 1960) recalling the hectic pace of the early 1960s at Lingdale:

> I joined the staff of the Clinical Theology Association at Lingdale in 1963. My seven years at Lee Abbey, North Devon, receiving about 4,000 guests a year, had revealed to me how often Christian workers, including myself, were handicapped by their inability to understand or cope with the emotional difficulties both of their clients and themselves. As one who had received much-needed help myself, I was keen to serve an organization which I perceived as doing pioneering work in training and sometimes treating these workers.
>
> My appointment was as Financial Secretary with responsibility for mailing and for occasional catering for conferences. Later I was relieved of the catering side; it seemed reasonable in theory but in practice the combination of catering with office work was difficult since the presence of conferences invariably increased demands on the office; I never mastered the art of receiving subscrip-

tions gracefully while dishing up a meal and it was trying when my failure to do so labelled me with a new neurosis!

The major part of the work was, however, the bookkeeping and mailing. The finances were precarious and Frank's vision expansive. My oft-sounded warnings about the bank balance were regarded as faithless and probably they were. Tutors covered vast distances between seminars, especially in the early days, and of course the travelling expenses were formidable. Failure to extract the expense sheets regularly resulted first in euphoria and later in huge claims which sometimes endangered but never quite invalidated the salary cheques.

During my first twelve months with Clinical Theology I recall that we sent out 13 mailings of pamphlets. There was a degree of catching up on material produced previously by doctor and clergy staff, and this level of distribution tailed off quite rapidly. This was a relief to me, working frantically to keep pace, but with hindsight the material should have been spread more evenly as subscribers who received a vast quantity of literature during their first year were disappointed never to receive as much again. Duplicating and collating the pamphlets (later printed) as well as addressing the envelopes was done in the cellar, prompting my predecessor, Olive Taylor, to classify herself as 'in training for a pit-pony'. The addressing of hundreds of envelopes had to be done with metal plates inserted into an ancient machine and thumped. We had not heard of word processors.

Lingdale had a large, attractive walled garden which was showing signs of neglect when I first saw it. On Saturday afternoons I undertook quite a large scheme of terracing by means of rockeries and then put the resulting level areas down to grass to reduce the maintenance.[14]

Nor should Sylvia Lake's role at Lingdale be forgotten either. She was a very significant figure to many, many people, not least to Frank. Her place for many years was beside him, offering a real contribution – with great dignity and enormous commonsense – which he valued deeply, despite tensions at times. All of these factors suggest that CTA was only what it was because so many people gave so much.

The seminar experience

The seminars were devised by Frank Lake as an effective means of learning and personal growth: and they are still so regarded by CTA today. They gave clergy an opportunity to evaluate and develop their own pastoral gifts so as to increase their effectiveness to their parishioners, while all – both clergy and laity – who wished to increase their understanding of mental dis-ease and human behaviour were amply catered for.

A general statement of the seminars' purpose is found in a hitherto unpublished CTA paper:

> The aim is to provide opportunities for growth as effective and competent helpers in human relations. We intend to provide conditions in which the members can experience a purposive fellowship, of Christians and those who are prepared to work with them, retrieving and focusing upon incidents, both satisfactory and unsatisfactory, which have occurred in their attempts to relate helpfully to others.
>
> To state this as our aim is, on another level, that of faith, to affirm that the seminars exist in order to explore together the personal and interpersonal dimensions of the love of God embodied for man in Christ. It has been the experience of many of us that the encounter with God through His Son itself creates a new beginning to life. These potentialities of the covenant of God with man through the saving and recreative work of Christ need to become actual in personal terms. This does come about within groups of persons who are responding together to an experience of the depth and extent of the love of God as it is reflected in the unconditional respect, deep understanding, and genuine caring which is shown to one another in human terms.
>
> The members become involved in a disciplined approach to achieving competence in helping relationships. They understand that this involves a willingness to submit excerpts of their work with others to the scrutiny of the training group. Levels of honesty and openness become usual. The task of the leadership is to model these attitudes and sustain them. The members find that energy formerly wasted in hiding from oneself and others becomes available for constructive living.

The behavioural and social sciences which deal with human nature tend to assume that the average man is the 'normal' man. We regard Christ as the man through whom we learn what it is to be truly human. In this view, man as we find him is largely alienated from his true nature. The recovery of that humanity in community is the task of small groups within the Church. We believe that the Holy Spirit assists those who stay alongside others in exploring together the depth of their need for reconciliation and integration. In this we recognize that human need is the focus of the redemptive activity of Christ.

The understandings of human problems and their conceptualization by the behavioural and psychological sciences are influential among those who have been given a mandate by our society to care for people, whether traditionally as doctors and nurses, or in the new patterns of social work.

Each has a kind of theology or ideology of man and his needs. In this they assist Christian pastoral care-givers in maintaining that primary focus. They press for a recognition that the training of representative helpers should be relevant, as God's help is to real situations of human need. They affirm that the method of training should be 'clinical' where the meaning of 'clinic' is, (as in Webster's Third New International Dictionary) 'a class, session, or group meeting devoted to the presentation, analysis and treatment or solution of actual cases and concrete problems in some special field or discipline'.

By this means the assumptions behind the various models of deliverance from need, sickness, sin or suffering are clarified and evaluated. Not all of them are compatible at all points with the nature of the Christian deliverance. At every turn, pastoral workers are choosing to act, for themselves and others, without examining these at times incompatible and usually hidden assumptions. This approach enables the helper to clarify his own grounds of action and to take responsibility for attitudes, methods, and goals which are responsibly chosen and consistently directed. The activity of the seminar is constructed to enable the members to become aware of the family and social context within which the action is taking place, to take account of cultural, congregational and theological factors. They seek, through a deepened knowledge of people under stress, of themselves under stress as helpers, and of God's dealing with them, as it emerges from the work of the group, to recognize where the structures of human organizations and of society are themselves in urgent need of change. They seek to exercise a 'prophetic' ministry, and to be agents, whether singly or corporately, of social change.

The course aims to provide opportunities for the members to develop these qualities of personality which are known to make for effective interpersonal helping, caring and counselling. These include genuine self-understanding and openness, together with a power of inner understanding of others, attention to and respect for them, and an ability to put those into acceptable words. The formula can be summarized as 'caring plus confrontation equals growth'.

Each three-hour seminar (in which the ideal number is between twelve and sixteen, plus two tutors) has three basic elements.

First, *growth group activities.* Experimental tasks, exercises (they are not games) and experiences offering opportunities for growth in self-awareness and awareness of others, are set up. These may, for example, consist of a 'play group situation', complete with balls, teddy bears, etc., in which one of the tutors behaves as an educationally subnormal child. The seminar members are involved in the experience, and very soon begin to identify with the child, moving on to their own experience as a child. This is then followed by 'story time' and lastly a debriefing session. The result is that the members share and focus responsibly, together, on the experience of childhood, rather than on a muddled memory of it.

By means of growth group activities people are moved, in a short period of time, towards a sense of community, mutual love, depth and intimacy.

Second, *practising effective counselling.* The members practise, in various settings, the offering to each other of those attitudes and acts which are known to make for mutually helpful counselling relationships. These are associated with the provision of empathy, respect, genuineness, concreteness, and of appropriately timed and expressed confrontation and 'immediacy'. The supervision of the counsellors in training is modelled by the tutor and communicated to the members of the seminar for use in mutual supervision.

Third, *relevant reflection and conceptualization.* This process involves one or more members being led into an exploration of themselves which, in turn, leads to a sharper perception of the ambiguities and options for change in the particular helping situation. The group thus operates as a supportive environment in which alternatives are tried and explored, and in which the risk is both justified and bearable.

It is possible to extrapolate from these elements some of the fundamental aspects of CTA's philosophy. There is the insistence, in the first place, on self-awareness, so that a person is equipped to be a better helper of others, and the validity of personal experience. Then, there is the principle of confidentiality: what goes on in the seminar is sacrosanct to the members themselves. Another is the crucial importance of listening. Unifying all these things is the sound theoretical basis undergirding what goes on in the seminars. The interpretative concepts are drawn from a wide spectrum of sources: the Christian pastoral tradition, systematic knowledge of human behaviour, growth and development, and the dynamics of personality.

Seminar members thus learn to grasp and articulate the nature and extent of their experiences, and the principles which they evaluate for themselves. In such seminars (graphically described by Peter van de Kasteele as a 'treasury of helping') there is an interface, a common meeting-ground between God's reality and the enormity of human suffering. In this way, emotional pain meets the unparalleled resources of Christ as they are embodied in the person of the helper (counsellor, pastor), who has a human commitment to the one who needs help and who is, in a practical and sublime sense, his neighbour. In this way seminar members are offered a satisfyingly balanced combination of the didactic and the experiential. In ultimate terms, they discover the truth of the incarnation:

> Incarnation means that God assumes our frame of reference, entering into our human situation of finitude and estrangement, sharing our human condition even unto

death. When the troubled person finds himself or herself under the care of someone with accurate empathy, someone who seems able to enter another's perceptual framework, he or she experiences a profoundly liberating feeling of being known, being understood.[15]

Frank Lake's successor?

The intense pressure of work, combined with the nature of Frank Lake's personality which tended to autocracy, precluded any serious thought and discussion about his eventual successor. His serious illness in 1978, though, ought to have led to a thoroughgoing consideration of the person likely to succeed him: this quite simply did not happen. But back to the story.

A Council meeting early in 1977 agreed to make it financially possible for Frank Lake to be granted a four-month sabbatical leave from October 1977 to January 1978. This was no more than he deserved. The latter part of this sabbatical was spent in Brazil, but about ten days after his return he was taken ill (in early March) during a weekend Primal Integration conference and was admitted to hospital. He had, in fact, suffered a brain-stem thrombosis, hardly a surprise after the pressurized life he had led for so long. The overall – and inevitable – effect was to underline the need for reorganization within CTA, and the Bishop of Sherwood, Chairman of the Council, outlined the changes in *Newsletter 31* (June 1978):

> CT, particularly in the person of Frank Lake, has amassed a wealth of expertise in the field in which we operate, and has done a vast amount of research which has not really been written up or fully translated into the practicalities of our work. It is now proposed that we should have two separate and clearly defined departments in our organization and that the accounts for each department be kept separately and that each should have its own budget.
>
> The two departments will be 1) Research and 2) Education. All seminars, conferences and counselling come under Education. The Research department will be shaped to provide Frank with the space, freedom and facilities to

> do the research and to bring it to the stage where the fruits of it can be passed on to the Education department.
>
> Frank remains overall Director of CT but his main activity will be in the Research department. The Pastoral Consultants will each take, and be in charge of their own particular section of the Education department with this co-ordinated at staff meetings under Frank's chairmanship.

And that is precisely what Frank did: press on with his research (which led to his writing on what he called the 'Maternal Foetal-Distress Syndrome'), his lecturing, counselling, etc., and in December of the same year he looked back over 'Twenty Years of CT Seminars' in *Newsletter 32*.

The end of an era

Early in 1982 Frank Lake was taken very seriously ill, and by February it became apparent that he would be unlikely again to work for CTA. A Council meeting was called for Friday, 26 February to examine the financial situation and to begin to formulate future policy. The then Chairman, the Bishop of Sherwood, wrote to CTA's friends and supporters with an 'Emergency Appeal':

> The crisis which faces CTA is that Frank's has always been our major source of income, through conferences, workshops, consultations and seminars. Now he must no longer be involved in any of these and we must now maintain him, instead of his financing us. Can you help us? To pay his way and provide the facilities such as secretarial help which he needs in assembling his notes we shall need £2,000 per month for the next few months. CTA lives on such a tight budget that this is beyond our means, especially as we have lost our major source of income, Frank, and it will take a few months to reorganize to a pattern of work without Frank.
>
> The Council of CTA is convinced of the necessity for continuing the work of the Association. We considered very seriously the implications of closing altogether or of merging with some other organization but felt that CTA has something unique in its correlation of psychodynamic theory with Christian theology, experience and faith. We

> offer this to the Church both in terms of training in pastoral care and counselling and in personal growth and consider we have not reached the stage where we could say that our work is done and can now be handed on to someone else. It is our intention now to build up the training and personal growth elements of CTA and to reorganize at Lingdale to cope with this and so to ensure our financial viability.

The response to the Bishop's appeal was overwhelmingly generous, thus enabling the Council to set up the research programme. Frank Lake left hospital on 9 March and died just over two months later. It was indeed the end of an era. How CTA reappraised its work in the post-Frank Lake period is dealt with elsewhere in this book (Chapter 6).

3

A Sketch of Frank Lake's Life

Frank Lake's life had four distinct (that is, primary) phases: his boyhood and adolescence in Lancashire; medical training in Edinburgh; in India as a missionary doctor with the Church Missionary Society (CMS); retraining in psychiatry, followed by his years as founder and first director of the Clinical Theology Association. They form a convenient framework for, and an introduction to, this sketch of Frank Lake's life.

Aughton, Lancashire (1914–32)

He was born at the Lake family home in Aughton, near Ormskirk, south Lancashire, on 6 June 1914, the eldest child of John and Mary Lake. Slightly less than a month later, he was baptized (5th July) in a temporary building while the parish church was being restored. He had two brothers, Ralph (born 1917), who spent his whole professional life as a schoolteacher, and Brian (born 1922), who became a consultant psychiatrist and worked closely with Frank in the formative years of CTA.[1] Both Ralph and Brian Lake now live in retirement in Yorkshire.

The Lake family had lived for generations in the country parish of Aughton, which by the time of Frank's birth had come to be regarded as an attractive exception to the otherwise rather uninteresting scenery in that part of Lancashire. Consequently, it tended to attract wealthy businessmen only too pleased to escape from nearby Liverpool.

Frank's parents were simple Lancashire country people, both churchgoers from their youth. His mother, Mary (*née* Tasker), was a teacher before her marriage, and John Lake worked in the Liverpool Stock Exchange, catching an early morning train into the city from Aughton. He was a keen gardener and would often rise early in the summer months to get a good hour's work done in the garden before leaving for Liverpool. He arranged his vegetables in beautifully neat rows, which he would proudly show to visitors, and to whom he would bring a basket of chosen vegetables, fresh and full of flavour, for their consumption. John Lake was for many years an organist and choirmaster of Aughton parish church, where, in their time, Frank, Ralph and Brian sang in the choir.

Later, after Frank's engagement to Sylvia, and his departure to India in November 1939, Mary Lake welcomed Sylvia warmly to go and stay with them, which she was glad to do whenever that was possible. Sylvia, in fact, became for Mary Lake the daughter she had not had, sharing many things with her. Sylvia was always glad in later years that she had had this opportunity to get to know the Lake parents better, perhaps more so than she would have done had she and Frank been together.

Dr Brian Lake has recorded[2] that in the first half of the 1900s, community life in Aughton was dominated by three major social groups. The first group, including the Lake parents, had its background in local trade, crafts and agriculture. The second, to which the Lake parents eventually migrated, generally worked in banks, insurance and other financial institutions in Liverpool and Ormskirk, after a grammar- or high-school education. The third group consisted of the more wealthy owners and directors of large businesses, together with such other professional people as accountants and lawyers. The outlook of these people was essentially conversative. This conservatism also characterized their religion:

> The major portion of these groups met in the old parish church on Sundays, to hear some reliable but restrained music provided by my father, who was organist and choirmaster. His father, our grandfather, sang baritone in the choir for sixty years and we three sons were all expected, and never failed to live up to expectations, to turn up at Matins and Evensong to sing in the choir in a barely restrained but reliable way too. For the whole of the period between 1914 when Frank was born, two or three weeks

before the declaration of the First World War until the ending of the Second World War when he was in India, the rector was Roger Markham, who succeeded his father as rector. He was a caring but somewhat autocratic and intimidating figure with a good mind. The hall and dining room in the rambling Georgian-styled rectory were covered with paintings of his forebears: bishops, admirals, explorers and judges, going back to the fourteenth century. Here the three groups met to see and hear the Christian beliefs and values demonstrated and enacted, and to experience a mixture of what was real and illusory, permanent and transitory, genuine and false.[3]

The Lake family's social identity was paradoxical. Again Brian Lake can explain:

> Our family both belonged and did not belong to the three groups; belonged because the church prescribed that we should; did not belong because each group kept more or less to itself in the social world outside the church.
>
> My parents had, apart from my father's work, rather little to do with the social life outside the church. There was a slight embarrassment and uncertainty in their approach to it. This led I think to an imbalance in our life. And it was reinforced in practice if not in theory, by the attitude of the rector, who had some difficulties in accommodating his social background to his surroundings. It was therefore a home and church, which excited possibilities and ambitions but left one in doubt about one's true value in the world.[4]

Nor was the home atmosphere, according to Brian, entirely harmonious either, because the Lake parents tended to communicate anxiety to their children: they were aware of this, 'but found it difficult to change'. The genesis of the inner pain which led Frank into a passionate need to draw other people's attention to the pain of relationships may be traced, I believe, to his home background. It is also the reason, in my opinion, why he constantly said that 'Father and Mother relationship is all important'. In fact, at the celebratory meeting[5] after his death, John Gravelle reminded those present of Frank Lake's obsession with 'mothers good and bad', an emphasis indicating that he never totally resolved his own interior wrestling with the matter. In Gravelle's graphic expression, 'Frank seemed to be walking over an abyss of dead bones, smiling as he did so'. Clear and unambiguous proof that he never fully reconciled himself to what was going on inside himself is found in part of a letter he wrote to the Revd Michael Green, then Rector of St Aldate's, Oxford, on 11 January 1978:

> My hardest task is to forgive myself. On the one level I can forgive myself and almost demand forgiveness of others in a shallow way that is false to the discipline of this moment in my life, and out of touch with the cost to a perfectly holy Saviour of coming into redemptive contact with the man I was shocked to find I am.[6]

The Lake parents were very proud of Frank, proud of his becoming a doctor, of his offering to work overseas as a missionary, and in later years Sylvia realized that it was the positive, successful, good things that Frank chose to share with them, preferring not to speak to them of things that had gone wrong, even to the point of not telling them when he was ill. Sylvia recounted to me how angry Frank was with her when she told them he was ill with malaria, with a temperature of 104, when on furlough. In contrast, Sylvia was always moving towards sharing what was really happening, and she would often argue with Frank about this.

During the war years before she went out to India to marry Frank, with her own brother a pilot in the Royal Air Force, and with both herself and her sister nursing under tough conditions, she felt that Frank's parents were cocooned from it all in their village life, and what is more, did not wish to know of all the terrible happenings, the bombings and the lives lost and, later, the news of Belsen and other camps of death. Mary Lake would hold up her hands to prevent Sylvia from telling her, and she would say that she did not want even to think about such terrible things. Perhaps it was typical too that when Sylvia's brother was killed at the age of twenty-three, it was Brian Lake who shared her heartbreak with her, and was able to draw near to pain without flight. Whereas in her own family Sylvia was able to share deeply all that happened to them, she noticed that Frank's mother had a way of foreclosing on those things which involved raw feelings, which drained them of their colour, their strength and vitality in her eyes.

Later in life, Sylvia heard Frank speak of his mother as a saint,[7] but she felt that was an idolizing of Mary Lake in an unrealistic way. Mary was certainly afraid of close relationships, a point confirmed by Frank Lake's comment on page 359 of *Clinical Theology*:

> I remember my mother saying, years after adolescent crises in my own life, how she had recognized that she would never be the person to meet my difficulties, so that all her urgent concern was directed to God in prayer, with the corollary that God would have to find the counsellors her sons would need, and produce them at the right time. This He did.

Mary Lake was also afraid of sex, which seems to have had a striking effect on Frank:

> My mother's handling of me has made me fearful and ashamed about my sexuality. The short misguided excursion into life with the maternal lid off makes it abundantly clear that my sexuality is strong and that I have spent a life-time inhibiting it. There too it was split.[8]

She was also able to arouse enormous guilt in the child who transgressed, to the point where the child hid his misdemeanours rather than risk her shocked reaction. Frank learnt to tell her a little and to say 'Sorry', knowing that that was all he was required to do to restore relationships, and this he enacted many times with her. In this way he learnt to hide his deeper struggles and fears, knowing all too well that he was far more competent to deal with them or not, as he wished. 'This pattern', says Sylvia, 'was re-enacted in his later life in greater or lesser extent, and even when he was aware of this, he never chose to break out from it.'

But doubts and anxieties regarding identity and self-worth notwithstanding, Frank duly and regularly attended the local parish church with his family, eventually joining its choir on 12 September 1922, aged eight, and being confirmed on 23 November 1928. In *Tight Corners in Pastoral Counselling*, he reflected on the church services he attended, particularly the eight o'clock communion service:

> [it] was reverent and quiet, useful for the chorister like myself who could be too attentive to the music to be able to concentrate on the meaning of the later services. You could rely, at this early service, on not being disturbed by others' looks. We saw only each other's backs, and the back of the Rector for most of the time. There was no sermon and no attempt at church-door *bonhomie*. There were no concessions at all to subjectivity, emotions, personal interaction, dialogue or meeting. We went home as untouched and unattended to humanly, as when we arrived.[9]

Then, in the same chapter from which the above quotation comes, there is this honest and revealing explanation:

> I would guess that most of us who found that early communion congenial were introverted types. It may be that some of us were even burdened with personality hurts which led to our disliking the kind of fellowship and extrovert activity from which that particular service protected us. For these reasons some of us found it hard to accept the parish communion when it became the central service of the day. The early service enabled us to keep in contact with some of the Christian realities without in any way disturbing our defences.[10]

So it was that in his adolescence Frank Lake remained unaware of the possibilities of meeting his fellow-worshippers either mystically or humanly, and had no conception, at that time, of the enrichment, both human and divine, that resides in the communion service.

The Sunday school in the parish church,[11] however, was a major influence on the lives of all three Lake boys. Two sisters, Dorothy and Marjorie Holmes, were its superintendents; it was their sister, Elsie Holmes, who published a volume of biographical poetry, *Margaret*, in 1936. Largely due to Dorothy and Marjorie, it seems, Frank and his brothers all became teachers in the same Sunday school. Later Frank and John Grindrod (now Primate of Australia) ran a Bible class together at the parish church, for young people. Even later, on 7 April 1939, Frank Lake and John Grindrod jointly conducted the Good Friday service at Aughton. In those early and far-off days Frank exhibited that trait of character which so marked out his later life: immense drive and boundless enthusiasm for a wide range of activities.

He received his formal education at the church school in the village, then at the Alsop High School for Boys, Liverpool, where he was admitted on 12 September 1923. He was not particularly successful at school; in fact, his non-academic achievements – for example, regular appearances in productions of Gilbert and Sullivan operas – were far more memorable and noteworthy. He did enough, however, to matriculate (30 August 1930), and to pass the exams for the then Higher School Certificate (20 August 1932).

Towards the end of his school career, the idea of being a missionary seems to have become firmly a part of his thinking. For example, on 23 November 1931, he was in touch with the Edinburgh Medical Missionary Society. This missionary interest may perhaps be attributed to Miss Eger[12] (formerly a missionary to India herself), who subsequently helped to finance his medical training at Edinburgh. Then, on 7 April 1932, he had an interview with the Church Missionary Society, and later that year attended (29 July) the Church Missionary Society summer school at Malvern.

Edinburgh (1932–7)

Frank Lake left for Edinburgh University and medical studies on 2 October 1932. This was, in a very real sense, a break with the Lake family because, holidays and furloughs apart, he was only infrequently at home again. The explanation for this is twofold. In the first place, there were sheer logistical and practical reasons. He had to cope with a lengthy medical course, as well as the many other activities he got involved with, while later there was the physical separation of life in India as a missionary. All this is valid and acceptable, but it does not, in my opinion, provide the real explanation. Rather, as Brian Lake has cogently suggested,[13] it was Frank's way of dealing with the admittedly 'modest psychosomatic symptoms' he had encountered in the Lake household. So he stayed away from home but dealt with the difficulties in another way: by writing almost weekly, detailed, lengthy and exciting letters to his parents who read them 'avidly' (Brian's word). Only on one occasion can Brian remember his mother being even 'faintly plaintive' about Frank's absences:

> He was staying on leave with us for a week when I was about twelve years old and he spent nearly all of the time with some friends in the vicinity. When a family rule was that you give your children into God's hands to do His work and you end up rarely seeing them, my parents were not the sort of people to be inconsistent and complain. Christianity demanded firmer self-control and sacrifice. There were, however, compensations. They could enjoy all the excitement and interest of Frank's penetration into a world they had not explored, secure in the knowledge that he stayed safely with them, inside the church.[14]

Ralph Lake (the middle son), however, does not entirely share Brian's emphases, either on the Lake family in general, or on Frank's relationship with it after leaving for Edinburgh. He recalls[15] a 'happy' home life; though, tellingly, he admits that his father could be 'hasty' and, at times, 'irritable'. He does see his father as a 'driven' man (a description frequently used of Frank in later life by his colleagues), who felt compelled to keep a sense of duty, and who took his responsibilities very seriously. Ralph views John Lake as a thrifty, provident and conscientious man (all worthy qualities in themselves), but feels that his father would have liked some of the frivolities of life which he was prevented from indulging by a steely sense of purpose.

Nor does Ralph see 1932 as the big cut-off point in Frank Lake's relations with his family. He amplified his opinions to me by pointing to the support given by the Lake parents to Frank's many and varied activities, especially his missionary interests, and recalled that a number of missionary events (after being held initially and briefly in some of Aughton's wealthier homes) gravitated more and more to the Lake family's sitting-room. He recalled too the impression his parents had of Frank as the 'golden boy', and also the fact that while pursuing a course in tropical medicine at Liverpool, Frank regularly visited the family home, on which occasions the fatted calf, to use a biblical example, was killed and laid out for him: red carpet treatment no less. There is no easy way of reconciling these differing views held by Ralph and Brian, and the wisest approach probably is simply to let them stand as representing differing perceptions.

Frank Lake remained in Edinburgh for the whole of his medical training, graduating MB, ChB on 14 July 1937, to which were later added DTM (Liverpool), DPM (Leeds) and MRC Psych (1973). But what of his Christian experience during his time in Edinburgh? This is what he said:

> My own commitment to Christ became articulate when I was a medical student in Edinburgh University. Medicals were not so harassed in those days. I remember stealing into the back of Professor Daniel Lamont's class in Apologetics, and John Baillie's on Systematic Theology. But it was Alexander White's writing, and J. S. Stewart's preaching that I think meant most to me in those days. The Edinburgh Medical Missionary Society was my home . . .[16]

Certainly he was a committed Christian when Sylvia met him in 1939, and he always said, like Sylvia, that he had 'been a Christian from the beginning, and that it was a matter of growth and deepening of the commitment after that'.

Two months after graduating (30 September) Frank began a tropical medicine course at the Liverpool School of Tropical Medicine, becoming a lecturer in Parasitology there in 1938. During the years 1937–9 he also maintained contact with the CMS through their summer school at Malvern (he attended there on 30 July 1937 and 29 July 1938), by means of consultations in London (3 January 1938), through recruiting stewards from Aughton for the CMS Exhibition in Liverpool (an event lasting four days), and by speaking at other CMS functions, including a meeting at Southport (11 March 1939), a CMS Youth meeting in Blackpool (25 March 1939), and by preaching: on 14 May 1939, for example, at Emanuel Church, Everton and at St Mary's in Bootle. During 1939, too, he met Sylvia Madelaine Smith, and before proceeding to chronicle his years in India, it is vitally important to chart her story, for she was to be his staunchest supporter for over forty years as well as being a most perceptive critic of her husband's work.

Sylvia's story[17]

Sylvia's parents (William Smith and Ellen Bullivant) had married in 1914, her father being at that time a widower with six almost grown-up children. Ellen was a hospital nursing sister, while William, Sylvia's father, was a miller and corn merchant with his own business, and a fine business brain too. He became blind early in his adult life, and never saw Sylvia, the eldest of three children born to him in his second marriage. William Smith died when Sylvia was nine years old, and an otherwise very happy childhood was overshadowed by this event: his death left her mother, brother and sister to face life on their own. Her father's blindness had impressed Sylvia greatly, and as the eldest child she learnt early to look out for him and to move obstacles from his path. She realized much later what a training this was for her in becoming aware of others and what was happening to them. William Smith was very musical, with a beautiful high-tenor voice, and when he got out his violin to play to the family, Sylvia remembers being so moved that she burst into tears on more than one occasion.

Not being able to see his children, William Smith would embrace them and gently pass his hands over their faces, their eyes and hair and shoulders, to familiarize himself with how they were. In this way he showed them the love he felt which could not be shown – as with most fathers – through his eyes. Sylvia's mother was a sincere Christian, and it was at her knee that Sylvia learnt to pray.

Eventually Sylvia went to the school of St Mary and St Anne, Abbotts Bromley, as a boarder, and was very happy there. She was soon put into the choir, which was her greatest joy, and she loved the many services she was required to attend. After leaving school she wanted to be a nurse, but stayed at home to be with her mother while her brother and sister continued their education. She did, however, join the Red Cross and completed all the training.

Already the rumours of war were reverberating. Her brother joined the Royal Air Force Voluntary Reserve, while beginning to train in the law. Sylvia was accepted at the General Hospital, Nottingham, to train as a nurse (a most convenient arrangement as the family lived in Nottingham).

She met Frank Lake, who was giving some talks at Swanwick Conference Centre, just prior to his going abroad as a CMS missionary. They met a number of times subsequently, as Sylvia's local vicar (of St Andrew's Church, Nottingham) asked Frank to become their own missionary. They became engaged about three weeks before Frank sailed for India.

Sylvia's home background was not troubled by the tensions apparent in the Lake family, and she recalls her formative years with unsullied pleasure. It is not difficult to see why she and Frank were attracted to each other. They shared many common interests: the Christian faith, music, serving others, with Sylvia particularly being prepared to put the interests of other people before her own wishes – witness her willingness to return home, after leaving school, to be with her mother while her brother and sister continued their education. The life of prayer was important to her too, something which has grown and developed since those early days at home when she prayed with her mother. Both families – the Lakes and the Smiths – were eminently respectable, and devoted to the local Anglican church. These common bonds were to be tested in the years ahead, not least while Frank was in India.

India (1939–50)

Dr Frank Lake sailed to India aboard the *Britannia* in November 1939. He did not see Sylvia again for four and a half years, and with letters taking anything between nine and sixteen weeks to arrive, it was a difficult period for both of them. After Frank's departure Sylvia was in the hands of the Church Missionary Society, and went to their training college, which was a marvellous time for her. She made many close friends then who have remained friends throughout her life. As she says herself, 'I was fortunate to have at the head Florence Allshorn,[18] whose teaching and example drove us deeply, to look at ourselves, and other people, and to look continually to God. She, with others, and all this training experience, set a course in my life which has only deepened and strengthened with the years.' It was Florence too who first prayed for Sylvia that great prayer of Søren Kierkegaard: 'To will one thing alone'.

The college staff and students were all moved at one stage when the bombing became too disruptive for them to work, to Ridley Hall, Cambridge, to a wing at that time unused because the young men had gone to war, and this was a wonderful time for Sylvia: the lectures she attended, 'Canon Charles Raven, and Paul Gibson on the Psalms, and of course all those Cambridge bookshops'.

As the war continued, the CMS eventually sent Sylvia back to continue her nursing training. She was very happy at the General Hospital in Nottingham. Then, in 1944, she was offered a sailing, one of the first to India of civilians since the war began, and three months later, after some amazing adventures in the desert of Egypt with fellow-missionaries of mixed denominations en route, she landed in Bombay, met Frank again and married him three weeks later in Poona, with Ralph Lake as Frank's best man (18 April 1944).

Frank's years in India were characterized by boundless energy and an involvement with a variety of activities.[19] He served as a missionary doctor in Bengal before joining, for military service, the Indian Medical Service (1940–45), becoming a lieutenant-colonel in the process. In June 1945, Frank and Sylvia's first child (David) was born in Poona, and when he was six months old they went together to the Vellore Medical Centre, where Frank was making diagrams and other visual aids for the Parasitology Department. When he was then asked to go back to Ranaghat to relieve Dr Mervyn Hatt who had done nine years' service non-stop, Sylvia came home to have their second child (Monica), and to get over amoebic dysentery which had troubled her for months and had defied all treatment. So Monica was born, in 1946, in Nottingham and Frank did not see her until she was fifteen months old.

Nothing was easy in the relationship between Frank and Sylvia, with Frank away so much and work always his top priority. He accepted every invitation to speak, wherever it was, and in the end she could not face India, with its heat and sickness, and the thought of taking two tiny children to the Bengal jungle outskirts, where it was suggested the family should build a cage round the stretch of land near the house to keep them safe from marauding animals.

So in May 1949 Frank went back to India on his own after

a furlough lasting a year. Sylvia remained behind in England, being already pregnant with their third child (Marguerite), and in July 1950 she and the three children settled on the Lincolnshire coast.

Meanwhile, back in India, Frank went to Vellore (1949–50) and became Superintendent of the Christian Medical College, Madras, meeting Dr Florence Nicholls who was Head of Psychiatry. He describes her appointment in the following way:

> My official task was to help her in the establishment of the psychiatric unit in the Medical College, but I caught something of her enthusiasm.[20]

The last phrase here is an understatement, because what happened in reality was that he became absorbed in the whole subject:

> My first contact with dynamic psychiatry and with a psychoanalyst enlarged for me the dimensions of medicine. It now had to include a variety of imponderable emotional factors which I had never been taught to think about seriously before. Moreover, I saw transformations of depressed and anxious people, not only with the aid of the primitive electrical shock machine we were then using, but in response to what I may vulgarly call a 'dose' of radical Christianity.[21]

This meeting, and his work with Dr Nicholls, is absolutely crucial for understanding the life of Frank Lake. In a sense it set the course for the whole of his future life, for psychiatry was not a passing fancy, or a momentary diversion from the real business of life: it became Frank Lake's dominating interest in so far as it was able to transform the lives of 'depressed and anxious people'. Canon Max Warren, of the CMS, realized the intensity of Frank's interest in psychiatry, and after deputation work for the society, suggested that Frank should either qualify in psychiatry and give himself wholly to it, or get it out of his system by getting some psychiatric experience.

This was timely advice because, as Frank Lake says in his Introduction to *Clinical Theology*, he was unable 'for various reasons'[22] to return to India. One of those reasons was that his post in Vellore had been terminated. A second reason was that since 1947 Indian society, for a variety of causes, had been afflicted by violence, and many years later, in the *British Weekly* for 9 October 1969, Frank Lake had this to say about the terrifying aspects of violence on a large scale:

> In 1947 I was in charge of a hospital in Bengal. During the war 2¼ million people had died in a famine that could have been relieved if merchants had released their stocks of rice at prices the poor could pay. Then, 40 miles away in Calcutta we had the Hindu–Moslem riots in which human beings were pushed into sewers, and the trains that passed the hospital gate were covered all over like flies on a jam spoon, with refugees passing in both directions. Ours was the only hospital with medical and surgical wards and midwifery for 5½ million people, at the junction of five railways. Violence and disorder were in the air, and in many desperate people.

The inevitable result of all these appalling factors was that Dr Lake and his staff were grossly overworked, medical cases could not be admitted to the hospital unless, in his words, 'they had six diseases at once', and the international staff of doctors, nurses and other ancillary staff were 'deprived of the time we would ordinarily spend in fellowship', while patients could only be treated in an administratively correct manner which was, again in his words, 'personally deficient'.

But then other political issues began to be apparent:

> A local Trotskyist group had established itself among a section of the nurses. They began to make demands which were, as we were to learn, designedly impossible to fulfil since they were planned to dismantle the hospital . . . We had to go. Weeks of conflict followed: 25 nurses committed to the communist cause, 75 eventually prepared, as they knew, to risk their lives to remain faithful to Christ. No one could sit on the fence.
>
> A week after I left on furlough, the doctor who succeeded me, and two sisters, were shot dead at their evening meal.[23]

The doctor referred to here was Dr Mervyn Hatt whose place Frank had earlier taken at Ranaghat: in fact, all three had been murdered before Frank's ship had landed in Britain again. Unable to return to Ranaghat because of the distressing incidents outlined above, and unable to return to Vellore because his post there had been terminated, Frank had to turn his life in a new direction, which, in the event, turned out to be re-training in psychiatry. His return to England also meant that important decisions would have to be faced which would affect the whole of the Lake family.

England, re-training and the Clinical Theology Association (1951–82)

So on returning to England, and after deputation work on behalf of the CMS, Frank Lake spent a year at The Lawn, Lincoln (1951–2), a period of re-training which took place under the supervision of Dr John Goodlad. From there he moved to Scalebor Park Hospital, Burley, Yorkshire, where he began his studies for the Diploma in Psychological Medicine, a course which took six years (1952–8). He was guided during this period by Dr James Valentine, whom he found both wise and compassionate. In the early years of this course, Sylvia was uncertain whether Frank would settle and as she did not wish to uproot the family unnecessarily from their secure base in Lincolnshire, they did not move to their new home in the Ilkley area until 1954. By now Frank was firmly embarked on his new career as a psychiatrist, but what was his relationship like with his children?

To David, during his childhood years, Frank Lake seemed somehow always too single-minded and too busy to be really interested in him. Although Frank would try, on his rare visits, to relate to David, as when he built the children a wattle hut in the garden, or when he built him a railway layout, David remembers his father in those years as someone who never seemed to belong, or to be at ease with him, his sisters or his mother. Although wonderfully willing to fetch water or dig the caravan out of the mud in pouring rain on summer holidays, Frank never ceased to appear something of an 'outsider'.

It was as an outsider that Frank viewed family matters too. This is what he said in a letter welcoming Metcalfe Collier as a professional associate of CTA:

I myself am pretty well able to commit to all kinds of

> situations and to some fairly deep therapeutic situations in which people come very close. But I am equally well aware that there are certain deep and obligated relationships, particularly, and this is the rub, in the family, where I find myself at times paralysed by an inability to become wholly involved.[24]

Perhaps even more honestly and opaquely, he told a fellow-CMS missionary on one occasion that he 'was not enjoying a happy and satisfying home life; nevertheless God was felt to have given him a wider family and the tremendous joy over the previous few months of leading some 150 persons to faith in Christ, or to a great deepening of their experience and commitment'. This hurt and pain was felt by his family too, and they did not have the compensatory factors of pursuing an exciting time in meeting interesting people, travelling, and so on.

Recalling his schooldays,[25] David remembers his father's love of books, an interest he shared. He was introduced by Frank to the works of George MacDonald when he was about ten, and to Tolkein's *Lord of the Rings* immediately it was published. He remembers his father's generous help with and loan of theological books whenever he went home from his school at Uppingham. This, and the love of the Christian mystics which he shared with his mother, encouraged David to choose to live at home for his theological studies at the University of Nottingham, after ten years away at preparatory school and public school. Although there were often heated arguments on theological and philosophical questions, David recalls those years as full and exciting, if also sometimes very painful.

The relationship between father and son was a combination of intellectual conflict and deepening mutual respect. Significantly, David felt that he had to 'find' his father, and that a real relationship became possible only after a process of painful wrestling intellectually and emotionally. They found it difficult to enjoy talking or reading together in a relaxed and restful way; his father simply had no time for that. But they did both really enjoy playing music together, Frank on the piano, David on the violin, and they would sometimes be joined by the womenfolk, all of whom had good voices and were musically gifted.

David also recalls his father's generosity and ecumenical tolerance: on one occasion, he supported David's desire to own a crucifix and rosary at his preparatory school, even though his own tradition was one that tended to frown upon such things. But Frank's all-consuming preoccupation with his work made it very difficult, David felt, for him to really 'hear' his son. David's interest in contemplative spirituality, and an approach that read the saints and mystics on their own terms, rather than psychologically, led to disagreement. But Frank's refusal to let his psychological reductionism come anywhere near his own evangelical convictions meant, in David's view, that in later years it was possible for them to meet on the common ground of real faith, however differently expressed.

David writes:

> I remember more than once falling into each other's arms weeping, after long, painful and often stormy disagreement. Somehow the ice had been broken, the distance was no longer there and we both stood face to face, tears streaming, overwhelmed. They were moments of rare tenderness and love. I believe the real mutual respect we came to feel for each other, in later years, somehow stemmed from those moments. Was all that struggle necessary? Looking back, the drama forgotten, the harsh words shriven, I still think perhaps it was. Rationalizations silenced, resentment spent and gone, suddenly love was present. That love remains.

A shared enthusiasm for the theology of St Gregory Palamas, and David's interest in Orthodox monasticism, flowered on a visit they both made to Mount Athos in the summer of 1965. A photograph of the Holy Mountain, taken at this time, was beside his father throughout the final weeks of his life, reminding them both of what they had loved and shared. In short, David was able to find his father after prolonged conflict, on the intellectual plane, though this interface was denied to him in childhood, as it was denied to his sister Monica.

Monica,[26] Frank and Sylvia's second child, first saw her father when she was fifteen months old, but for the next seven years met him only occasionally, as he was either in India or pursuing his re-training in psychiatry in Lincoln. Thus she has no early memories of him, except as a fleeting stranger who sometimes came to stay with Sylvia and the three children. To her, her mother was the sole parent, bringing up the children almost single-handed. And even when Frank did live continuously with the family, Monica, like David and Margi, found it difficult to accept his authority, because she, like them, resented this stranger telling her off; and so she continued to turn to her mother for advice, reassurance and encouragement. 'Dad', she says, 'was always too busy with his work to bother about us much. He didn't mind making things for us when he had the time, for example a large garden swing or putting lights on our dolls' house, but he didn't know how to play games with us and was always very serious.'

She has some vivid memories of family holidays:

> Whenever we went to church – even the remotest 'wee highland kirk', Dad seemed to find either somebody he knew, or someone who knew somebody he knew, and we used to spend hours waiting for him to stop talking, so we could go and have our lunch.

Later, when Monica went to boarding school, it was Sylvia who wrote every week to keep in touch with her, although she did persuade Frank to come with her sometimes, usually to the more important occasions like Confirmation or Speech Days. But:

> Even then, he seemed to think it was more important to converse with the more influential parents there, than it was to hear how his daughter was getting on.

After leaving school Monica lived at home for two years while doing her nursery nurse's training, before starting her SRN course at Guy's Hospital in London. This is how she remembers those years:

> David was also living at home while studying Theology at Nottingham University. On Sundays Brian Lake and the young curate from our church in Nottingham (St Mary's) would often come to lunch. The theological discussions

> would last throughout lunch and most of the afternoon. It was all way over my head and I would disappear when I'd had enough, and let them get on with it. Sometimes the arguments would get very heated, especially between my father and my brother David.

She comments like this:

> I know that Dad valued the work I was doing as a nursery nurse, because he knew the vital importance of loving and caring for the very young – especially the deprived ones that I was looking after – and he was proud when I became a nurse. But I don't feel he valued me as a person, as much as David or Margi, because I couldn't talk and discuss things on his level, so we didn't have much in common.

There were occasions when Monica forced her father to take notice of her, or tried to, but colleagues or patients always seemed to her to be more important to him. In this respect, she has one particularly poignant memory:

> When I was about thirteen I went into his study to say 'goodnight'. He was sitting reading, so absorbed that he hadn't heard me from the door. So I went and stood in front of him and repeated my 'Goodnight, Dad'. No reaction. So I knelt in front of him and with my hands on his knees said 'Goodnight, Dad'. He was in another world. With tears pouring down my cheeks, I went to bed and cried myself to sleep. I didn't try again. During my late teens, I felt much closer to my father's brother, Brian. I became very fond of him for I felt that he loved, understood and valued me as ME, and I shall always greatly value his fatherly caring for me, when I really needed it.

Marguerite[27] (now called Margi by all the family), like Monica, did not see her father until she was about fifteen months old, and her earliest memory of her father is of a family holiday on a camping site in the north of Scotland when she was five years old:

> My mother had suddenly been summoned to England in the event of her own mother's death and for the first time in living memory, my father had to cope with all three children alone, a task which he was somewhat at a loss to

> fulfil. Seeing as cooking was never one of his strong points, and socializing with the other campers was, he proceeded to accept a string of invitations to eat out every night with 'friends'. Having been accustomed to the homely fare and security of my mother's cooking, this represented an insurmountable problem for a sensitive five-year-old whose mother had suddenly disappeared for no apparent reason and abandoned her to the care of this man called 'daddy', but who was in effect a stranger who occasionally entered her life, but who rarely stayed for long and was certainly not to be depended upon. The upshot of this state of affairs was that she was filled with horror and retreated to the toilet tent and flatly refused to come out again. My father became angry and impatient and lectured her at length on the discourtesy of offending 'such good and generous people'. Fortunately, her brother and sister rallied to her aid and tried to explain the situation to their exasperated father, who eventually left her to nurse her insecurity in peace.

Incidents like this are all too well known in the routine of family life, but it does show that Sylvia was regarded by the children as the secure foundation of the family, and she needed to be, with Frank away so frequently. It also shows that he lacked the sensitivity to deal with the needs of his youngest daughter, whose confidence could probably have been won had he bothered to, say, boil her an egg in the privacy of their own caravan instead of putting her in a situation of facing strange food among strange people, and with her mother absent too. The effect of this incident was that it set the tone of Margi's relationship with her father for the next ten years or so:

> He was not a father who displayed any real pleasure in relating to us as small children; we were very much the children of 'my good wife', as he would describe my mother to other people, and as such, her responsibility to love, discipline, educate, provide for, in whatever way she thought fit. When he could be persuaded to come on family outings, it was with reluctance and little enthusiasm. I still have a clear picture of him sitting in the tent which was designated as his working area on caravan holidays, spec-

tacles perched on the end of his nose, scribbling away from early morning to late evening (he was writing *Clinical Theology* at the time), emerging only to eat meals and pass or fetch water as the need arose. He seemed to have an innate dislike for all natural exuberance, joyful expressions of fun, or the kind of lively, playful humour which naturally occurs in healthy families. In the event that circumstances prevented him from escaping such displays of unreasonable pleasure, he would accuse us of 'daddy baiting', as if our enjoyment of life was at his expense.

In later childhood, Margi associated his presence with restriction and unpleasantness, and she remembers the sense of relief rather than regret or disappointment when he found an excuse not to participate in family events. The times she remembers being at peace with her father were rare:

> They occurred when I was in bed with measles or mumps or some such children's disease, at which time he would read stories from mythology or fairy tales, or draw pictures for me, or sometimes on 'runs' in the car, he would ask my mother to stop the car (she always drove, on account of the fact that my father's attention was rarely on the road, which made his driving somewhat erratic, besides which the family car belonged to my mother), in order to 'just have a look inside' the local church. At such times he was possessed by an austere calm, a certain reverence mingled with curiosity which I could relate to. This was a sort of safe communication ground, as was a discussion about architecture or history, but the essential experience, the sense of the presence of something beyond human comprehension, he was never able to dwell quietly in or recognize and confirm in me, almost as if he feared that I would see that he was moved and translate it as weakness.

From an early age, Margi made a point of not looking into her father's eyes, which she considered to be 'cold and distant', and in them she perceived an emptiness which terrified her, even to the point of inducing nightmares:

> In the light of this I found it significant that in later life he wrote so extensively on the importance of the mother's look of love for her child.

In her early twenties, and by now possessed of a stronger sense of self and self-worth, Margi would try to look into his eyes:

> The result of this was that he either turned away, or if he met mine, the depth of his pain and emptiness inside would cause tears to well up in us both, and he would sigh and say, 'Ah, dear Margi', as if for a moment we had both recognized what he had always missed, a kind of core sense of connected strength and well-being.

Margi was always mildly surprised at how impressed others were by her father, and often wondered what on earth had attracted him to her mother in the first place, seeing as the various women he appeared to find interesting were either blue-stocking intellectuals or hopelessly confused *femmes fatales*, whereas her mother was, and still is, an extremely sane, practical, competent sort of person who radiates a great deal of warmth to those she cares about. Her father also struck Margi as being embarrassed, ashamed and at the same time moralistic on the subject of sex:

> I do not remember sex as having ever been a subject which it was possible to approach him with in terms of personal experience, though he was ready, always ready, to expound on Freud, projected fantasies, unnatural relationships and suchlike.

Frank Lake, in Margi's eyes, was not a man who recognized and confirmed a woman's sexuality in a warm and supportive way, and she believes that he did not particularly like mentally and physically strong and healthy members of the opposite sex, or that he felt adequate as a man in their presence. Later, he preferred to turn a blind eye to her rather 'bohemian' existence in her early twenties, though when confronted by it, he expressed downright disapproval from the perspective of Christian morality. As a growing woman, Margi seemed increasingly to represent a threat to him at close quarters, and she was only acceptable to him when discussing intellectual issues:

> Perhaps the latter is one of the reasons I studied Theology and the former (dislike of strong women) why I gave it up

once I had graduated. My father had an intense dislike for warm, full-blooded emotion and all forms of romantic expression, be it music, art, poetry, love or mysticism. His derision of it was dogmatically final. He was attracted by the accurate, cool, ordered, unemotional, intellectual approach in all things.

This is how Margi sums up her view of her father:

His boundless energy and dedication to the task at hand was formidable and nothing, be it bishops, colleagues, friends or family was going to stand in his way if he could help it. If you were with him, you were guaranteed a place on his surfboard which was carrying him at great speed into the future, if not, he would drop you off at the first convenient rock in the ocean and never look back.

Frank Lake was clearly less than ideal as a father, the primary burden of the family's welfare and upbringing devolving onto Sylvia. This was a task she was well fitted for and which she discharged with integrity and much love. She provided the children with stability, and she needed to, because Frank was so frequently away pursuing his own path, his own interests, his own ambitions. It is not just that he found the presence of three children inhibiting, even frustrating: most fathers do from time to time. It is not just that he was selfish in following pursuits outside the immediate confines of home and family: selfishness is, after all, an inherently human failing. Rather, it is the feeling – conveyed by the Lake family in general, in conversation with them – that he was prepared, in an utterly ruthless and frequently insensitive fashion to neglect his family while he got on with his work. Hardly surprisingly, such a response led to much emotional hurt in the Lake household, pain which is admitted quite openly by the members of the family: Sylvia, David, Monica and Margi. And perhaps what made their pain all the more difficult to endure was Frank's inability to consider constructive criticism in relation to personal grievances as far as family matters were in question.

None of them, however, doubted his ability, either intellectually in general or in the realm of medicine and psychiatry. In 1958 he achieved the Diploma in Psychological Medicine from the University of Leeds. After this award a consultancy post was suggested, but then occurred another of those meetings which radically affected the course of Frank Lake's life, this time with Donald Coggan, then Bishop of Bradford, and together they provided the energy behind the setting-up of Scargill House near Kettlewell.

Sylvia remembers Donald and Jean Coggan sitting in her lounge at Ilkley, listening to Frank expounding on the lack of training the clergy had in preparation for their ministry to so many people in every kind of need, a lack which had brought many of them to Scalebor Park Hospital in breakdown, and therefore into his care during those years of training. In Frank's eyes they needed not only preparation in theological colleges, but post-ordination training too, and Donald Coggan turned to him and said: 'Well – who could do this? Have you ever thought that God may mean it to be you?'

So the seed was sown. The family decided to move to Nottingham, which is ideally placed in the middle of the country, and a letter went out to all the bishops asking them if they would allow seminars to be held in their dioceses. As the answers came back, Frank Lake realized that there was more than enough work being offered, for him to dare to begin, so he moved away from the health service and receipt of a regular salary into an unknown future. It would not have been possible to do this financially had not Sylvia's father left her some money at his death, a legacy which had accumulated through the years, and with which she was able to purchase the house in The Park, Nottingham, where Frank saw the first clients and where the first Nottingham seminar was held. She was also able to cover school fees regularly. The rest is history, including the beginning of the Clinical Theology Association. The year is now 1962, and Frank Lake had started on his life's work.

'Treasure in a large earthen vessel' [28]

Four years later, in 1966, his huge tome, *Clinical Theology*, was published. It represented the distillation of many years of work, analysis and meditation. Its content will be examined and evaluated in Chapter 5, but here mention must be made of the considerable attention it attracted, especially in the Christian press, by way of reviews, reference to it in clergy conferences, and letters to denominational journals. This approach will have the advantage of pinpointing its significance within the biographical framework of Frank Lake's life.

Though couched in different language, and also with differing degrees of analytical skill and expertise, the reviews were united in emphasizing the *uniqueness* of Frank Lake's contribution to the dialogue between theology and psychiatry (*The Times Literary Supplement*); the essential importance of clinical theology for the pastoral training of ordinands in the Anglican (the *Church of England Newspaper*), Roman Catholic (*Catholic Herald*), and the Free Churches (*Free Church Letter*); its significance for pastoral care and counselling in general; clinical theology's carefully defined conceptual framework and its deep commitment to the Christian Gospel; and the fact that clinical theology had, in the words of the reviewer in *Regina* (the magazine of Queen's College at Birmingham), 'led many to a deeper knowledge of Christ as truly human and as active now in the integration of persons: both amongst the clergy and the laity'.

Reviewers were equally decisive and forthright in identifying those problems associated with a movement Bob Lambourne (*The Christian*) dubbed 'a byword in church circles . . . and a spectacular work in pastoral training of the ordained ministry'. These problem areas included (though not in any order of priority) the controversial nature of Frank Lake's widespread use of lysergic acid (LSD-25) in the treatment of patients at all stages of human agony and need; the poorly organized and repetitive nature of the material in the book; the psychologizing of religious writings and mystical experiences which caused offence, as Professor Pond of The London Hospital said,[29] 'among some of even the more liberally minded Christians', though he generously added: 'Such is the common fate of pioneers, especially of those who try to bring together fields of interest that are regarded by many as totally different or even antithetical'; the uncertainty perceived in Frank Lake's methodology: 'He is inhabited by a most powerful impulse to explain himself and the range of his preoccupations in terms of the ministry he has accepted, and clinical theology bears the stamp of his unresting imagination'; the pervasive doubts about the importance of birth trauma in dealing with psychic wounds: 'It may be so, but the thesis is as yet unproven' (Norman St John Stevas);[30] the fact that Clinical Theology (both the book and the movement) 'seems to lead the parish priest into a type of pastoral counselling which requires more expertise than he normally has and more time than he can afford';[31] and lastly, what some considered to be the 'hotch-potch' nature of Frank Lake's attempt to integrate psychology and religion: 'a mixture of analytical psychology, Pavlovian psychology, and a mystical kind of Anglicanism'.

The most devastating criticism of *Clinical Theology* came from Bob Lambourne. In *New Christian* (December 1966), Dr Lambourne welcomes the book as 'an original, provocative contribution to pastoral theology' but says that as a standard textbook for pastoral study 'it will not do'. He then points to its 'fundamental defects', and his reasons for his stance on the issue, by making four criticisms:

> Firstly, it assumes that an adequate theology of pastoral care can be gained from the study of psychotherapy and that redemption is to be understood by a study of sin and practice of its removal.
>
> Secondly, it is a theology of a *mental* Cross which does too little justice to deliverance through contemporary *incarnate* deeds. There is a thread of Gnosticism, of superiority of mind over body, which seems to fear deliverance by neurophysiology, psychopharmacology, and biological research.
>
> Thirdly, Dr Lake's use of descriptions of mental states in infancy and illness as if they *are* the events, and that their similarity proves a causal relation, is a misunderstanding of both science and art.
>
> Fourthly, this book is intolerant of doubt. It creates enthusiasm at the price of a proper uncertainty.

Dr Lambourne ends his review by expressing the hope that the book would, both by its successes and its failures, 'direct the Church's attention to the deplorable state of much of current practical education for the ministry', but concludes that 'Clinical Theology's concept of pastoralia is too narrow, too closely related to psychopathology, and too dogmatic'.

Clinical Theology, then, was accorded the sort of detailed critique, rigorous and analytical, which important and serious books deserve. Part of the problem was undoubtedly related to its enormous bulk, and the fact that it is really several books in one – as Professor Pond said: 'It is a System of Psychiatry, a comparative study of psychotherapy and spiritual direction, an account of psychological disorders found in clergymen and ordinands, and a volume of sermons.' He also drew attention to the charts it contained, and described them, at their face value, as 'highly misleading'. On the other hand, *Clinical Theology* amply fulfilled Bob Lambourne's hope that it would call the attention of the Church to its deplorable state of practical education for its clergy. It also performed the extremely valuable function of pointing to ways in which psychiatry and theology can be brought together. It is equally true, too, that many evangelicals were given cause to think deeply and perceptually about their faith. The Revd Roy Ackerman, for example, wrote: 'As an Evangelical I have always stood firmly on the great doctrine [justification by faith], but the fresh light revealed by Clinical Theology has brought to me greater release from bondage of sin and inhibition, deeper self-knowledge and a more exuberant faith.'[32] Others, like the Revd Robert Vokes, found that Frank Lake's treatment of scriptural passages was 'powerfully therapeutic for those deeply distressed and disturbed by emotional and personality problems', and that the book provided 'insights into the resources of the Gospel' from which one could draw 'relief as well as comfort'.[33]

To summarize, *Clinical Theology* was a challenging book which throbbed with missionary zeal. That psychiatrists and theologians, as well as clergymen and helping agencies, should have subjected it to minute scrutiny – and should question Frank Lake's claims vigorously – was only right and proper. Indeed, it was a high compliment that reviewers should have taken the book – Frank Lake's first – so seriously. What was not entirely clear, however, was for whom reviewers could recommend it. Certainly its indigestible parts could have been jettisoned so as to preserve it for students of psychiatry, psychotherapy and counselling. In time, of course, its use as a companion volume to the work of the Clinical Theology Association meant that its more idiosyncratic emphases were balanced and qualified in the light of counselling practice.

Whatever its limitations, however, *Clinical Theology* has been in continual demand since its first appearance, while Martin Yeomans's 'eminently practical abridgement' (Neville Ward in *Church Times*, 12 September 1986), has had two important effects: it has made the book more manageable, and it has introduced it to a much wider (and often new) public.

Frank Lake confessed to 'deep disappointment' at the reaction of reviewers, and in a letter[34] to the Revd Leland V. Eliason, Bethel Theology Seminary, Minnesota, claimed that they had 'uniformly failed to grasp what I was getting at', though he adds: 'And yet, in writing a book of that length, I could not expect to be understood except by those who would sit down, and spend months of hard work digging out, from a rather rich supply of ill-assorted ore, what could be regarded as gold from the pastoral point of view'. He seems to have felt particularly frustrated that many people trained in strict theological or scientific discipline 'reacted strongly against this attempt to work across the frontiers of disciplines'.

The pace of Frank Lake's life during the years up to and after the appearance of *Clinical Theology* was, to say the least, hectic. His correspondence contains many, many references to the intense pressure under which he worked, much of it owing to the nature of his own personality. On 11 December 1970, for example, we find him writing to Paul Ballard of the University College, Cardiff, to apologize for the delay in forwarding the typescript of a talk he had given at the Theology Faculty there: 'At the moment I am absolutely jammed up with other work of an urgent nature. I promise to get on with it as soon as I can.' Frequently, too, in his correspondence there are copies of letters apologizing for having missed deadlines. On 11 April 1975, the following note accompanied an article for *Renewal*: 'I am sorry that it is late. I hadn't realized the deadline.'[35]

The demands on his time were enormous, but it is difficult to escape the conclusion that he quite simply took on far too many commitments and assignments. But what is perhaps more interesting is to ask how he was able to achieve so much. A clue to this is found in a letter to the Revd John

Stacey, then Chairman of the Methodist Publishing House's editorial sub-committee:

> Oh dear. I have been getting up at 5 in the morning and writing for some weeks now with urgent material for our tutors, and your letter arrives as I am packing in the preparation for four 5-minute talks on ATV which must be in on Monday. I have done the article on The Mental Health of the Clergy in draft, but I cannot have it with you before Friday 22nd. This reminder has got right up against the final date, and I am afraid leaves me with the unfortunate necessity of disappointing you.[36]

This extract mirrors, effectively, the whirlwind life of Frank Lake throughout his years at the head of CTA. He was able to work for many, many hours at a stretch, frequently getting up early in order to cram as much as possible into the day. An obvious drawback when working in such an intense and sustained way is the lack of time to reflect upon the work, or, as above, on the written material he poured out. Had he had more time, some of his writing would have been less discursive and less verbose than it is.

On the other hand, and like many creative people, he seemed to need the stimulation of working against time. This was especially true of his sermons, as Sylvia told me: 'Frank usually wrote a sermon over the night before and up to the very last moment before leaving. He seemed to need this high tension to bring forth what he wanted to say.'

The closing years

It was inevitable, in the end, that Frank Lake's body would react against all the strains imposed on it. This occurred early in March 1978 when he suffered a minor stroke.

On 17 March 1978, he wrote a lengthy letter[37] to Basil Hobbes and colleagues from the Nottingham General Hospital. In it, after describing the physical symptoms of what he called his cerebral vascular 'accident', he pondered the possible consequences for himself, for Sylvia, and for the whole thrust of CTA's work:

> As I looked at my diary from now until August . . . I

realized that, as usual, earning for CTA has overridden every other consideration . . . I should probably be wise to change my style from the strong physical involvement in strenuous primal work, and direct others rather than do it myself. I would like, if possible, to keep our mutual options open until we see how this physical disability resolves.

The shock of realizing that I had made no provision for Sylvia, except for some life insurance, the value of which has plummeted through inflation, caused me to ask, if I have six months to live, how do I want to spend it: in earning for CT by doing conferences, or by writing books which, hopefully, will bring in some income for Sylvia in the coming years?

The letter concludes with this request for advice:

Do you now have any sense of what I should now do that would commend itself to you as wise and sensible, for CT, for me, for Sylvia, and for any wider kingdom issues that seem to you to be relevant?

Nothing was resolved immediately, but the future was very much in his thinking as he neared his sixty-fifth birthday (6 June 1979), as his letter (dated 27 March 1979) to the then Chairman of CTA, the Right Revd Richard Darby, makes clear:

I have come to the conclusion that it would be best for CTA and good for me to mark my 65th birthday or thereabouts by resigning from the Directorship of CTA, while retaining the Research Directorship if the Council agrees.[38]

He gave two reasons for this conclusion. One was the strain he felt of carrying the directorship, with its large correspondence, which, as he said, could not be fitted in without 'neglecting other available gainful work'. The second was that it would make the 'succession and ongoingness' (his words) less difficult and problematical.

In reality, no preparation was made for the future transition of the work when Frank Lake ended his directorship of CTA, and his schedule went on unabated: lecturing, advising, counselling, reading, preaching, writing. The effect of the failure to prepare for the post-Frank Lake era was all the more dramatically highlighted when he died in 1982.

But, for the time being, life carried on much as it had done since 1958. In 1981, *Tight Corners in Pastoral Counselling*, which he himself described as 'orthodox in its Christianity and ethics' and 'avant-garde in its findings about psychological origins',[39] was published.

The slowness with which the reviews appeared seemed to irritate him, and this led to a frantic burst of letter-writing (the letters being accompanied by free copies of *Tight Corners in Pastoral Counselling*) between September 1981 and the beginning of 1982, to about thirty people. A number of these letters ran into many hundreds of words, and one ran to almost 2,000 words. Replies to them were received from a small but appreciative number of people, though interestingly some of them were from high-ranking Anglicans who applauded Lake for his work and its effect on the Church of England. Here is the Bishop of Liverpool's reply: 'It was extremely kind of you to send me a copy of *Tight Corners in Pastoral Counselling*. I was most interested to look at your chapter 9 on Violence. I have frequently said that I cannot begin to understand what is happening when people mug an old lady or smash an empty house to pieces. My first reading of your chapter interests me a great deal. I will go back to it at rather more leisure sometime soon. Thank you again for your kindness – and for your ministry, whose results I thank God for in a number of circles.'[40] The Dean of St Paul's reply was briefer: 'How good to hear from you again, and thank you so much for sending me *Pastoral Counselling*. I am going to have a few days in the country and that will give me a chance to read – and also think. Of course, you are right about the need for the Church to cure itself of what disorders it can and you have helped us enormously in that direction.'[41]

In a more personal and less detached letter, a woman wrote from West Wales:

> I have just received your *Tight Corners in Pastoral Counselling* and really want to thank you. I couldn't have received it at a more appropriate time, and reading through has helped me to steer a way through a very turbulent week.
>
> Your book has been such a source of insight in its clarity

> in stating the truth of so many of man's difficulties, and I have taken from the pages what I most needed. My own adult belief has been affirmed and what I knew to be the truth you have expressed and expanded so well. I am just so glad that you have devised such a system for relating the results of your research and theology. I'm glad you didn't retire and leave the book unwritten.[42]

Eventually, of course, the reviews themselves began to appear. Sean Fagan (*The Universe*) welcomed the book's 'most satisfactory balance', applauded its integration of psychology and theology, and strongly approved of Lake's vision of how the 'Christian faith can be an integrating factor in the achievement of wholeness'. He was hesitant, however, about the 'development of this theory [the influence of pre-natal life] in certain areas'.

The *British Weekly* reviewer hailed Frank Lake as a 'pioneer in pastoral counselling' and as someone with a 'faithful shepherd's heart'. The theoretical basis to the pre-natal emphasis and experience is perceived as a 'mixture of enlightened common sense and bold imagination'.

The review carried in *The Tablet* was positive yet cautious: 'There is a great deal to admire in this book with its sound counselling advice, the fruit of many years' practical work. There is also much that is controversial. The author is convinced that many emotional disturbances and attitudes spring from pre-natal experiences in the womb and the birth experience itself . . . the case for the theory is clearly made and interested readers must make up their own minds.'

Some of the journals concentrated on the controversial aspects of *Tight Corners in Pastoral Counselling* (for example, *The Methodist Recorder*), while others, like Tony Baggot in *The Sunday Press* (Dublin) emphasized its practical implications: 'The book is deep and merits the time required to absorb its contents. It implies counselling and helping on a level not yet widely available. Throughout there are valuable and realistic insights on counselling. The short last chapter could well be required, repeated, meditative reading for all in the helping professions.'

Richard Holloway, in *Church Times*, was almost alone in choosing to comment specifically on what he saw as a minor theme of the book: Frank Lake's link with the Charismatic Renewal Movement:

> He does not offer any extended discussion of it, however. One simply discovers that he has found that renewal has an integrating and unifying effect on the lives of those influenced by it. Nevertheless, some of his most powerful criticisms are aimed at the emotional superficiality of much renewal piety. Alas, few of us have his skills or his patience, though this book may strengthen our feeble knees somewhat.

In *Health and Healing*, both *Tight Corners in Pastoral Counselling* and Frank Lake are generously praised: the book as 'a very useful guide round some of the problem corners of pastoral counselling, and a readable introduction to the work of the Clinical Theology movement now'; and Frank Lake for his 'pastoral wisdom' and for his ministry the reviewer saw as remaining 'strong, and biblical and humane'.

These reviews caused few ripples, either within CTA and its adherents or in Frank Lake's personal response to them. The same could not be said of Alastair Campbell's review in *Contact 74*. Dr Campbell describes *Tight Corners in Pastoral Counselling* as 'provocative' – for both positive and negative reasons. The bulk of Campbell's review centres on the question of 'primal experiences', about which he has grave doubts; he sees them as 'epistemologically confused and of dubious theological relevance'. He then develops his case in the following way:

> So far as epistemology is concerned, Dr Lake seems to be making statements which are impossible to substantiate (or refute), yet for which he claims the status of scientific fact. Examples of such claims are that his subjects can 'reconstruct the relationship within which they were conceived' (p. 27); can recapture the (sometimes blissful) feelings of non-attachment of the blastocyst prior to implantation in the womb (p. 15); can experience the foetus's 'delectable (or detestable) participation in the mother's bodily experience of sexual intercourse . . .' (p. 27); and, generally, can gain such a full picture of the emotions passed from mother to foetus through the umbilical cord in the first trimester

that 'before she (the mother) knows that she is pregnant, the foetus *knows* what sort of a person this is, in whom he or she is fortunate or fated to be' (p. 15, my italics). In making such assertions Dr Lake uses freely the terminology of science – evidence, hypothesis, syndrome – and he claims more than once that 'the hypothesis continues to resist attempts to nullify it' (p. 38).

But (one must ask Dr Lake) what could possibly nullify such claims? Our only access to what the foetus 'knows' (a strange word to use of the human organism prior to full cerebral development) is the experience of Dr Lake's (and other therapists') subjects. We do not need to doubt the sincerity of their belief that they have returned to a primal state in pointing out that such a belief cannot be proved. These claims are fantasy, in the strict sense of that word, since what has been reached through the imagination cannot be empirically verified in any conceivable way. In view of this I think it is significant that Dr Lake professes an interest in metaphor (Introduction, pp. 1–3). The title of the book is itself a metaphor, referring to the uterine analogue of many of our counselling dilemmas. Throughout the work the insights which come from the author's therapeutic experience carry this poetic quality. (A particularly fine example can be found on pp. 25f. under the heading 'Stitching'.) Yet, like Freud before him, Dr Lake wants to be recognized as a scientist, offering irrefutable data. I do not understand why he does not accept that – like Jung in spirit at least, if not in detail – he is treading the mystic path well beyond science.

These comments on the metaphorical character of the writing lead naturally to the second area of difficulty, the relevance of all this to theology. The book is sadly deficient in providing any clear definition of the 'pastoral counselling' to which its title refers. This lack stems from a basic unclarity both about the nature of pastoral care and the correct method to be employed in pastoral theology. Taking the last point first, we find Dr Lake describing his method as follows:

> Approaching the theological task *inductively*, my concern must be to take up 'an issue in the present situation' and

> then to analyse it in depth, to see what is at stake in it and *how Christian truth may be related to it* (p. 53, my italics).

Later on the same page he states that he and his colleagues as 'clinical theologians' must be selective in their advice, but "the whole pharmacopoeia of the Gospel as medicine is open to our use'.

Whatever this approach is, it is not 'inductive theology', as that has been defined by Hiltner, for example. Rather, it appears to be the *deductive* theology and 'pastoral medicine bag' approach which Hiltner specifically opposed (see his *Preface to Pastoral Theology*). Dr Lake seems to believe that bits of the Gospel or Christian truth can be 'applied' to specific situations, without themselves being affected. The inductive theology movement, on the contrary, wished to *reconstruct* theology from the ground up. Earlier in the same chapter we find another confusion, when the author is suggesting correspondences between peri-natal catastrophes and the Crucifixion. The heading for this section (supplied by the editor presumably) is 'A Theology of Correlation', a reference, we might suppose, to Paul Tillich. But there is no correlative theological method evident. All we have is *juxtaposition*, with no indication of the nature of the symbolic relationships, so carefully explored in Tillich's work.

Such a failure to tackle the basic issues of theological methodology leaves the religious language in the book in a state of profound disarray. At places we are offered some very orthodox-sounding references to the Cross, the Resurrection and the Holy Spirit, reflecting perhaps the Evangelicalism of the author's own religious background. Yet elsewhere there is a very different atmosphere. A notable example is the chapter entitled 'Infatuation and the Divine' (to my mind quite the most creative piece of writing in the book). Here the theology is adventurous and imaginative, and the images derived from therapy are vivid and of obvious practical application. In this chapter (and in parts of other later chapters) we do in fact have an inductive theology, a theology growing from praxis. Interestingly, there are far few references to Primal Therapy in these chapters.

We may suppose that this theological unevenness is at

least partly responsible for the book's lack of clarity about pastoral care and pastoral counselling. Are 'clinical theologians' the same, or different, from pastoral counsellors? What is the distinction, if any, between pastoral care and pastoral counselling? Who should offer pastoral care and/or pastoral counselling? How does primal therapy (or any other psychotherapeutic method) relate to pastoral work? None of these questions is adequately dealt with in these essays, yet, without clarifying them, Dr Lake has left the field open for people to misunderstand or (worse) misapply his ideas. Not only is this unfortunate from a theoretical perspective, it has considerable practical dangers. Anyone reading the description of the author's therapeutic method (pp. 26–28) can see how damaging it could be if applied without proper training or safeguards. It is a great pity that Dr Lake does not make it clear how the *non-professional* helper, not trained as a therapist, might use his ideas without emulating his methods.

This book offers us the developing thoughts of one of the most important figures in the contemporary pastoral care scene. It is obvious that Dr Lake's ability to synthesize apparently disparate bodies of knowledge makes his work essential reading for anyone interested in pastoral theology. But it will be very sad if the quasi-scientific dogmatism in the book remains a dominant influence, and we find the Clinical Theology Association in thrall to what might be called 'First Trimester Fundamentalism'. The imagery of the book is its lasting worth, and one hopes that the author will take to heart some advice he gives his readers – pay heed to the right hemisphere, trust your intuition, remain open to the alogical as a true source of insight.[43]

Ordinarily a review of this sort would be taken as a routine matter, as it is precisely the free-ranging and hard-hitting analysis expected of an academic like Alastair Campbell. Unfortunately he was not writing in normal times, because Frank Lake was seriously ill with cancer – indeed, it was clearly understood that a very limited time remained to him. Campbell, knowing that his review was critical, wondered if it ought to be published, but the editorial board of *Contact* decided to go ahead with its publication. To complicate matters further, of course Frank Lake had always found it difficult to accept constructive criticism of his work, and undoubtedly extreme physical weakness made it all the more difficult for him to accept Campbell's strictures, which were carefully and incisively argued, with a panoply of supporting details. And in fairness to Campbell, his review is a mixture of criticism and generous praise. Hindsight confirms what many people involved with the whole area of pastoral care felt at the time: that no blame can be attached to Alastair Campbell, whose review, quite rightly and properly, applied critical objective perspectives to *Tight Corners in Pastoral Counselling*.

Frank Lake, however, looked upon this review with considerable *angst* and, on 7 May 1982, he sent a lengthy letter[44] to Dr Kenneth Boyd, Editor of *Contact*, rebutting many of Campbell's points, though characteristically he begins by describing the review as 'tendentious', and claiming that it could be 'deeply humiliating'. Neither of these claims is true, nor is he correct in saying that later in the review (in the section in which Campbell deals with Lake's theological premises), the reviewer's criticism is 'flagrantly irresponsible'. I think the kindest verdict is that Frank Lake saw something very close to his heart (in many ways his life's work) as under threat, and so he responded from a 'defended position', which was made all the worse by terminal illness. His response to Campbell's review is *not* particularly well argued; the wonder is that so near to death he could write this letter at all. It is painful even now to read the correspondence between Frank Lake and Alastair Campbell, because Frank seemed unable to see that beyond Campbell's critique lay real and genuine admiration for what he had achieved in the realm of pastoral care, and that Campbell viewed him as a man of stature and importance.

The furore must not be allowed to obscure *With Respect: A Doctor's Response to a Healing Pope*, which had been published on 1 April 1982. An explanatory gloss on its contents is found in a letter, written the very next day, to Sister Jane Scott-Calder, of Stanbrook Priory, near Worcester:

> Yesterday a book of mine on John Paul 2 was published. It has got off to a good start. I hope that you will be able to read it – and that it will be good for English Catholics

in many ways. Of course, it really is for the good man himself and Archbishop Heim at the pro Nunciature has sent him a copy. Pray he may be drawn to read it.

I was saddened to read recently that many feel that he is turning away from the God-given newness of Vatican 2, trying not to see it as a great new beginning, and 'wanting to turn the clock back'. If that is the case, my book is a powerful reminder that it was not always so. Too much of him belongs with the open Church, with respect of the emotional growth, without chivvying from ecclesiastical governesses, of individual Christians, gathered for fellowship of a spirit-authenticated kind.

While all Church life was congregational and priest-focused, Rome could call a world-wide Church to heel, and local growth communities really couldn't exist. But now the Basic Christian Communities of Christians exist in every country. Their sense of spiritual authority and authenticity is too well established, and is so solidly the outworking of Vatican 2 with all that that means of renewal under God and the whole episcopate, I believe that even should John Paul pull back, which God forbid – it would be a betrayal of his younger, truer self – the true Church will continue on two levels. And it would be the Basic Christian communities – and so many of the renewed religious orders have become such – that will be the attraction points for pagans and alone can survive into the persecutions that may well come.

A little over a month later, Frank Lake was dead. The closing months of his life had undoubtedly been strenuous and emotionally testing for his immediate family and close associates. They witnessed his bodily pain which was, at times, excruciating. Writing to one of his regular correspondents, he said: 'This morning for an hour I was writhing in the ghastly pain of a sharp attack of pancreatitis. It is so easy to be "distracted" by the intensity of the pain – just howling for it to stop. But I discovered that it *is* possible to direct my attention rather to God and Christ's sharing of the pain. So what could be a faith-shattering experience becomes a faith-strengthening one.'

A contributory reason – in addition to his physical pain

and generally weak condition – was his determination to finish all the writing he wanted to do. For example, while still in hospital he wrote (on 3 March 1982) to some senior colleagues within CTA with this specific request:

> Would you be able to give time to helping me do a corporate job on the revising of the First and Second Year Seminar materials, with a view to the publication of two 'Training Manuals'? Darton, Longman and Todd are keen to have these, and it would be a good foundation to the Council's decision last year to keep CTA together after my demise, believing that through seminars and in other ways, Clinical Theology has a distinctive Christian slant on pastoral counselling and some depth insights into spirituality which haven't yet been accepted by the Churches, though individual Christians and other 'seekers' have been seized by their importance. They could be a launching-pad for new seminars – some perhaps self-sustaining with a spontaneous leadership – others more closely related to our tutorial hierarchy.[45]

Two of his books, *Tight Corners in Pastoral Counselling* (1981) and *With Respect: A Doctor's Response to a Healing Pope* (1982) had analysed the significance of maternal tranquillity or distress for the developing embryo and foetus. He felt, in his own words, that 'an additional small book was needed to set out what [was known] of the healthy and pathological psychodynamics of the first trimester (the first three months in the womb), the inter-reaction between the mother's emotional state and the needs of the foetus'.[46] This was, in fact, a manual long projected by him, indeed going back to the year 1966.

Between February and May 1982 lengthy parts of Frank Lake's days were lost in deep 'stuporous sleep' (his description), followed by four or five hours of profuse sweating, after which he would emerge, with a mind clear and organized and with a body energized, ready to write steadily for anything up to ten hours. By May the volume was completed,[47] though another volume, which would graft the pre-natal element on to the first-year seminars run by CTA was simply not possible. The completion of the manuscript (entitled *Mutual Caring*) left Frank a 'happy man' (again his words).

Nor were Frank Lake's iron-clad will and determination

diminished either. Incredibly, on the day before he was supposed to have a total gastrectomy, he left his hospital bed to give a lecture at Mapperley Hospital, one that he did not want to cancel. He returned, exhausted, for a two-pint blood transfusion. This courageous determination was apparent to the end, as Monica recalls:

> Dad was determined to complete his writing. Three nights before he died, when he had slipped into one of his semi-comatose states that were becoming increasingly more frequent, my mother was sleeping in the room with him and heard him call out: 'No, no, not yet. I haven't finished. I must get back.' Next morning when he came round again, he told me that he had felt his body lose all sensation. He had dreamt that he was floating up in the sky, looking down onto a shadowy, dark world. He could see the moon, but he was floating to a much more brilliant light. He was being drawn towards it. He suddenly remembered that he hadn't finished the writing he wanted to complete, and had to force himself to come back down. He remembered saying the words my mother heard him say.

Amidst all the tensions and strains of those difficult months there were also quieter, more soothing moments. They were, for example, a particularly healing time for Monica, who was able to provide in her house at Rushden the nursing care her mother could not possibly provide on her own:

> Dad was very grateful and for the next seven weeks until he died, I was closer to him than ever before. It was a very important time for me. For once, he really needed me. He actually listened to what I said and accepted my nursing advice with a grin. 'Yes, Nurse, anything you say.' We spent hours together, quietly listening to the church music tapes I made for him, and I was able to help him with his work – doing his photocopying and posting his letters.
>
> The telephone seemed to ring constantly with relatives, friends and colleagues anxious to know how he was. I felt he was greatly blessed to have the love and prayers of so many people. We received hundreds of letters and many beautiful flowers which filled his room with the fragrance of spring that he was missing outside. All this made me

realize how much he must have meant to so many people and I felt privileged to be his daughter. I began to understand why, when sometimes in life a person has to give his 'all' to the world, he will have nothing left to give at home. There just isn't enough of him to go round. Sacrifices have to be made. At last I could learn to come to terms with and accept that my loss of a fatherly figure, presence and support meant a gain for hundreds of others.

Also, late on a Sunday afternoon (9 May 1982) Frank had a long conversation on the telephone with Barbara Lake (Ralph's wife), whom he had taught almost fifty years earlier in the Sunday school at Aughton. They speculated together about the features of the after-life, and he expressed his hope that he could still, in some way, be involved with the family. He also wondered whether hurts and anxieties would be a part of eternal life, or whether an integral aspect of it is the rising above and triumphing over such problems. Barbara feels now that their metaphysical talk made up for a lot of wasted opportunities during all the years they had known each other. Frank also had a friendly conversation that same afternoon with Ralph, who recalls that his brother's spirit was as unquenchable as ever. Frank told him: 'I have finished my work.'

David writes:

I shall never forget that final evening before my Father died. I had spent part of the morning with him, and he had been speaking, among other things, of an experience, a day or two before, of looking down towards the earth and upwards into light. Now, he was asleep, in a deep semi-coma sleep. My sister and her husband, nurse and doctor (though not his official doctor) had retired to bed for some much-needed sleep. They were to rise to tend and turn him later in the night, with my mother. She, exhausted, was asleep on a small bed in the same room. I waited awake in the silence, praying the knots on the prayer-rope, to the balanced rhythms of heavy breathing. With both father and mother asleep, like exhausted children after a long day, I watched and listened, silently praying. That is all, all that words can say.

Eventually I slept. Next morning he passed away, my

mother on one side and I on the other. We prayed the Lord's Prayer, Psalm 23, and other things. I held his right hand, his writing hand. 'Lord Jesus Christ, Son of God, have mercy upon him.'

He was buried on Friday, 14 May 1982 at Southwell Minster. At this service the address was delivered by the Bishop of Sherwood, whose tribute was realistic, generous and perceptive:

I do not know exactly why you are here, but I am here to thank God for the life of Frank Lake. If I am to do that, I really ought to know what I am thanking God for. Frank could be the most cussed, awkward, frustrating man imaginable, and yet he was a man I loved and respected. While sitting thinking about today, I had a picture in my mind of sitting with Frank and saying, 'What shall I tell them, Frank?' and he seemed to be answering, 'Tell them what I was all about.' So I am not going to eulogize on Frank's lively faith and deep sincerity, nor on his frustrating or infuriating characteristics.

This is Frank's funeral, and he was looking forward to it because it is part of what he was all about. We have just read that passage of St Paul's about building God's Temple, and being built *into* God's Temple, and this was Frank's concern (I Cor. 3:10–23). That we should be able to come to terms with this strange business of building and being built at the same time. In this process, most of us spend our lives scurrying to and fro, never quite certain where we stand in it until we are vouchsafed a vision, an understanding which transforms us from hod-carriers dashing up and down the scaffolding with a hod full of bricks, into what St Paul calls a 'skilled Master Builder' who sees what it is all about, and sees this strange paradox of building and being built at the same time. There, upon the foundation of Jesus Christ to build and be built into an inner place. Frank's whole ministry was to help people towards this vision and understanding to the realization that 'surely you know that you are God's Temple where the spirit of God dwells'.

So much of the rubbish we carry about with us; our anxieties, our tensions, our neuroses, are so out of place in

God's Temple. Frank's mission was to help us unload the rubbish and enjoy the Temple. Frank has helped so many of us to find and to recognize our own inner place, and to appreciate the privilege and glory of being part of God's Temple. But to sit there then would be so much less than that to which our Lord calls us, and Frank the slave driver would have none of this, and in his spritely little way he would almost say, 'Ah, so you have found it. Now I will tell you how to go out and help someone else to find it.' Frank saw all the rubbish we carry about with us, not in terms of wasted energy or marred lives, but in terms of human suffering, and his whole life was dedicated to trying to understand people's suffering, and to take them out of torture into peace.

He belonged to so many people. How much it must have cost his loved ones, in strain and tension, and love and care. They have had to give so much to a world which needed Frank and many more like him. To them I would say, 'Be proud now, of your ministry, and his.' There are so many people all over the world who have reason to thank God and Frank's ministry for the quality of their lives. His loved ones bore the tensions which made this possible.

I know now why I want to thank God for the life of Frank Lake. And now he has found his own deep, inner place, and the truth that 'Everything belongs to us, yet we belong to Christ, and Christ to God.'

God rest his busy, active, vibrant soul.[48]

The Bishop of Sherwood also conducted the service of interment at Wilford Hill cemetery. Two months later a service of thanksgiving was held at All Souls', Langham Place, London (7 July 1982). The closing hymn on this occasion aptly summed up Frank Lake's dynamic, confident brand of Christianity:

The day thou gavest, Lord, is ended,
  The darkness falls at thy behest;
To thee our morning hymns ascended,
  Thy praise shall sanctify our rest.

We thank thee that thy Church unsleeping,

While earth rolls onward into light,
Through all the world her watch is keeping,
And rests not now by day or night.

As o'er each continent and island
The dawn leads on another day,
The voice of prayer is never silent,
Nor dies the strain of praise away.

The sun that bids us rest is waking
Our brethren 'neath the western sky,
And hour by hour fresh lips are making
Thy wondrous doings heard on high.

So be it, Lord; thy throne shall never,
Like earth's proud empires, pass away;
Thy Kingdom stands, and grows for ever,
Till all thy creatures own thy sway.

4

Some Personal Viewpoints

> Frank Lake was in many ways a genius, a visionary, and his work is of profound importance.[1]
>
> Like most geniuses, he had an obsessional way of working which excluded concern for others or their feelings.[2]

This book is not an official biography of Dr Frank Lake. Still less is it hagiography or, in any way, to be regarded as a monument to his theories and achievements. It is, though, important to record how other people, especially those colleagues in CTA who worked with him in whatever capacity and to what degree of closeness, viewed him. There were also many others who came only fleetingly into contact with him in a particularly significant or stressful or helpful fashion. How he impressed, affected and even altered the lives of these people is of considerable relevance to the overall thrust of this study. In this chapter, therefore, I include the recollections of a variety of men and women, both clergy and lay, specialist and non-specialist, whose lives were influenced, for better or for worse, by Frank Lake, about whom John Bunyan's words describing Mr Valiant for Truth are pertinent: 'His wounds and his scars he carried with him.' We turn now to the personal viewpoints themselves.

The Right Revd Michael Hare-Duke, Bishop of St Andrews

He first came across Frank Lake when he was beginning the ideas of his seminars. This occurred at a promotional meeting in Manchester and then within a group that met regularly in the Revd John Grindrod's vicarage in Salford. These are Michael Hare-Duke's thoughts on Frank Lake and the movement he initiated, though it must be remembered that he left

CTA many years ago, and that the association has changed since his day, as evidence in this book suggests.

Frank Lake was not an easy colleague to work with because he was always so totally convinced that he was right and endeavoured to deal with argument by inducing guilt. He found it very difficult to operate on an adult basis. He had either to be the charismatic leader holding parental authority or else he swung into the role of the child. I remember two crucial occasions, one at a big planning meeting in Scargill and another in the staff meeting when we were debating the rightness of his trip to India, when he simply burst into tears and it felt as though he was seeking to manipulate the meeting. There was about him a curious lack of personal insight. He had himself never been analysed. The staff persuaded him to go on a Grub-Tavistock group training course. He came back having enjoyed it very much because he had set himself up as a kind of counter-consultant to the staff.

As a therapist he had great gifts of intuitive diagnosis and the descriptive skills which also underlay his theoretical formulations were fascinating and evocative. He was always quick to interpret a negative transference but seldom perceived what was happening in a positive transference and was never at pains to resolve it. In his use of LSD as an abreactive agent he was a pioneer and achieved some amazing results by working with patients under its influence. When other psychiatric members of staff felt uncomfortable with it and saw it as far too powerful an agent, he tended to interptet this as their lack of ability to cope rather than a gentler model operating with the patient's needs in mind.

In setting up the work of the clinical theology association, he was unsparing of his own time and energy. He was impatient of demands for more careful training and assessment of tutors. He wanted to see the work expand and if the full-time team of four staff members, himself, Brian Lake, Tony Bashford and myself were unable to fulfil a teaching schedule which at one point had one hundred seminars dotted around England, Wales and Scotland, then he was prepared to use anyone who had been through the system. He was so convinced of the efficacy of the theory based on his charts, that he felt that anybody who simply expounded them was adequate to the task of leading a seminar. In this there was a kind of gnostic belief in the value of the formulae. He did not see that he had evolved one possible way of describing the external symptoms and the inner dynamics of mental illness and that what mattered most was the quality of relationship rather than the information imparted. He used to make annual visits to the theological colleges at Warminster where men from King's were finishing their last year. As the priest of this team I was always invited to do a follow-up visit. Early on in this arrangement I said to the students: 'You must realize that the plates from which these charts are printed were not delivered on Mount Sinai.' The principal declared to me in private that this was a remark which must be made every year, whatever else I might wish to contribute.

Part of Frank's drive and energy came from his missionary zeal. Temperamentally he was somebody who worked with a desire to convert. In clinical theology he changed his message but not his style. In the initial stages of waking up the Church in its various denominations this may well have been a very necessary method of operating. Clinical theology took off where the more reflective and tentative approach of Jungian-based groups of clergy and doctors in London never broke out of their own small circle.

The price of such enthusiasm is, however, the inability to reflect critically upon one's own basis of thought. Nor does one want to be associated with colleagues who provide that kind of approach. For this reason it was noticeable that over the years Frank changed the group who worked with him time and again.

In all this, he was essentially the 'charismatic leader'. It was interesting that, at a later stage, he became much enthused by the charismatic movement and particularly its emphasis on exorcism. Essentially he was a lonely person. He lacked friends who could laugh at him and with him. He was somebody who, at the right time, produced a very important collection of insights for Christians to work with. It was not in his nature to be part of the on-going process which he had initiated. People passed through his area of influence, gained much from it, but needed to go on to develop. For this reason the clinical theology association did not become the forum for an exchange of ideas which it might have become.[3]

Dr Roger Moss

He first met Frank Lake in 1966 when working in Derby as a Senior House Officer in paediatrics and then neurology, prior to starting his career in psychiatry the following year. Currently engaged in writing a book on primal integration, this is how he recalls the founder of the Clinical Theology Association:

> Frank acted and breathed like a doctor, even though later he absorbed and shone in many other fields of activity. He had a very deep longing that his work should be accepted by the medical profession, and I suspect he was disappointed that he did not enlist many more in the fields of exploration he opened up.
>
> He could be an intense listener, and he could convey a sense of a very special personal interest in somebody with his profound, fascinated comment, 'really'. I knew him best in the last few years of his life, and I think that then more than ever he impressed and scared people with his intensity. He was well aware that his intellect was his greatest psychological defence. Latterly, he seemed not to allow social, family and leisure pursuits to balance the fierce, burning ardour of his intellectual pursuits; everything quickly turned to the primal viewpoint.
>
> He had an unusually strong personality, so much that many felt overwhelmed and invaded by him. In the personal therapeutic work I did with him, I needed that strength to anchor my own – I felt deeply secure in his medical, Christian and fatherly experience. But if he suspected a truth about someone, which turned out to be inaccurate or premature, he purged it relentlessly and sometimes destructively.
>
> Having said that, he won the affection of many who allowed themselves to get close to him by his unusual capacity for love. His love undoubtedly made his insights

and discernment therapeutic when they might have been destructive.

Frank classified his personality, in the psychodynamic sense, as schizoid, and this must be a major reason why he devoted so much thought and space to the subject in *Clinical Theology*. He undoubtedly experienced a considerable measure of healing of his personality in the course of his lifetime, but both he and those around him recognized areas in his character which never fully aspired to the wholeness he strove to find in so many others.

His mind moved quickly, sometimes rather abstrusely, though by no means always oppressively. He could call on an immense knowledge, and increasingly used his right hemisphere to call on images and colouring in his talk and thinking. To a considerable extent, conversation tended to go in the direction he steered it. There was perhaps a sense that everyone he encountered was a kind of subject in his laboratory of life: this could be experienced as intense personal interest or being passively manipulated, depending on how you chose to take him. He stimulated many, angered not a few, but I guess he left most who worked with him wondering how they could keep it up.

As a psychotherapist, he became unusually percipient, skilful and successful. As a psychiatrist, he was eccentric and individualistic, and quite unlike the mainstream of British psychiatrists. Very few psychiatrists (as contrasted with psychoanalysts or psychotherapists) in Britain have remained anything like as psychodynamic as Frank Lake.

As a scientist, he came under fire because he chose not to think in the accepted fashion. Actually, I think he strove harder than most to cope within the framework of basic scientific principles. For the most part, however, he did not present his results in the accepted journals or with impressive statistics, and although most psychiatrists would agree that these are not the only measures of a behavioural scientist's professionalism, they are the common yardstick of acceptability. Moreover, the way he communicated his findings was a good deal too abstruse and verbose, and probably too laden with images for those used to the parsimonious and dehumanized communications of science. Overall he was very competent in the areas he concentrated upon. Simply because his effectiveness was not measured in conventional terms, should not detract from the help he gave very many people.

The Revd Tom Smail

He got to know Frank Lake through his work as General Secretary and then as Director of the Fountain Trust (1972–9). He was responsible for publishing Frank's articles in *Renewal* magazine, and both he and his daughter consulted Frank professionally. His courteous view is representative of many other charismatic renewal leaders in the 1970s.

I liked him very much for his warmth and concern and profited greatly by his wise advice. I did, however, become increasingly concerned by his ever-growing obsession with primal therapy which, in his magazine articles, was presented almost as a universal panacea and something like another gospel, a new key to human salvation. It was for this reason that I asked round other qualified psychiatrists to find that it was in fact a very controversial and speculative area and I found an excuse to bring the bimonthly articles to an end.

I can remember when, together with a number of other leaders in the Anglican renewal movement, I met Frank in London to convey to him our concern about all this and to beg him to not to go on suggesting that the text 'You must be born again' in John 3 could be validly exegeted as meaning, 'You must relive your birth experience'. We cannot have convinced him because he went on doing it.

That made me ask whether the association was much more clinical than it was theological and just how much theological as distinct from psychological criteria operated in Frank's later presentations of it, where the patient was seen almost exclusively as innocent victim and not as the one who made sinful reactions to the wrongs done to him in or out of the womb.

When I became vice-Principal of St John's, Nottingham, where Frank taught, I found that students tended either to swallow all his theories whole or to react violently against them. It was very rare to find a reasonable and considered response to him. Emotional reactions were much more common.

I said all this to Frank himself many times and, although we did not agree about it, we never ceased to like and respect each other.

Louis Marteau, The Dympna Centre

He was on CTA's Council for a number of years, though never a member, and his grateful recollection dates from the early days when Frank Lake was just getting started:

> My abiding memory is that every time I met Frank he was in the throes of new discovery. His mind was bursting with his latest development of theory or method in the process of therapy. I was influenced by many of these, those which resonated within me. However, I really left the Council at the time of his development into re-birthing which I found too much to take.
>
> I think Frank had only one real problem – he was too humble. He was restless in his search for the ultimate answer and travelled through many avenues in its search. He was ready to try out any method which seemed to go deeper into the problem and tease out its solution. However, I feel that Frank was too humble to realize that the real reason why each of these methods worked was 'Frank'. I have always thought that if Frank had been convinced that skipping for ten minutes a day was the answer, it would have worked for him.
>
> Frank was never able to accept that it was not so much the method that he was giving but himself. His humility drove him to think that it was all due to the theory or method which he was using.
>
> From this you may gather that I have reservations about many of the theories and even more about their possible success when undertaken by those who are 'less than Frank'.
>
> At the same time I have the utmost regard for Frank as one who was prepared to spend himself in pushing forward the boundaries of knowledge and understanding. I hope that he has left with us that restlessness of spirit and mind

which is never content with what we are doing at the present and is ever aware of how little we really understand about the complexity of the human state.

For this reason I would hope that CTA enshrines his spirit rather than creating a museum of his theories.

You may quote any part of the above as long as in its final form it brings out the gratitude I feel at having known Frank himself.

The Revd Michael Jacobs, University of Leicester

He edited *Tight Corners in Pastoral Counselling* for publication. He also saw Frank Lake once a year at an editorial board meeting of the journal *Contact*:

> After the editorial board meeting of *Contact* I would journey home on the train with him. At the meetings themselves he was always full of ideas, but tended to get carried away in talking about them rather than being involved in the main business of planning future issues of our journal. Hence he was fascinating to talk with in such a group, but it was a time-consuming exercise, and did not make it easy for the chairperson. I also found on my journey home with him that he would talk all the way. I rarely said much, but when I tried to point out alternative ways of interpreting some of the phenomena he was mentioning, I do not think he really heard me. He used to thank me courteously at the end of the journey for listening to him, as though he needed to talk, but as though it was difficult for him to hear others' views with any seriousness.
>
> His special gift was vast reading and absorption of material. His failing was the wish to integrate everything he read as soon as he could, without really digesting it, or looking for alternative explanations. His other failing was that he was too verbose.
>
> The Clinical Theology Association started many clergy and laity off in the direction of looking at psychodynamic ideas, and counselling skills. This cannot be underestimated as being a most effective start for this whole area of work. But it began to go wrong, I felt, with the rapid undigested introduction of the newer therapeutic ideas, and

it has, I think, had to get back to basics in order to survive Frank's death.

While I am happy to accept that there are influences, of which we yet know little, in the womb, I have always entertained the most profound doubts that these can be reached in weekend workshops, in the way Frank felt. I think he went for more complicated explanations when he could have looked for simpler ones, for the effect on people on the weekend workshops. Why go for this womb explanation, when I think some of it was sexual? I remember one observer of such a weekend saying that she had heard people say, 'I must have another primal', as though it was an orgasm.

Mrs Mary Maslen, Nottingham

She worked with Frank Lake in a secretarial capacity for fifteen years, and was the typist who coped with the vast manuscript that became eventually *Clinical Theology*. Her memories go back to the early 1960s when, with her family, she went to live in Nottingham Park, about two hundred yards from Frank's home. She clearly remembers him with much affection, though implicit in her version is the fact that he made extensive, even exorbitant, demands on other people:

> We had joined forces with my elderly parents and for many hours I was tied to the house. At this time Frank Lake was in need of some secretarial help and my name was given to him by one of the local rectors (Canon A. Inglis).
>
> At first it was just letters and medical reports, but soon the work grew considerably. He caused havoc, in the nicest possible way of course, with my domestic timetable, as I tried not to work in the evenings when my husband was at home. He was a man who seemed to have ten days in every week, and twice as many hours in his working day, and was surprised when other folk could not match him. But his way of asking and his appreciation of work done was such that it was impossible to refuse him.
>
> I have known him telephone saying he could be round within ten minutes to bring a letter he wanted typing, and would really like it to go off in the afternoon post. The ten

minutes stretched to two hours or more, and the letter (earlier described by him as 'little') would cover many typewritten sheets.

Typing *Clinical Theology* was a vast undertaking, and I now wonder how I managed to get through all those pages. My husband and I did the index, at a time when it all had to be done the hard way, no computers or word processors then, and we could have done with two more dining tables to take all the sheets of paper.

I stopped working for him in 1972 or thereabouts, but he always sent a Christmas card, usually with a note inside. He helped us after the death of my parents within two weeks of each other, and I came to look on him as a friend more than just an employer.

The Revd David Bick, Gloucester

He never worked closely with Frank Lake, though he attended, from time to time, seminars, conferences, primal therapy and growth groups. In the early 1970s he became an assistant tutor with CTA, and in the late 1970s was a tutor, in his own right, for the Gloucester and South Wales area. His submission concentrates on Frank Lake's personality and dedication to the work of CTA:

> He was an intense and single-minded man who would give his whole self to whatever he felt was the important issue for him at any one time and pursue it with vigour, totally ignoring everything else. It was this quality which enabled him to set up CTA, but the negative side of this was the hurt and offence he caused to any who worked very closely with him. I sensed this very early on. I joined his seminars and received much help, but after a few years I distanced myself from close relationship with him.
>
> During the late 1970s and early 1980s I frequently spent time at St John's College, Nottingham, doing some of my own research. Frank Lake was lecturing there at the time so I frequently met him, often at lunch. At these meetings he often inquired most enthusiastically how I was and especially what work I was doing. It interested me that work was the only way one could get into a deep conver-

sation with him, and such conversations were usually long and demanding. On one occasion I told him of some of the work I was doing for Bristol University Extra-Mural Department which was on CTA lines. This work had a sociological basis and one course was on small group leadership.[4] He asked me to let him have a copy of my rough notes, which I did, fully expecting to see something of them appear in his own work, but it never did. This must have been about 1979. I think it was because this area of work had no meaning for him. He certainly did not know how to lead a group because he was primarily a one-to-one person. However, he was a past master at using other people's work and bringing it together in his own particular way.

Mrs Evelyn Halliday, Lancashire

Her brief recollection of Frank Lake pinpoints someone she describes as a 'very caring man':

> In the 1950s I was given authority by the Bishop of Ripon, the Right Revd George Chase, to administer the Laying on of Hands within the diocese. When he wrote giving his authority he said he was taking steps to get together a group of clergy and doctors to advise him on the ministry of spiritual healing. It was because the Bishop started this group that Dr Frank Lake became involved with what we called the 'Fellowship of Prayer and Healing'. The fellowship was an ecumenical group and in addition to meetings for prayer we arranged more than one series of public meetings on related subjects.
>
> Dr Lake was the first speaker at a series on 'Anxiety', and he also gave generously of his time to help and to train members of the groups.
>
> On a personal note, Dr Lake was always accessible and willing to help us. Reading between the lines of a letter I wrote him, he gave me a verse to cling on to which I cherish to this day: 1 John 3:2;[5] and on another occasion he answered my appeal for advice to give a young mother who thought God was asking her to sacrifice her baby, by

making an appointment with her and dealing with it himself.

The Revd James Cotter

He knew Frank Lake slightly in a personal capacity through friendship with Dr David Lake. He recalls a deeply compassionate man who wished to heal others and, as he said in a letter to me, 'was willing to pay the price of that himself, not least in the quality of his presence':

> I remember being mesmerized by Frank Lake as a preacher: I was an undergraduate at Cambridge when I first heard him, and he preached for nearly an hour, and you could have heard the proverbial pin drop throughout. I use the word 'mesmerize' deliberately, for I think you did have to shake yourself awake when you listened to him, and take care that you did not abdicate your critical faculties. Nevertheless, I was greatly helped at the time by his pioneering work on the boundary of theology and psychology: what he was saying and writing, together with the addresses of Paul Tillich and Harry Williams, just about kept me a Christian.
>
> Later I became more wary of his powerful and powerfully communicated convictions, in that he did seem to me to be often in the grip of the latest theory. I suspect it was the combination within him of pioneer and fundamentalist. I clearly remember one public occasion, I think in the mid-1970s and at a meeting of the association for Pastoral Care and Counselling, when it seemed to me that he was categorizing all same-sex relationships as compulsive, and he did affirm this on questioning.
>
> I think a verbal facility ran away with him, not least in the length of the tome. Certainly his words often helped, but I feel sure they hid something more problematic in his make-up connected with the emotional and relational.

The Revd Derek Atkinson

He was part of CTA's seminars in Canterbury in the early 1960s.

We had both Frank and Brian Lake, and other of the 'founders', coming to the seminars in those days. We were not expecting Frank on the day he first appeared. I have forgotten who the regular tutor was (we met for a whole day once a month), but we were quite a 'mixed' group – a few clergy, a 'religious' sister, a hospital almoner, a Samaritan. We gathered in a church hall, and were joined by a slightly dishevelled little man in a polo-necked pullover. None of us knew who he was. The hospital almoner glared at him. 'Who are you' she demanded fiercely. 'Um . . ., I'm Frank Lake,' he said. And he proceeded through the day to delight us by explaining very charmingly just what those intriguing but difficult-to-understand charts were all about.

For one flash of enlightenment that day I shall be for ever grateful. It was a personal reminiscence from Frank that when he was getting tired he would sometimes become aware of 'the little frightened child within'. The phrase immediately 'rang bells' for me and provided at once an explanation, and the comforting thought that it was not only me, but great ones like Frank, who still suffered 'the little frightened child within'.

And, of course, the seminars themselves completely changed the course of my life and thinking.

Canon J. E. Swaby

His recollections of Frank Lake stretch from the late 1940s right through to the 1960s.

I first met Frank Lake when he was attached to CMS but had been allowed leave to follow the line of study which led to the foundation of Clinical Theology. I was then Vicar of Scunthorpe. It was probably in the late 1940s when he came with a CMS deputation. I don't remember anything about his sermon in Scunthorpe Parish Church, but I was deeply impressed by the way he was up early in the morning to find much time for his personal prayers. He stayed with me. On the Sunday evening he gripped a meeting of young people by his insistence on self-surrender. He was quite uncompromising. Later that day the discussions I had with him quite altered the way I looked at problems over the ministry in the United Church of India.

In the early 1950s he preached at the Good Friday evening service (at my invitation) convened by the churches of the borough of Scunthorpe. As often happened, he spoke for a long time, but he held a very large audience. Again his theme was surrender and he quoted the Methodist Covenant service to great effect. When the service was over a group of people gathered round the platform wanting to discuss things with Frank. I noticed a Conservative councillor, who was a prominent businessman and rarely attended church. I noticed also a Socialist councillor, who had imbibed the Marxist philosophy and with whom I had debated. Frank was certainly making us all think.

In the 1960s I met Frank again. A clinical theology group was being started in Scunthorpe to which I had returned in 1960. A short time afterwards I wrote asking if he could call to see me about someone who was deeply troubled. He broke a journey back to Nottingham, coming quite a distance out of his way to help. That he was able to do.

I am glad to have known him, even if only briefly. He was perhaps too much given to quoting from what he read, *but he really had a message*. Personally I am grateful for the quality of his life and for the fact that he, whom I would regard as an Evangelical, added width and depth to my Catholic outlook.

Judith Weston

Her contacts with Frank Lake took place between the years 1970 and 1974. Initially she heard him speak at an international Fountain Trust Conference at Westminster, entitled 'Joy in the City'. Shortly afterwards she went to Lingdale to a small group conference called 'The Charismatic Prayer Group and the Healing of Forgotten Pain'.

At this conference Frank's sensitivity to the Holy Spirit's activity in the group as we 'worked together' was most apparent, as was his own deep trust in God his Father – shown by the simplicity of his prayers. His praying for guidance seemed somehow to flow quietly in amongst his listening and speaking to the one who was receiving help.

It was while someone else in the group was 're-birthing' that the Lord began to release deep and hidden grief in me. Up to that time I had no awareness of my own need for inner healing at all. Before I left that session Frank had been used as a channel of God's love which was the beginning of a process of healing and growing inner freedom for me. Part of that time was a 're-birthing' experience.

The 'lack' for me after that session was explicit prayer into the situation of 'loss' that I was experiencing. Frank himself was ministering the love and acceptance of Christ in a very tangible way.

After this conference I did the Clinical Theology seminars in Leeds but they were not led by Frank and although I found them informative and helpful, there was no prayer in the group at any time. The lack of prayer made a great difference to the 'feel' of the teaching and the effectiveness of the group work. I recognized then that Frank's own deep spirituality was responsible for the whole ethos of the work done at the Nottingham centre.

I was also a participant at one of the Clinical Theology annual conferences at Nottingham University. There we had 'growth groups' and I was glad to be in a group led by Frank Lake himself. There was also in the same group a psychiatrist whom I had met at another retreat, and I remember being very impressed by Frank's willingness to admit his own lack of experience in the field of deliverance ministry, and his readiness to learn from someone who had some experience. After that conference I was invited to attend several short 'group' conferences at Lingdale as an assistant. Frank was again very willing to share his work and to encourage others to participate in the counselling so that they learnt by 'doing'. My experiences and contact led me to appreciate Frank's friendship and to realize that he too had known and knew deep sadness in his own life experience. He was a man who cared about others, intellectually very clever, single-minded and often misunderstood.

Mrs Patrick Keeley

Her recollections are mainly to do with primal therapy, at a time of quite considerable personal difficulties.

> In the space of eight months I suddenly lost an adopted baby, a close friend from cancer, a husband to another woman, a much loved father and the mother I knew to pre-senile dementia.
>
> Floundering in a sea of grief, madness and depression, I put in for a week on Primal Therapy and met Frank Lake. My two children were six and ten and their losses too reverberated on their primal pain. A context was discussed for our strange behaviour and Frank enabled me to help them and recognize what their behaviour was externalizing. Chemically he helped me to discover the nut's and bolts of my madness, and to discover in the group the greatest discovery I made during that week-course on Primal Therapy – that I was myself and that it was okay. The months that followed were very hard as my mind felt like shifting sand. The place of prayer was helpful, but the befriending and caring given by Frank to me and my children affirmed us and helped us to trust in love again. I had his personal telephone number and that enabled me to keep my head above water. A year later when I moved to Wales, 250 miles away, he came to our farewell pot-luck supper. He was concerned that I was moving away from support.
>
> The telephone line reached him on a number of occasions when he made sense of my madnesses, by placing them in the context of what was happening.
>
> My daughter is now twenty, and at medical school – she has a strong sense of identity. She worked with me at ten and primalled. My younger daughter is sixteen now, and did a lot of primal work in play form. She is well motivated and adjusted. What Clinical Theology gave me was a skill, and Frank along with the others gave me the confidence to visit the depths and rise again. Having a skill acquired by visiting the depths, with Frank on the other end of the telephone, has given me a lot of confidence to be more fully myself and to live.

The Revd Dick Reeve, MB, ChB, MRCGP

In 1974, Dr Reeve and his family left a general medical practice in Norfolk, and he spent nine months working with Frank at Lingdale. He also attended the course for the 'Diploma in Pastoral Studies' at St John's College. He recalls his experiences with affectionate gratitude:

> On a personal level, the acceptance by Frank and Sylvia of my wife, Moira, and I into the daily workings of Lingdale, and into the growth group for counsellors, had far-reaching repercussions in our development and relationship. I can only describe my own experience as 'release' – an increased freedom in relationships, and a loss of the fear of emotion being released in dealing with patients. Moira remembers that following our time at Lingdale I was no longer embarrassed in holding her hand in public! Moira was opened up considerably in the groups, and says she was given a glimpse of the wonder of healing and wholeness that is there for those willing to work through their pains and insecurities with an accepting group. The healing process was started in us by the love and acceptance we received from Frank and Sylvia at Lingdale.
>
> One of my memories of that time is of Frank giving three lectures to the students and their wives at St John's. After this, many of the couples realized the weaknesses and insecurities in their own relationships. Frank directed the couples to Moira and me, and two groups were formed in which we worked with them on their problems.
>
> We left Nottingham in 1975 to start a New Town practice in Runcorn, and will always be profoundly grateful to Frank and Sylvia for the opportunity of sharing the Clinical Theology experience, which helped to equip us for coping with all the personal problems we met in the New Town, and later in parish work.

Dr Brian Lake, FRCPsych

Last, but certainly not least, Dr Brian Lake was intimately involved in the work of CTA between 1961 and 1969. His reflections are fascinating, not only because they go back to the earliest, visionary days of the association, but because they are so wide-ranging; also, because they show, with piercing clarity, that CTA's success was not just due to Frank's unquenchable zeal but, additionally, to the sterling work of many, many other people too. Though twenty years have elapsed since Brian Lake left the association, he remains convinced of the value of the work he was able to execute in conjunction with his brother:

> I shared an ideal with my brother Frank from the mid-embryonic stage of the development of CTA in 1961. Its broad outline was his creation but it was one I identified and recreated as my own. At a practical level it was concerned with the development of two schemes. One was the development of psychotherapeutic centres in Britain in which people could explore and if necessary look for help in resolving their psychological and religious problems. The second was educational. It involved sharing with clergy and interested lay members some of the relevant psychological understanding we had learnt of the nature of man, of his psychological disorders and their treatment and exploring its relevance for Christian theology and particularly for the practice of pastoral care. Our presupposition, as I understood it, was that each system of thought and practice could profit from the other and lead to a more creative and usable interpretation of our own and, we hoped, others' experience and behaviour.
>
> The presupposition had clearly been in the mind of others and the planning and execution of this vision over the next few years became the work of a small group of interested people, who were committed to this venture, and became either members of staff, members of council, tutors and members of the courses or the contributing members of the Clinical Theology Association.
>
> The details of the early development and working out of these plans have already filled a plethora of pages in many pamphlets, booklets, books and reviews. Most have been written by Frank whose ability, fluency, and desire to communicate was certainly much more evident than that of other key members on the staff of the Association. I doubt whether our diminished need to explain what we were about would have reduced Frank's desire to communicate

his own wealth of ideas but it does make us responsible for the general perception that the CTA was Frank and that other members of the team were merely ghosts in the machine! And having been in part responsible for this misleading perception it is time to remedy it.

I doubt that the work of CTA would have seen the light of day for some years if it had not been for Frank's vision and his powerful drive to fulfil it, and for the vision and deep commitment of the staff to his and their own understanding of its guiding purposes.

Most of those who became members of the training group in the earlier days came in regular contact with Frank, Tony Bashford and myself as psychiatrists, Maurice Clark and a year or two later Michael Hare-Duke as pastoral director, Peter Caporn as warden of the Centre, Isobel Debney our first secretary and Edna Clark our first financial secretary. At a later stage John Gravelle and Brian Hawker were to serve as pastoral directors.

In those days the three psychiatrists and Michael spent two or three weeks treating or counselling our respective patients or clients, dealing with organization issues, giving training courses to tutors, and speaking about the work of the organization. The following week or part of it we spent on visits to training groups in different parts of the country. These were shared out equally among the four of us and we interchanged so that throughout the year each group had a range of tutors. In this way, whilst keeping to the curriculum, we hoped to modify each other's emphases and idiosyncrasies.

The three-hour session consisted of two one and a half hour periods in which two separate but related subjects were presented and then discussed with the introduction of relevant pastoral issues. There was a half-time break for tea. I notice from an old 1963 diary that in February I took five separate groups in London, some in different parts, and five other groups respectively in Eastbourne, Croydon, Leatherhead and Guildford. Two weeks later I was travelling to groups in Manchester, Burnley and Keighley, later to Stockport, Crewe, Chester, Liverpool, Birmingham and Coventry and at the end of May to Cambridge, Ipswich, Chelmsford and St Albans. In June it was to Durham,

Newcastle, Stockton-on-Tees, then Middlesbrough and home to Nottingham. Between October and December I visited each of them once again. In the interim periods they would have seen Frank, Tony or Michael. The next year would involve visiting groups in different parts of England, Wales, Scotland or Northern Ireland.

The work and the pace was demanding. New groups were springing up every year and more tutors had to be selected and trained at the Centre to meet these requirements. These too were built into our timetable. In later years each group had its own local tutor and had supplementary visits from the Lingdale staff. The finances of each separate group and of tutors training at the Centre and the organization of smaller and larger conferences involved a lot of work for all of us and particularly for the secretarial and finance staff. As the work grew, Frank was increasingly called to speak, or attend other conferences in Britain or abroad and the resulting volume was carried by the rest of us, and as deputy director for some years many of the problems came to me. But we survived and worked well together.

All of this work had its intensely interesting, enjoyable and even exhilarating side. For although in the early 1960s the number of clergy and church workers in Britain who had any training in modern forms of pastoral counselling were minuscule there was clearly an immense desire for it. And despite the scepticism of most of the medical and psychiatric profession there were some who had been deeply influenced by the earlier work of Freud, Jung and Adler and the later writings of Suttie, Fairbairn, Guntrip, Bowlby, Dicks, Balint and Winnicott. New books such as Laing's *The Divided Self* and Guntrip's *Personality Structure and Human Interaction*, both published in 1961, were challenging the established wisdom. The Americans who already had university and college degree courses in clinical pastoral care were also generous in their response to our request to draw on their knowledge and expertise. Professors of clinical pastoral care came over to give short courses to the tutors and to speak at the yearly CT university conferences we initiated. They taught and recommended a variety of shorter and longer term counselling processes and psychotherapies and advised us on training. So in a number of areas we were psychotherapeutically well in advance of other services both in the breadth of our theoretical training, and for example in the use of a number of modern techniques of role play. Our standard of supervision of the members' counselling was limited but at least it existed and was generally valued. In 1966 I wrote and published a review and assessment of clinical theology training based on the response to questionnaires of members of the groups who had just completed their second year of training. In 1964, 230 members responded out of an estimated 312 members. In 1965 201 members responded out of an estimated 337 members. The questionnaire was constructed with the help of Leslie Harman, a social scientist who also analysed it, and discounting for subjectivity and halo effects we found the results very encouraging.

However, as time went on the problems and divergencies of view between Frank and any two or more of the team which had initially seemed resolvable became more entrenched. There were long and occasionally heated exchanges at council meetings. They centred around some of the therapeutic approaches that were being used at the centre and discussed in the seminars; the high rate of growth of the seminars and the effect on the level of qualification of tutors; and the perpetual difficulties we experienced in keeping to our budget and getting financial support.

I was particularly aware of the growing unease of some sympathetic psychiatrists and psychotherapists and of the uncertainties being expressed by the church hierarchy over Frank's increasing interest in and propagation of the concepts of birth and prenatal traumata. He felt passionately about what he believed to be its significance. As the subject and the treatment associated with it was at this stage speculative and at a prenatal level of development I thought that whatever its merits, its introduction into a course for clinical pastoral care was ill advised. I wholeheartedly supported many of the essential features of the training scheme and particularly Frank's choice of object relations theory as the theoretical and clinical base for the course and I felt that the increasing irruption into his writing and lecturing of a theory and therapy which at that stage could muster little empirical support, was beginning to and would continue to undermine our credibility. But this was just a symptom of a deeper malaise. As members of a team we seemed less able than ever, and there was never much success, to influence Frank over some important issues of present and future policy. He held resolutely to views which to him seemed the most rational and caring. Others of us either individually or together would argue what we felt to be a stronger case, but were rarely able to influence his determination to proceed along lines that he was convinced were right. What had started with a joint vision and as a co-operative venture was becoming steadily more monocular and idiosyncratic in its expression. It was agreed in principle to call in a management consultant from the Grubb Institute but for a variety of reasons it did not happen. It was distressing, and some of us felt that we could do nothing to change it.

In 1969 after considerable discussion I decided that there was no possibility of a genuine compromise. It was either collusion or resignation and I chose the latter. Michael Hare-Duke resigned from the staff a month or so before I did and left to become Bishop of St Andrews. Tony Bashford was soon to follow. Others continued the work until Frank's death. I don't think Frank or any of us lost the vision we started with. And despite the disagreements and eventual separation I thought and still think that we made some striking achievements together.

A comment

The views reflected above have an impressive range: from Anglican through Methodist to the Evangelical, on the one hand, from Catholic to Charismatic, on the other hand. Their time-span too is significant: from the formative days of the Clinical Theology Association right through to the 1980s. While the full implications of Frank Lake's career (in all its main aspects) will be assessed in a later chapter headed 'In Retrospect', it is only right and appropriate to draw some *initial* conclusions about the effect of his life, teaching, counselling and therapy on other people.

Clearly, Frank Lake was a man of *abundant energy* who could work full tilt for many, many hours, which, inevitably, was exhausting for those whose metabolic rate required more rest and relaxation than he seemed to need. This frenetic activity was off-putting to many of those who came into contact with him.

Equally clearly, he was not an easy man to work with or for. In fact, several people wrote to me, when they knew I was preparing this book, to say that it was almost impossible to work with him, and, in such circumstances, they either accepted it as part of the price to be paid for working with a highly gifted man, or just left and went their own way. This was regrettable, for it denied CTA the valuable insights and perspectives of a number of able, well-intentioned and distinctly motivated people. But perhaps few other options existed when working under the guidance of a man as demanding and as ruthless as Frank Lake; for ruthless he had to be – and absolutely single-minded – in setting up something like CTA.

A third stress in these viewpoints which gives unity to the picture of the man and his movement is that he was prepared to give of his time and abilities in a sacrificial manner, frequently driving miles out of his way in order to help someone going through a traumatic experience. This also applied to the hours he would patiently spend in counselling and therapy.

Inevitably, too, not all the viewpoints given above cohere; many indeed are divergent, but this is only to be expected in assessment of someone who was so dynamic and charismatic a figure, whose movement aroused such strong reactions in general, whose work on primal integration brought forth ridicule, even scorn, from some; while advice to people undergoing stressful circumstances is highly personal and subjective, being successful with some people, and totally failing with others.

Many people were greatly helped by Frank Lake, and when this happened they felt not only enormously grateful to him, but also showed a very real sense of personal loyalty to him. One example of this only needs to be cited to substantiate the point: 'Frank Lake was a very great help to me personally, as to many, many others who found themselves in the 1960s with incomprehensible psychological problems and personality difficulties which seemed for a long time to be at variance with their professed Christian faith. I did not know him closely, as many did; but to me he was always totally generous and kind: a sort of surrogate father-figure who taught me more than any other man I know, for which I remain everlastingly grateful.'

Against this powerful testimony, there were those who did not find his ministrations so beneficial. One person wrote describing how she had been suffering from persistent (though mild) depression, and was advised that 'half an hour with Frank Lake' would sort her out. This is what actually happened:

> Two hours with Frank Lake left me feeling *shell-shocked* for about a week and then more and more depressed until I was able to get help from Dr Brian Lake, who I must say worked wonders for me. I think Frank was misled about the depths of my problem. I also think that he made a bad professional judgement in probing so deeply when there was no possibility at the time of following the session up with any further help.

The latter half of this statement highlights one of the most persistent and fundamental problems associated with CTA and Frank's therapeutic work: the lack of an adequate follow-up system. That he had a very deep insight into the way a human being grows and develops is indisputable. That his understanding of the doctrine of the cross as it applies to individual suffering, was deep, is also indisputable. That he carried people along with him on a tide of enthusiasm is also beyond question. Why, then, did he not provide for any continuation of the vital process he had set in motion? Perhaps the most basic explanation has to do with his own personality: as a virtuoso performer, he wanted to be all things to those who approached him for help. With such people he did not merely expose their pain, he was prepared to stay with them *in* it, which, unfortunately, made them feel all the more bereft on returning to home situations where such compassionate understanding and attention was simply not available to them. This lack of integration between what occurred in the counselling room with Frank himself and what happened subsequently often left people in a very bad state for long months (and, in the most extreme cases, years) afterwards. A second explanation is a matter of logistics, but is consistent with *his* view that he was CTA: namely, the lack of decentralization in his lifetime in the organization of CTA. Like a juggler he had to keep all the balls in the air himself.

But, warts and all, working for Frank Lake was never dull. Frustrating maybe, extremely annoying at times, yes, but not dull. As the Revd Ronald File told me: 'It was both an exciting and frustrating experience working for Frank. He was always bubbling over with new insights and new material. My memory of tutors' conferences over the year was of Frank always having something new to introduce to the tutors. The frustration arose out of his habit of doing things without consultation and sometimes without thought of the consequences for other people.'

Autocratic and a law unto himself, he needed people with administrative gifts to translate his fertile ideas into practicality. Another less polite way of putting all this is that he had a large vision but that others were often left to clear up the debris scattered in his wake. Whether he was aware of this chaos or blithely regarded it as only right, is not entirely clear to me, but I do know that his responses often surprised and appalled his colleagues and those working for him. One of his administrative staff at Lingdale recounted to me the shock she felt on coming across several cartons of unanswered mail in a cupboard. 'Because people write to me doesn't mean that I have to answer' was Frank's airy and unsympathetic reply. This seems to be in marked contrast to his ability to make people feel special and understood when talking to them. The tragedy for him, and perhaps for many of those influenced by him, was that he often aroused expectations that he could not fulfil.

An *enigmatic* man, therefore, whose darker sides could be destructive, as his own family were only too aware. Sylvia Lake told me: 'Frank was a man of paradoxes, and it seemed that the closer one got to him, the greater was the possibility of hurt, and the negative destructive force felt more keenly. Living out love for him through a lifetime was hard work.'

5

Listening and Helping – a Guide to Frank Lake's Seminal Ideas

Serving others

> Atticus stood up and walked to the end of the porch. When he completed his examination of the wistaria vine he strolled back to me.
>
> 'First of all,' he said, 'if you can learn a simple trick, Scout, you'll get along a lot better with all kinds of folks. *You never really understand a person until you consider things from his point of view* –'
>
> 'Sir?'
>
> '*– until you climb into his skin and walk around in it.*'[1]

Frank Lake's life was one of dedicated service to others: first as a missionary in India, then as a psychiatrist. His driving motivation was to understand people's afflictions and suffering, and by taking them out of the torture of wasted lives, damaged emotions, frustrated ambitions and debilitating habits, to lead them to a position of well-being, peace and fulfilment. In other words, to a place of harmony internally, to wholeness psychologically and spiritually.

He pursued this aim with an apparently inexhaustible zeal, and at great cost to himself and his family. It is no exaggeration or a loose use of words to say that the work of the Clinical Theology Association consumed his life for almost a quarter of a century.

Three introductory quotations, two from *Clinical Theology* (1966) and one from *With Respect* (1982), pinpoint this fundamental driving force in clear, unequivocal terms. The first is part of a tribute Frank paid to Dr Tony Bashford and to his brother, Dr Brian Lake:

> They have kept me more faithful than I alone could have

> been to the tensions inherent in a clinical theology, that it is substantively theology, putting faith, ultimately, not in human wisdom but in the love and power of God, yet, meticulously observant of the sound practice of psychiatry and psychotherapy, with the restraints upon religious (or anti-religious) influencing which are properly implicit in them.[2]

The second defines the role of the clinical theologian:

> Like all caseworkers and professional men whose work is to understand human beings in the extremities of stress, he depends on the behavioural and psychological insights which are common to us all. He will learn in the same way to subject his manner of interviewing to the supervision of more experienced workers. He will learn how to bear with the pain of his own personality at its most unreliable moments, irrational resistances, and compulsive needs to remove the client to a less threatening distance. He goes through this discipline so that he can remain loving and open to all sufferers, however disturbed or disturbing they may be. Finally, and only here does he diverge from the others, he has learnt how to communicate this or that out of his own specific or general theological and pastoral resources in an acceptable way, a way which takes precise account of the road blocks which this or that distorted personality is likely to erect against him.[3]

Implicit here is the price the clinical theologian is called upon to pay in order to bring disturbed, unhappy or neurotic beings out of their trauma. Frank Lake saw this role and duty as part of the 'transforming power of the Gospel'. A necessary corollary is that the helper has to experience for himself or herself the creative darkness 'which we are all liable to enter when we have been given the courage to abandon our defences'.[4]

The third quotation illustrates what became for him a life-long quest:

> . . . to find theologians able and willing to enter into dialogue at depth with doctors,[5]

after which he makes this personal statement:

> Four years ago the research to which I was committed as a dynamically orientated psychiatrist led to findings which pressed me into a shocked awareness that pre-natal distress in the mother was distressing also to the foetus. We could not avoid the conclusion that the primal trauma, and so the origins of psychosomatic and personality disorders, were reliably attributable to displacement and containment of foetal distress during the first three months of life in the womb. When, professionally, you have put yourself 'out on a limb' but 'can do no other' than stay there, any measure of support from medicine or theology becomes particularly reassuring.[6]

He did achieve a measure of support from both medicine and theology, but never to the extent he wished for. Part of the explanation for this state of affairs – which left Frank Lake towards the end of his life disappointed and feeling let-down – was his obsessive emphasis in the last four or five years of his work on 'primal trauma', primal therapy, etc., a controversial area at best considered to be speculative and uncertain by general practitioners and psychiatrists. This specialized interest also caused some to feel that he had gone away from the main work of CTA. This is not an entirely fair or accurate verdict, though the relationship between pastoral care and primal integration is a continuing debate within the association.

The transformation he so eagerly and passionately desired in people's lives was very largely achieved through supportive groups in which there was 'shared life, shared pain, and deep caring and personal therapy':[7] that is, personal therapy in the form of in-depth counselling. Before coming, however, to that vital aspect of Frank Lake's work, it is necessary to define what is meant by the expression 'clinical theology'.

What is clinical theology?

Many people I have consulted in the preparation of this book simply said 'Frank Lake' in reply to the question. This is only to be expected in recollection of someone who founded CTA and who presided over it with such panache and with such obsessive attention to it for so long a time. It is not to be wondered at, therefore, that clinical theology as a concept and as a movement should be so readily and closely identified with Frank Lake himself, whose volume *Clinical Theology* – perhaps even more so in its abridged form – remains *the* textbook of the movement.

But clinical theology is more than one man, however dominating and able he may have been. The reason for this has nothing whatsoever to do with personalities, but with another much more fundamental fact: a 'clinical' 'theology' has been part and parcel of the Church's outreach and witness since the days of our Lord, who knew and cared for his sheep (John 10:11–15).

'What is Clinical Theology?' is a question both posed and answered by the Revd Peter van de Kasteele, currently General Director, formerly Administrative Secretary of CTA, in the third issue of *Contact* (The Interdisciplinary Journal of Pastoral Studies) for 1985. He shows that the basic connotation of 'clinical' is not a medical one. Instead, 'clinic' is to be understood in terms of 'a class session or group meeting devoted to the presentation, analysis and treatment or solution of actual cases and concrete problems in some special field or discipline'. As a parish priest, van de Kasteele had frequently found himself overwhelmed by his parishioners' expectations of him: nothing short of what he calls 'omnicompetence' was expected of him. Visiting the sick and bereaved, the lonely and the afraid, the emotionally disturbed, and those with failing marriages, he felt ill equipped, on the one hand, and without the necessary pastoral skills, on the other hand, to cope meaningfully or even adequately with the many and diverse stressful situations that came his way. This lack of pastoral and counselling skills in the Church in general was alluded to in Chapter 1 of this book.

Nor had he realized that 'there was strength in sharing the load with others who similarly cared'. This was – and is – the 'clinical' part of the title, but what of 'theology'? The CTA syllabus puts it like this: 'Theology denotes the intention to be explicit about basic assumptions, values and meanings.' He found this less satisfactory as a statement and as a working definition, so he turned to other dictionary definitions, including this one: 'Theology is the systematic study of Christian revelation concerning God's nature and purpose.' But, theology is about God and his revelation to us. Without God, theology does not have precise meaning, while theology divorced from the idea of God's revelation is simply not possible.

In its broadest application, therefore, clinical theology offered priests like the Revd van de Kasteele two sorts of resources: first, the resources of the Christian faith for enhancing pastoral care; second, the collaboration of like-minded people. To enable these didactic and experiential elements to operate purposefully and competently, Frank Lake devised a pattern of seminars as a means of learning and of personal growth. There is no need to repeat here the features of the seminar experience, as they have already been dealt with in Chapter 2.

Clinical pastoral care

Frank Lake's theological and psychiatric ideas relating to clinical pastoral care are set out in enormous detail (1,200 pages, some half a million words, plus ten teaching charts) in *Clinical Theology*, first published in 1966; a severely abridged version of this volume appeared in 1986, edited by Martin Yeomans. The earlier vast book had grown out of Frank Lake's experiences, both as a missionary and as a psychiatrist.

The publication of *Clinical Theology* fulfilled a prophetic statement made almost a century earlier by Archbishop Frederick Temple. He wrote, in 1857: 'Our theology has been cast in a scholastic mould. We are in need of, and we are gradually being forced into, a theology based on psychology. The transition, I fear, will not be without much pain.' This massive volume was intended primarily, but not exclusively, for theologians and psychiatrists:

> Unless I am mistaken, I have been brought to an empirical knowledge of the truth and power of the central facts of Christian theology. I rely for myself, and for my work, on the Incarnation of the Son of God, the Crucifixion and Resurrection of Christ, and the giving of the Holy Spirit within the continuing life of the universal Church in the Word it proclaims, the sacraments it celebrates, and the fellowship which anchors it in human society in every age. This divine–human fellowship and destiny I take to be

> central to the meaning of human history. It is relevant, therefore, both to the healthy (who seldom recognize their need of Christ as Physician) and to the sick, whatever form their disorder or distress may take. I am a theologian only in the sense that every Christian layman could be a theologian, committed to think about the ultimate meaning of the knowledge and the skills he commands.[8]

An eclectic work, therefore, it contains many case studies which illustrate Frank Lake's theses but which would probably be considered insensitive under today's stricter conventions governing publishing. Its pioneering quality loses none of its essential importance in the considerably reduced version published twenty years later. In fact, Martin Yeomans's excellently crisp editorial work has made it accessible to a whole new generation of readers, as its sales have made demonstrably clear.

Clinical Theology enshrines Frank Lake's main ideas, and it is to an analytical overview of these perceptions that we must now turn.

Listening and dialogue

The indispensable starting-point for all his subsequent ideas, and for the whole of his pastoral care, is the ability to listen attentively and seriously, which is why Chapter 1 of his monumental work, occupying a hundred pages or so, is so vital for an understanding of Frank Lake's thinking.

He saw pastoral listening and dialogue as the 'very language' of the Bible and as the chosen method of Jesus Christ. Thus, in discussing our Lord's communications to men and women he distinguished between Christ's *general* communications for all people (for example, the 'Sermon on the Mount'), his *group* communications (for example, to the disciples or to the Pharisees), and thirdly, his *dialogues with individuals*. These latter occasions (for example, with Nicodemus or the Syro-Phoenician woman) he viewed as 'specific communications which could not be transposed. Few would argue with this contention either.'[9]

> What made the apostolic band into witnesses was not their ability to comprehend and expound a system of religion, it

> was their personal knowledge and observation of Jesus Christ Himself. What qualified them as witnesses to Christ was rather a simple power of observation, of listening, of faithfulness to the concrete and historical details of the life of the Master, the manner of man He was, the things He did, and the things they had heard Him say.[10]

At the heart of our Lord's approach was this deep interest in people rather than in ideas, and of course more than half his treatment of individuals was taken up with listening.

Such non-directive listening has a definite therapeutic function for the human spirit in its anxieties, and Lake at least was in no doubt about the correct order of listening and witnessing:

> I believe that every Christian working in this field, not only the pastor or psychiatrist, must wait until he has the freedom to speak which the Holy Spirit gives, before he advances from the universally acceptable human task of listening to his specific task of witness, namely to saying that Christ is also the great listener to every human conversation.[11]

Indeed, Lake found that 'the freedom to speak' was not always given, and he records this personal experience:

> I remember having a strong sense of being restrained from speaking of God or Christ for a whole year or more to a certain young psychopathic patient with a long record of crime, with whom I was working very closely. Not a word passed between us about God. Over a year after he had left the hospital I chanced to meet him in the town in which he lived. He accosted me with some enthusiasm and informed me with a great guffaw that he was being prepared for Confirmation. He told me then that if I had attempted to speak about God, while treatment was on, I would have ruined the whole free progress of his spirit towards God.[12]

He took seriously the responsibility incumbent upon all of us to listen, one of the most eloquent descriptions of which is found in these words from *Life Together*, by Dietrich Bonhoeffer: 'One who cannot listen long and patiently will presently be talking beside the point, and be never really speaking to others, albeit he be not conscious of it.'

The listener, Frank Lake perceived, is quite literally representing Christ, and thus requires both great charity and great humility; but when properly and effectively carried out, listening brings about ontological and theological results:

> God has not only spoken through His Son; what is perhaps more important, He has listened through His Son. Christ's saving work cost Him most in its speechless passivity of dereliction. It is this which gives Him the right to be called the greatest listener to all suffering. It is this which gives His listening its redemptive quality.[13]

'In pastoral dialogue,' Lake taught, 'initiated by the pastor's willingness to listen to one of his fellow-men and concluded when both of them are listening to Jesus Christ, we have an epitome of that for which the world exists. Preaching without listening may fail to create the communion of saints. The deep mutuality of pastoral dialogue costs more, involves the pastor in more suffering, but its endurance in the presence and power of Christ is an indelible event in the divine order.'[14] Such listening is particularly needed by people who, in Lake's words, 'have serious doubts about their solvency as persons',[15] and thus require considerable reassurance. Listening of this sort is the very antithesis of that defensive isolation which wishes to avoid commitment. But this form of listening involves a basic psychodynamic understanding of the whole area of anxiety:

> The mental pain of a breakdown is the echo of the pain of long-lost relationships. The echo resonates through into consciousness because a painful loneliness has descended again upon the person. The sound of friendly voices is lost, or is felt to be lost, or is feared will be shortly lost. If we can see no companionable looks as we search around us in the present, and hear no friendly voices, to be afraid of actual loneliness is quite a reasonable fear. Neurotic anxiety is the addition to that reasonable fear of strange, unreasonable terrors, that is, of the long-repressed separation-anxieties of infancy. Patterns of loneliness in the present tend always to invoke their prototypes lying dormant at

> the roots of being. Working this way, the buried past turns a tolerably fearful present moment into an intolerably anxious one.[16]

This particular type of awareness has an inherent logic:

> Now if we understand anxiety in this way, as a painful diminution of the power of 'being', due to loss of relationship with the personal source of 'being', it is simply the most logical step that a therapist or pastor could take to provide just this quality of accepting and undemanding relationship.[17]

Thus, by offering a sufferer attentive listening, he is drawn back into a place of safety, or what Lake calls 'personal bondedness'.

Frequently in his published and unpublished writings, Frank Lake emphasized the importance of non-directive 'client-orientated' listening by referring to the Old Testament prophet Ezekiel as a model:

> So the Spirit lifted me up, and took me away, and I went in bitterness, in the heat of my spirit, but the hand of the Lord was strong upon me. Then I came to them of the captivity at Tel-Aviv, . . . and *I sat where they sat*, and remained there astonished (dumbfounded) among them seven days.[18]

He was equally fond of quoting, with total approval, Søren Kierkegaard: 'And if you understand the art of making yourself a nobody in a conversation you get to know best what resides in the other person.'

The two key ideas in the extracts quoted above, are, first, 'I sit where he sits' (that is, identification with the suffering person), and, secondly, the subjugating of one's own personal identity in order to help (therapeutically) the person who needs counselling. The paradigm in this second instance is, of course, our Lord himself, about whom Isaiah wrote: 'He emptied himself, and became of no reputation' and 'He poured out his soul unto death'.[19] This act of self-giving is something which Frank Lake did with countless scores of people over the years, thereby establishing a caring and accepting relationship. He was prepared to stay with the sufferer down the often excruciating road of memory, letting the troubled person retain the 'steering-wheel' in the conversation. Lake taught that the counsellor must not attempt to alleviate his *own* anxiety by regaining the central direction of the conversation.

He also returned, time and again, in his lectures, speeches and writings to highlight the obstacles to good counselling:

1. *Premature solutions:* offered before the point of the problem has been reached. The counsellor is in a hurry to establish his own confidence as a man who can grasp the point quickly.
2. *Pre-judging the issue in a moralistic way:* as if all suffering followed directly on sins committed by a man, and never on evils endured through the sins of others. Are his responses a direct or implied judgement and condemnation of the sufferer?
3. *Preventing the expression of strong feeling:* because the counsellor cannot bear the powerful, all-or-nothing emotions of the infancy to which all people in breakdown regress. His manner *pre*cludes 'catharsis'. His *pre*monition is that strong feelings are dangerous.
4. *Predominating personal need to be the man with the answers:* The educational system punishes those who do not have ready answers to all problems. It is hard to realize that the opposite is true in opening up a counselling relationship. Failure as a counsellor automatically punishes us when we come up with ready 'answers', and expect to be thought well of. Maybe this man cannot get away from the ideal image of himself as the good college student.
5. *Preference for*, if not insistence on, *clearly stated problems* briefly told. He forgets that all our earliest and deepest feelings are pre-verbal. Accidents and injuries are stored in memory without explanatory tags. Finding words to fit confused primal states takes time. Romans 8 speaks of 'agonizing longings' and 'groanings that never find words'.
6. *Preconceived idea that his own experiences provide the clue.* He cannot stay with the sufferer's own tale, which may not have a happy ending. So he distorts it to fit his own tale with its successful conclusion. It seldom is relevant or

helpful. The troubled person is made to feel inferior to the counsellor.

7. *Prevalent pastoral habit of giving 'practical solutions'.* He suggests 'geographical escapes', transfer, domestic re-arrangements, bits of 'practical advice' which are not relevant to the emotional distress or the dynamics underlying it.

8. *Pressure of religious talk to avoid bad feelings.* ('But don't you know Christians should be joyful; you mustn't give way to sadness') – or to avoid the counselling relationship ('You should take it to the Lord in prayer; not now, but when you get home') – or to show off ('By prayer and reliance on Bible texts and promises I have avoided such troubles').

9. *Pre-existing fear of silence.* Silence grates on the ears of some talkative counsellors, who must fill every possible silent moment with good advice. Depressed and apathetic people think very slowly and need long silences. His embarrassment cannot permit this.

10. *Predictable attitudes*, from the man who has to be true to type; true not to himself or the 'good shepherd' role, but to the expectations of the critical people with influence in the congregation. He cannot deviate from the public expectation of him in his role as the bold preacher, the firm administrator or the stern disciplinarian.

11. *Predilection for scandal*, that makes a man pursue and probe into the more sordid aspects of the story yet to be told. He who has a nose for dirt has a dirty nose, though he will deny it strenuously.

12. *Pre-arranged scheme for typing people, for quick disposal*, destroying the troubled person's sense of being a free, self-determining individual. It traps both in an impersonal mould and destroys the spontaneity and humanity upon which the counselling relationship depends. The provisional use of personality reaction patterns in diagnosis does not depersonalize the relationship.

13. *Pre-learnt and highly practised counselling techniques*, in which the pastor has too much confidence. These get to feel mechanical and frustrate the free flow of dialogue in counselling. A good technique is the habit of attending at

all times to the relationship, sensitive to the above technical errors which block or destroy the counselling relationship.[20]

Clinical pastoral resources

To Frank Lake the whole thrust of clinical theology depended on the truth of the Christian claim that 'in fellowship with God, through Christ and his Church, there are available personal resources which transform relationship and personality'.[21] The obvious link here is with the teaching of the Apostle Paul on the 'fruit of the Spirit' (Galatians 5:22) which, Lake constantly stressed, psychoneurotic persons need above all else. Anxiety, immaturity and proneness to gloomy feelings can be cured by the availability of love, joy, peace. He believed absolutely that nothing less than the divine energy, demonstrated so supremely in Christ, and which his resurrection makes open to all who have a relationship with him, can cure people who have lost their way in life and who seem to have no meaning in their existence. In the cross of Christ, Frank Lake believed as did St Paul, all the resources of evil are replaced by the power of the new birth, and it is this event which Lake perceived as 'the primary source for the ultimate transformations of human personality'.[22]

Christ's person, therefore, becomes the ultimate resource, the very antithesis of neurotic attitudes, but that person, in turn, bestows an unchanging vocation on his Church:

> Take up again His ministry to those who suffer from personality disorders and mental distress. Our danger is probably a too wordy analysis without the power of synthesis. We need interpretation, but more than that, we need integration. We have less need of advice than of the power to carry out what we already know to be true in human relationships. 'For the Kingdom of God is not a matter of a spate of words, but of the power of Christian living.'[23]

The implications for clinical pastoral counsellors, as Lake saw, were enormous:

> . . . as its introduction, the task of listening to a story of human conflict and need. This listening may be indistinguishable from that practised by non-directive

> counsellors. This is, in itself, a therapeutic resource. To the extent that our listening uncovers a human situation which borders the abyss or lies broken within it, we are nearer to the place where the cross of Christ is the only adequate interpretative concept. And this concept is historical fact, not ideology.[24]

His views on this particular resource are aptly summed up as follows:

> Just as it is the total work of God in Christ which is the ultimate source of man's total redemption, so we have learned to look to specific aspects of His Death and Passion for the specific medicines of the spirit in its particular evils, both those which it has actively done as sin, and those which have been passively endured as affliction.
>
> The Spirit of Christ, in spite of flinching, did bear all the extremities of persecution and affliction. That is what His Cross and Passion assure us of. He carried this unique experience of patient endurance of human suffering, through death, into the risen life God gave Him. The very same Spirit of Christ 'descended' on the Church at Pentecost and has been with us and in us as Christians ever since. It is this Spirit of God, able to endure all things with the fortitude of the Son, who has sustained the martyrs and upheld the afflicted. He is our first and final resource, when, in clinical pastoral care, we encourage Christians who seriously 'want to get to the bottom of their trouble', to turn and face the emergence of whatever threatens the self from within.[25]

The whole Church, therefore, is 'in solemn trust to the afflicted' to mediate to them through pastoral care all that is to be obtained through 'the merits and death' of Jesus Christ, God's Son, and 'through faith in his blood'.[26]

Other pastoral resources, in addition to the norm of the life of Jesus Christ, included, for Frank Lake, the following: the insights that come from out-patient psychiatry; the common life of the Body of Christ; prayer, both as end in itself and as a resource in mental pain; the sacrament of Holy Communion; the preaching of the Word of God; and clinical conferences with members of the healing professions.[27]

Giving cohesion to all of these ideas for people on the edge of nervous breakdown, Lake believed, was the communication of empathy: 'The troubled person cannot be reached except by someone who can see and feel with him the strange, limited universe into which his spirit, crabbed and confined, has shrunk'.[28] To communicate empathy with a person whose experience seems utterly alien from that of the listener is not a natural endowment or aptitude. It requires both careful study and costly identification. In precise terms, there is the recognition that each person is unique, with needs that are peculiar to him or her. For Frank Lake special clinical care meant 'sound knowledge and personal training in the interpersonal relationships of parents and their effects on infancy and childhood, of psychodynamics, and of the mechanisms which the mind employs in denying or defending against these primary injuries to the identity of the ego, the being, and the well-being of the human person'.[29] The technical expression for this is 'the healing of the memories', especially the repressed memories of personal injury, 'however early in our life history they came upon us and were imprinted'.[30] This subject will be dealt with in more detail later in the chapter. Suffice for now to say that Frank Lake saw this task as belonging to the Church, and not as medical function except in the severest of cases:

> In the established Church with its parochial system, this standard of care is possible only for the gathered congregation and a few fringers from the unshepherded thousands who live within the territorial boundaries of the parish. There is not the slightest suggestion in Great Britain that the medical profession has any serious intention of occupying this field or providing these services. No national health insurance can be extended to cover all the risks implicit in every unhappy home. We are speaking here of the Church's responsibility to her own members and to those who appeal for help.[31]

Problems of identification with the client

Frank Lake fully realized that listening to an anxious person is an arduous and demanding process. This is so because the listening is meant to be a 'demonstration of empathy', and may lead to anxieties within the listener himself. He taught that Christian therapists (be they medical or pastoral) ought to regard themselves as essentially different from their clients: 'We have to step out of our role of professional superiority and stand with them, before the cross, at the place of help. If we retreat from this, both we and our brother face spiritual disaster'.[32] Nor must the physician betray his *own* anxieties about the encounter with the patient:

> We cannot help an anxious person to the peace of God if that peace has not been given us by the Holy Spirit, making real Christ's justifying grace. We shall not help the depressive to handle his rage consciousness to drag it forth in all its red-handed murder before the cross of Christ, if we have not so learned to handle our own. We shall not help the schizoid person to face his own complete inability to believe that there is any beneficent Being behind the universe if we ourselves are rigidly defending against the emergence of just that quality of utter unbelief in ourselves. We shall not help the hysterical person to come to terms with intolerable loneliness if we are using that need and our profession, in a dual collusion of attention-seeking, to engage in flight from separation anxieties common to both.[33]

Thus, and this was absolutely vital in Frank Lake's view, the physician, whether his focus of attention be to body, or soul, or spirit, must recognize that the primary task which will prepare and equip him for the life of therapeutic dialogue 'is to have faced and dealt with his own anxieties'.[34]

Lake was, of course, clearly aware of difficulties inherent in this whole area, and he categorized some of the more pressing ones as follows:

COMPULSIVE PERSONAL DETACHMENT AND INTELLECTUALIZATION

It is a commonly held view – and with considerable justification – that authority figures retreat behind their office. So a clergyman masks his anxiety behind his cloak of priestly office, while the general practitioner either demands obedience or issues authoritarian prescriptions, or both. Such approaches are only partially efficacious, but there comes a point 'when the patient realizes, whether the physician does or not, that they are merely childish evasions of his own inability to understand the disease or cure it'.[35] Indeed, the counsellor must 'remain faithfully and fully present, as a person, in order to evoke, on this occasion, a better and more durable response', and here the emphasis is on a particular type of relationship and on a particular type of physical approach too:

> If the conclusions of analytical studies are tenable, this would be possible only through a personal relationship, mediated by direct confrontation of the needy person by the one who cares, and whose genuineness of caring is manifest in the light of his countenance, which primarily is in the eyes. All the other sensory modalities by which the spirit of a person is made manifest to another needy person are important. Tone of voice is as important as the words spoken. The attitude of the spirit is expressed in the posture of the body and the movements of the face.[36]

COMPULSIVE OVER-ATTACHMENT

Lake viewed this as the obverse side of 'the underlying experience of panic-provoking uncertainty about human relationships in depth'.[37] These over-attachments can take many forms, for example to pretty women or to pretty boys. The result of such attachments is blocked communication between the listener and the client. One senses Lake's heart in this extended comment:

> Difficulties in ourselves as listeners may block communication just as effectively if our personality, not being so stressed so severely as in schizoid persons, has none the less been sufficiently threatened to make us adopt compulsive, rigid moralistic attitudes. There are many fine clergymen whose religion is based on compulsion rather than freedom. They take great pride in their work and become depressed if not appreciated. Being perfectionist, they tend to be sensitive, touchy, resentful of criticism. They cannot accept their own brokenness, nor admit failure, nor the need for any other than a very general confession. Outward expressions of anger with those in authority upon whom they are dependent have long been suppressed, rage has

been repressed even from their own consciousness. To a variable extent their acquaintance with the sexuality of their own minds is also repressed. If so, their attitude to sexual misdemeanour becomes as harsh and rejecting when it occurs in others as when it occurs in their own deep mind.

Intolerant of weakness in themselves they have no welcoming word for those in whom weakness has broken out in undesirable ways. Since they have never overcome the difficulty of accepting their own bad side, whether of rage or truant sexuality, they have an insuperable difficulty in accepting the persons of those who manifest such morally undesirable drives overtly.

When a Christian minister becomes primarily a moralist he is creating insuperable difficulties in the way of pastoral dialogue.[38]

OUT OF DEPTH IN THE ABYSS

A clever but inadequate subheading for the dread, terror, despair and affliction of this very dark place. In the contemporary pastoral counselling scene, one of Frank Lake's great contributions was the recognition of it and thereby his personal ability to stay with those experiencing this (terrifying) darkness.

Psychiatrists, general practitioners and priests all know of the defensive desire to remain within the role of professional detachment, as did Lake, of course. But broken relationships can only be healed by the counsellor entering into them as fully and as deeply as the need demands: there can be no opting out of the responsibility:

> If we believe in truth, we shall need to listen at one and the same time right down to the truth of this desperate person's history, and right down to the Truth himself, hanging in the darkness, crucified upon his cross.[39]

DISINCLINATION FOR RADICAL CHANGE

Most clients, as Frank Lake rightly claims, would rather have the effects of sin and their deep pains palliated or tinkered with as opposed to having them 'faithfully and radically dealt with'.[40] Thus the duty of the counsellor/pastor/doctor is quite explicit: 'The transformation of the troubled person's attitude to life'.[41] Essentially, resistance to change is a fear of giving up well-tried and cultivated defences against deeply repressed mental pain. This is the case whether the client is an hysterical sufferer with separation anxiety, a schizoid personality, a depressive, an obsessive person, or a homosexual.

Lake saw that to deal with such issues, whether as pastor or laity, three requirements were indispensable: first, openness towards God in a life of close obedience towards God, arising out of a persistent prayer life; secondly, openness to one's fellow-beings about one's own unresolved fears and struggles, etc.; and thirdly, openness towards others, 'which they can usually recognize before we can'.[42]

The dynamic cycle[43]

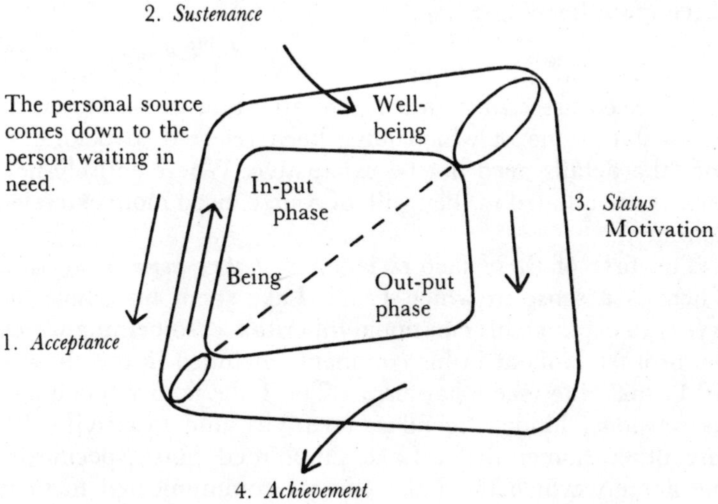

This conceptual model is the very heart of clinical theology, its nerve centre no less, and must be treated seriously and comprehensively. It is an amalgam of psychiatric – not just, but also more basically – psychological and theological understanding, the knowledge of human personality growth and development, of the disorders that affect them, and was based on Frank Lake's experience as a Christian and as a counsellor over many years.

What he had been looking for was a model that correlated the clinical and the theological, but which avoided either classic psychiatric models (because sickness-dominated) or pastoral and ascetical models (because sin-dominated). He delineated the requirements of such a model like this:

> We need a model which will correlate the dynamics of relatively well-functioning personality and of spiritual health, in its formation and maintenance, before it turns to the clinical conditions in which this integral wholeness is lost and replaced by deprivation, anxiety, conflict, defences, distress, and various forms of disorder. By inference, the model must point the way back to health and wholeness, showing why the various therapeutic forces are effective.[44]

It will probably be most helpful to examine the model under three main headings:

1 GENESIS OF THE METHOD

A balanced assessment must give attention to six factors in particular, some of which have been referred to before, so that the details need not be exhaustive. Where entirely new factors are alluded to they will, of course, need more extended comment.

The first of these factors is *Frank Lake's home background.* There is a sense in which Frank Lake spent his whole life trying to expunge his emotional inheritance, something which his brother hints at in his comments included in the chapter on Frank's life (see Chapter 3). The Lake family home had its tensions, hidden agendas, creativity and negativity like any other home. Brian Lake pinpointed quite specifically the anxiety which the Lake parents communicated to their children. For Mrs Lake it took the form of excessive worrying in a fussily obsessive way, while Mr Lake varied between detachment and irritable impatience. There was no doubt that the parents *cared*; but the home, in Brian's phrase, was 'a safe but rather anxious place to live'. It seems too that the somewhat authoritarian church life did not ameliorate these tensions; rather, that home and church life were lived in compartments: a split, in other words. The Lake family life lacked integration, and the Lake children were aware of inner troubles, collusional blind spots. These, for the most part, were kept shielded in a defensive way, or in Frank's case (certainly once he had gone to Edinburgh) by detaching himself from the immediate environment apart from extremely long letters describing his various exploits. In later life, too, when in discussions with people who brought up issues that threatened his defended position, he would retreat behind the simple, if obvious, device of saying 'I missed that', or 'Could you repeat that again?' The model was as much for Frank Lake as it was for those he wanted to help.

The second factor was the *occupational stress he observed among the clergy*. This was, as Chapter 1 demonstrated, the background against which Clinical Theology was developed in the first instance. This was true of his home parish of Aughton, where the home rector was formidable and autocratic in demeanour. It was also true of many of the priests he came into contact with in his early days as a psychiatrist in Yorkshire. So many priests simply could not fulfil their parishioners' expectations of them, and so they retreated into a 'bunker mentality', a heavily defended position which would not admit of any questioning of their role, their attitudes, or their theology. Partially whole themselves, they were called upon to minister to people whose dark sides mirrored their own, often in startlingly similar ways. To admit to these dark inner regions, of course, would be tantamount to an admission of failure, maybe even a denial of the truth and power of the Gospel in its ability to transform lives and emotions.

The third factor was *Frank Lake's meeting with Emil Brunner*. This important meeting with the Swiss theologian took place when Lake visited in Vellore in 1950.

At that time Frank Lake had been asked to compile a Bible study course for fifth-year students at the Christian medical college there, on the interrelationship between the Christian faith and medical practice. He worked from the basis that psychiatry (the study most closely bordering on theology within medicine) lacked 'those models of normality which would be acceptable to a Christ-centred view of man'.[45] On pressing Dr Brunner to show him where Christian theology could find a model of people's understanding of themselves, he was directed 'to a long and repeated study of the dynamics of our Blessed Lord, as they occur in St John's Gospel'.[46] Out of that study arose the ontological analysis embodied in The Dynamic Cycle. Thus our Lord in his 'perfect humanness'[47] is the norm against which the dignity of all people can be viewed and measured.

The fourth factor was the *Christian tradition*. Frank Lake affirmed that 'our understanding of our psychodynamic model [is] that the Holy Communion is a sacrament which literally carries ontological and so spiritual strength and sustenance into the life of those who participate in it'.[48] He linked this resource with the preaching of the Word of God, and applauded that 'genre of preaching which can reach down to the heart of psychoneurotic and psychotic problems and open them up to the resources of God'. But he was illuminatingly specific on *how* Scripture should and should not be used:

> The dominant factor in the neurotic mind is the regressed mood of infancy, pre-verbal now, as it was then. While faith is dominant the Scriptures will continue to be used however much the mind is overturned by uncovered repressed affliction. And it is in precisely such turmoil as the spirit is thrown into dark nights of flesh and spirit (actively or passively endured) that the Word of God is an effective counsellor to the Christian. It measures up to all the extremities to which the soul is driven.
>
> However, to quote or not quote Scripture to a distressed person is a matter of delicate balance. Sometimes the appropriately addressed word of searching authority is most apt. In another case it is better to withhold the direct quotation. God is healing the whole personality of the sufferer, the worst affected parts being those still sore from the earliest years, before words had any meaning. God may wish to express his loving parental care through us by what we are and do, rather than by what we say. To insist on quoting Scripture may be a neurotic compulsion in the helper, with hints of superstition, almost magic, with an unwillingness to let patient befriending precede verbal witnessing, as parents must do.[49]

Another potent – and fifth – factor was the influence of the *Object Relations Theory*. This is the understanding of the infant person's responses to 'objects' and ultimately in relation to his/her mother as a whole person, and also in relation to other siblings. The leading British theorists are Ronald Fairbairn, Melanie Klein, and D. W. Winnicott. The latter defined the essence of Object Relations in the following terms: 'There is no such thing as a baby – meaning that if you set out to describe a baby, you will find you are describing a *baby and someone*. A baby cannot exist alone, but is essentially part of a relationship.' In addition, Harry Guntrip, who belonged to the same school of psychotherapists, and who had been Brian Lake's analyst, is referred to on sixteen pages in *Clinical Theology*, though all the references are to his books.

Lastly, there was Frank Lake's *clinical experience of LSD-25*. When he used it, between 1954 and 1970, for therapeutic purposes, it was an entirely legal process; when later it was banned, Dr Lake ceased to use the drug. Initially he used LSD-25 as an abreactive agent to enable patients to re-experience the first year of life, 'whether normal or abnormal'. A particular interest was its use with those classified as schizoid personalities, and he justified its use like this:

> In order to establish the origin and nature of this schizoid syndrome scientifically, the subjective experience ought to be reported on by sufferers during, or shortly after, its occurrence in the early months of life. This is impossible. We would be in an impasse were it not for the fact that traumatic infantile memories are split off, dissociated, and repressed into the unconscious mind. They are then preserved unchanged. All the components of the experience, as they affect interpersonal relationships, the psyche, and the body, are held in suspension. They are unaffected by the passage of time. In a sense they are outside time. The impasse is overcome because, under favourable circumstances, and using an abreactive agent such as LSD-25, these experiences can return to consciousness. Accurate and discriminating recall of the total experience is possible.[50]

The second stage in his use of LSD-25 was related to the question of birth trauma. His findings are described in *Clinical Theology* and summarized in an article in the *Journal of Psychosomatic Research* (vol. 22, 1978) entitled 'Treating Psychosomatic Disorders Relating To Birth Trauma'.[51] In this paper he draws together evidence to show that 'birth trauma does, at times, provide that degree of severe pressure or tension which, acting upon those parts of the nervous system which are fully functioning and competent at birth, triggers off the mechanisms of stress'. Then he adds this explanatory note:

> This stress reaction generally subsides when the emergency is over, but if it has been so severe as to demand splitting off from consciousness and repression, then by definition it remains latent. In later years, similar pressures and tensions of living are perceived as evoking the return of the trauma, as it was in the beginning. Added to the normal body–mind responses to present trouble, resonance with the archaic element of birth injury triggers off identically the same somatic sensations and psychological emotions as at the beginning. All the specific defensive reactions that were originally aroused and recorded occur again. But whereas, on the first time round, the end of the birth process brought about a measure of demobilization of those defences, now, the common enough perpetuation of life stress means that no demobilization is ordered. The mistaken sense that the perinatal injuries and the defensive reactions to which they gave rise are still relevant and have to be faced again in the present, guarantees the chronicity of the disorder.[52]

In this respect, Frank Lake follows the work of Otto Rank who, in 1924,[53] referred to the trauma of birth as the first experienced anxiety. He perceived it as the prime source material for '*all* (my italics) the neuroses and character disorders'; further, it was, he claimed, 'the original emotional shock underlying all personality dysfunctions'; and he affirmed that there 'we have recognized the neuroses in all their forms as reproductions of, and reactions to, the birth trauma'.

Frank Lake's conclusions from all this research may be expressed in the form of two generalizations. First, that difficult births leave emotional scars. He believed that before we can search the Scriptures for the appropriate word 'in the redemptive work of Christ for the matching identification with the patient's suffering, we must listen more intently to the predicament itself as it is stated by those whom it has attacked'.[54] This predicament, in Frank Lake's view, came up 'in pure form' in the statements of persons under LSD-25, who are reporting 'on the spot' their 'fixated experiences' from which the coverings have been lifted. These he conceived of as statements of people who are in a state of double consciousness:

> They know all the time who they are, where they are, can get up at any time to relieve themselves, or to change position. There is nothing hypnotic about this. At the same time they recover many of the painful experiences and fantasies (and some of the blessed experiences) of infancy. These are relived as if they were a tiny infant again, with a small body, hands that cannot reach above a few inches, feet that can only kick but not walk, eyes that can see and remember detail with eidetic imagery but cannot interpret, ears that can hear but understand only the emotion behind the words. Sometimes the patient will relive the whole experience in silence and report upon it afterwards. Others are able to report on the experience as it goes on, usually commenting that although they are now using words, no words accompanied the original experience. A few are able to write it down in the doctor's absence.[55]

This is how one person (an unmarried businessman) abreacted under LSD-25:

> There's no strength in me at all. Utterly squeezed out. (The patient is shaking in fear.) As if you're choking the life out of me, as if you are squeezing a secret out of me. I'm in your power, I don't know if I am hiding any more. I couldn't possibly conceal anything from you, you could accuse me of anything, and I'd admit it. I've no will. I have a feeling of utter dependence. It could never depend on me. It's much bigger than me. Whatever it says I've got to do. I've got to tremble and debase myself before something much stronger than me. Please don't treat me like this. What have I done? (Very marked trembling.) Why can't I love? It is as if you are telling me I am naughty, and you are telling me off. They don't love me, why should I love them? I feel cheated. I am a little thing with giants surrounding me. I am just a little grain of sand

that has come into the world. What more do you want? Just let me sleep so that I can get some peace. Then I can forget about you. I have admitted you are stronger than me, and I'm not happy, so let me sleep. I feel as if you are being very cruel to me. Why can't you be kind to me? I've admitted I'm only a little grain of sand. I'm a worthless little grain of sand, so please be kind to me.

The very nucleus of me seems to be in my genitals and bowels, as if that's a unit of me in there. I'm being melted up, there, now, completely melted up. (Legs shaking.) There's somebody cruel behind it all. There's some cruel fate in store for me. I've admitted you are stronger than I am; you don't want to kill me, I suppose, so why can't we be happy? I'm tired of telling you you're cruel, and you are still cruel, so I'll just have to go along with you. I want her to reassure me that she loves me. If she did that she could have all the love back in the world. Now you are making me tremble like a little bird. I can't stop my teeth and pelvis from chattering, as if I'd had a terrific fright, overwhelmed, horrible feeling. Wrung out, wrung out, a terrific thing trying to kill me. I've got to fight against it. Yes, I think I can beat it. Again this terrifying presence and I've got to grovel. It might still kill me. There's no way of avoiding it. I feel like a mouse hiding from a cat, seeking ways to get peace from you.

Now I've just been thinking of my mother. I get a burning feeling as if I'm embarrassed in the face and sexually. A feeling, watch, you may be caught doing something I oughtn't to be doing. Now I'm screwed up, wrung out with great lobster claws, a gigantic female lobster, not friendly, a cruel presence going to hold me to account. I'm a small, dependent, screwed-up little thing on the kitchen floor. Everything bigger than me. No love, just cruelty. You won't love me. Deadness. And when I'm searching for love I can feel the hardness in the skin, embarrassment and hardness, tightness of the skull, repels me, like touching someone who's dead. If this is love I don't want to know about it. It is all one-sided. Well, perhaps not. Someone did put me in here in the first place. So I'm content with all that. Now I've got a feeling of getting to despair. No love, just cruelty, female cruelty. Nasty, strict presence of a woman, strict,

> sexless, flat-chested and nasty like an eagle. (Teeth chatter, and shakes.) Like a witch, one would rather have a man. Nothing at all from that sort of woman. (Shakes.) Cruel, treating me like that, making a convenience of me. That's strange. I've always associated a bird of prey with a woman. I've always done.
>
> Now I get the feeling that I want to take my mother, or a woman, and melt in her. To be at one with her, but there is a kind of hardness, and every time I try I feel disillusioned. It is as if there is a fright between women and me. Now I'm trying to please mother. And then I say, why bother trying to please her if she is going to be like this? Just be limp, be nothing, now I feel a kind of love behind it all, saying, come on, try your best anyway. Yes, I'll do that. That's how I feel. . . . Now I have a female presence trying to strangle me. My throat and penis together. I can't feel love anywhere. Just a strict female presence. I can hardly believe that I came from a woman. One can hardly believe that they could treat one so badly, and give one this screwed-up feeling. A cruel female presence and a terrific consciousness of my penis. . . . I feel just like a little baby, just born, waiting for something nice to happen, and it doesn't. . . . A feeling I mustn't wet myself, don't make a mess. As if I can produce something dirty. Now I feel my penis being screwed out of me, just pulled right out. As if that woman wants just that part of me. But there isn't anything else of me. I'm conscious I am just a sexual thing. A glow all around me. I'm thinking of a very small baby, just a little being, I feel I've got to push my maleness forward to some woman who isn't satisfied. I feel I've got to prove it. It is not as cruel as it was before, now. Synthesis, synthesis. You know, I can remember when I was young, I would talk in a woman's voice to the pillow. I used to do this when I heard my stepmother and father rowing. I'd feel very insecure. I'd hug the pillow and I'd act, with a woman's voice, and yet I'd be the man.[56]

The second generalization derived from his research with LSD-25 was that difficult births also have somatic effects later in life, and where the two disorders (psychological and somatic) are indissolubly combined, it is also true of psychosomatic disorders too. To illustrate this point Frank Lake recounted the case of a priest who was prone to severely explosive outbursts of rage in which he would, in his frustration, smash chairs:

> In his later thirties at the time I first saw him, he had suffered from severe atopic dermatitis from a fortnight after his birth. Every summer from May to September he was covered with the rash which he scratched, leaving a blood-flecked sheet whenever he got up from a bed. His photophobia was intense. Travelling with me in my car he insisted on having his mackintosh over the car window. Worried at the chronicity, his dermatologist encouraged us to go ahead. On one of his LSD sessions he began to relive a four-day dry labour. He experienced intense frustration and a mounting rage at the lack of progress. His skin was burning hot. For many hours he was apparently in a transverse position and the right chest was crushed. The struggle to live switched, at the peak of the pain, into a struggle to die. The death wish became profound.
>
> Eventually, after four or five hours sampling these four days of wretchedness, he was 'born'. For three or four hours he cursed and swore at the misfortune of being still alive. 'Why the bloody hell', he yelled, 'couldn't they let me die?' The murderous rage at being alive eventually spent itself and he decided that since the good God had got him here he had better become reconciled to it. This was in June, when the condition was at its worst. Within a week the skin was clearing and by a fortnight it had totally cleared. For the first time in his life, that August he went to the seaside and could take his clothes off. The photophobia disappeared. I spoke to him the other night and he tells me that after nearly forty years of annual eczema he has been totally free for fourteen years. The diathesis is still there, however. Ten years ago when his mother-in-law was putting some pressure on the family he suffered some return of the itching for a fortnight. However, he was able to recognize the underlying tendency to deal with this present-day frustration and anger by reactivation of the birth trauma and its concomitant burning skin. Since both the present rage and the old experience of birth were now quite

conscious, he was able to keep them separate, deal with the mother-in-law issue firmly in its own right, and forestall the reactivation of the dermatitis.

He reminded me that he had also suffered from severe migraine before we tackled the birth trauma. He still has attacks, not so severely, and only a couple of times a year when there has been pressure about. It is quite likely that in reliving the relevant parts of the birth, he opted out of this particular nasty corner on the occasion of the major abreaction. More primal work would probably have reached the 'original' migraine attack, which is usually identified by the patient as a particularly nasty tight spot towards the end of the second stage of labour.[57]

What LSD-25 did was to blow through the collusional defences of people independently of the analyst. It also alerted Frank Lake to the possibility that birth trauma could be vividly relived. Indeed, his use of the drug from the very beginning as an abreactive agent was intended to evoke powerful memories, for this therapeutic reason:

> . . . for it is these that distort the face of 'god' in the ground of personality, creating difficulties in the conduct of daily life, distorting relationships, and making trust of God difficult in the here and now, because 'god', small 'g', then, was so devastatingly unreliable.[58]

But at this point it is worth recalling one of Frank Lake's oft-repeated qualifications:

> So severe are these memories of evil days, passively endured in the uncomprehending innocence of babyhood, that they cannot be recalled to mind, even with the aid of an abreactive agent, unless the spirit be fortified to meet them. The nature of this fortification is partly personal, in that the patient must have a high level of trust in the therapist, who must be present during the full four or five hours of the abreaction, and partly theological, that is to say, Christological. For it is the Holy Spirit who sustained Christ in Gethsemane who makes the ultimates of commitment anxiety tolerable, and on Golgotha who makes the ultimates of dereliction anxiety also bearable. That God suffers with us, and in us, in our worst stretches of mental pain, of

whatever sort, whether acute and agonizing, or long-drawn-out and exhausting, is the central theme of Clinical Theology.[59]

One of the most radically interesting applications of the constriction of birth idea has been propounded by David Wasdell, Director of what was formerly the Urban Church Project, who worked with Frank Lake in the latter years of his life (1978–82). He concluded that the traditional urban congregation, under pressure of social changes, develops a too-rigid boundary structure and suffers from dwindling pastoral and other resources. This actual, realistic impasse, he observes, is apt to develop into a more serious risk of regression to primitive levels of anxiety. These, in his opinion, do not derive from post-natal events, but from the stress of birth and earlier experiences of a similarly frustrating kind in the months between conception and birth.[60]

2 PHASES OF THE MODEL

The model is an ontological analysis of interpersonal relationships expressed in infancy, and is based on a study of the life of Christ as 'the norm' for dynamic studies of man. It has four phases: two dynamic in-put phases and two dynamic out-put phases (see the diagram on page 121). These phases are, in Frank Lake's words, as follows:

1. *Acceptance* of the potentially isolated and, as such, anxious individual, by at least one other person, primarily by the mother, subsequently by the father, the rest of the family and society, is the primary ontological requirement. This access to human relationships ensures, on the personal level, his very 'being'. Without this he 'dies' as a person or as a member of society. Personal life is possible only when the seeking 'I' finds a 'Thou'. This alone makes possible the emergence of selfhood, of a steadily functioning 'I-My-Self'.

2. *Sustenance* of personality. Whoever *enjoys* relationships of a generous and gracious kind is enhanced by them in his power of 'being'. The quality of 'well-being', good spirits, courage and personal vitality is a reflection of what has been communicated from others in this phase. 'Existence', in the form of good personal relationships, produces, in

the person who responds to this donative experience, a worthwhile spiritual 'essence'. These two phases constitute the dynamic in-put of personality. Ontologically speaking, 'being' and 'well-being' are achieved by an adequate response to an adequate personal source in this phase of absolute dependence.

3. *Status.* The two in-going dependency phases are normally followed by an out-going movement, back to involvement in self-giving relationships in the place where tasks are taken up. At this point, the essential quality or *status* of the personal spirit that has resulted from (1) and (2) can be observed by introspection and inferred from the analysis of behaviour. If the in-put phases have gone well, *motivation* is strong, surgency is characteristic, the flow of energy is free, the mood joyful, the powers of concentration and decision adequate, with a readiness to invest interest in persons and concerns outside oneself. The natural desire in such persons is to care for others as they have been cared for, to love as they have been loved. Under these circumstances, mental processes function at their optimum. The quality of spirit that has been induced by the experiences of the first two phases is passed on to others. This person is in good heart, and is able to enjoy, as a gift which has not been earned, the status of a courageous person. Standing in this large room, with ample psychological space, the fourth phase of work and service to others can be readily faced. This phase implies that status includes freedom from the dependency of phases (1) and (2), to go out, on one's own, without 'smothering'.

4. The *achievement* of the task appropriate to the person. Purposeful activity is required of every human being in society, whether it be the acquisition of skills in childhood or the performance of work and service in adult life. This involves the expenditure of ontological resources, that is, of the resources of the powers of 'being' and 'well-being' which have been derived from previous phases of the interpersonal cycle. 'Ideally' when the cycle is functioning normally, work is done with sustained application and concentration, with fair tolerance of frustration, with realistic adjustment to difficulties, but with steady persistence of aim. Personal relationships with others are characterized by

outgoingness, openness, generosity, kindness, tact, warmth and reliability of commitment, peacefulness, hopefulness and patience.[61]

Frank Lake saw these phases as being present in the life of Christ, in the following way:

1. For Christ, His Spiritual 'Being', as Son of God, arises in a relationship between the Father Who attends with love, mediated by the Holy Spirit, given to Him without measure, and the Son Who responds to the Father by the same Spirit. *Acceptance*, for this Holy Son, is always assured. The Son responds by withdrawing alone for prayer, with instant access.

2. His 'Well-Being' is reached as Christ abides in the Father who gives *sustenance* to Him on all levels of His Being. The Father, with whom He is united, in prayer and worship and communion, conveys to Him the plenitude of love, glory, joy, grace and truth.

3. The dynamic outflow of personal 'being' and 'well-being' occurs when the Son of God proceeds forth from the Presence of His Father, full of grace and truth, deeply conscious of His *status* as the Son of God, to work among men. His motivation is to love as He has been loved.

4. His *achievement* has all the characteristics of the Holy Spirit's in-dwelling. It is the fulfilment of His redemptive destiny in history.[62]

The theological paradigm (from acceptance to achievement) is that of justification by faith, which, according to Leon Morris, 'means the according of the status of being in the right. Sin has put us in the wrong with God and justification is the process whereby we are reckoned as right. It is the great teaching of the New Testament that we are justified, not by what *we* do, but by what Christ has done.'[63]

The result of this justification is freedom for the individual who, because he is accepted by God, is accorded the status of sonship/daughterhood which, in turn, expresses itself in voluntary acts of worship, holiness and neighbourly service: the idea of 'good works'[64] which runs throughout the New Testament.

3 APPLICATIONS OF THE MODEL

The model is the theoretical basis for clinical theology seminars. Its significance is explored and related to real-life situations in the first-year course. This study leads to self-awareness and personal growth, in which the emotional, the physical and the intellectual are integrated. Peter Cousins, Editorial Director of The Paternoster Press, has recorded what he gained from his two years of seminars:

> I gained immensely from the two years, both in terms of insight into human nature and the springs of personality, also in respect of counselling techniques, particularly listening and responding. The two years revolutionized my perception, in terms of my own motivation and that of other people, grasping the importance of relationships, heightening awareness of other people and their feelings, and showing me how much our relationships with one another and with Jesus are grounded in feelings. The in-put/out-put cycle, his understanding of relationships between Father and Son, and the relevance of separation anxiety to Christ's experience on the cross are indelible.

The model, thirdly, illuminates the work of pastoral care. This is how Peter van de Kasteele reflected on the model in relation to his work as a parish priest:

> A woman used to telephone me most Sundays at lunchtime, beginning her conversation with, 'Vicar, I know you have had a busy morning'. On a Tuesday when she telephoned if she had not done so on a Sunday, she began: 'Vicar, I know it is your day off, but I *do* need to speak to you.' After I had begun to recognize my own hysterical reaction and glimpsed its roots within my inner world, I was less threatened and more able to bear the manipulative demands of this 'Mrs Lever'. I was also more able to forgive her plain untruths about me, and other people, which she gossiped around endlessly.
>
> One summer I returned from holiday to find two elderly men were angrily not talking to one another because of something that had happened (I cannot remember what, but it was nothing significant in itself). One was sacristan and the other treasurer, both of longstanding; the

> atmosphere was far from worthy of worship, though both knelt at the Communion rail together. Each one blamed the other while oblivious of his own shortcomings, and I received considerable blame too. As with 'Mrs Lever' who makes me feel horribly 'bad', so 'Captain Parry Noyes' (the paranoid) makes me feel guilty and impotent. The Clinical Theology model helped me to separate my own material from what belongs to other people, and that has freed me for the work of pastoral care and to love more truly.[65]

The model also gives insights into the trauma of inner pain. This is achieved, in Frank Lake's view, because it locates its roots in infantile experiences;[66] and he saw these primal experiences in terms of the suffering of the innocent and of our Lord's passion in particular:

> The Spirit of Christ, in spite of flinching, did bear all the extremities of persecution and affliction. That is what His Cross and Passion assure us of. He carried this unique experience of patient endurance of human suffering, through death, into the risen life God gave Him. The very same Spirit of Christ 'descended' on the Church at Pentecost and has been with us and in us as Christians ever since. It is this Spirit of God, able to endure all things with the fortitude of the Son, who has sustained the martyrs and upheld the afflicted. He is our first and final resource, when, in clinical pastoral care, we encourage Christians who seriously 'want to get to the bottom of their trouble', to turn and face the emergence of whatever threatens the self from within.[67]

From this understanding must, inevitably, come empathy.

Fifthly, the model offers an understanding of the helper–helped relationship. The therapeutic process depends on a healthy interpersonal relationship, as Frank Lake knew only too well.

It also offers an analysis of the mother–baby relationship: 'We are assured that dependency, unconditional acceptance and sustenance are vital in-put phases which make for a normal healthy selfhood in infancy.'[68]

Finally, it offers an analysis of the essential biological processes:

Acceptance. This is analogous with the journey of the venous blood from the tissues (to which the life-sustaining oxygen has just been imparted) along the great veins to the right side of the heart, thence to be pumped into the lungs, the place of renewal. This is the route back to 'revival'.

Sustenance. The blood 'abides' in the lungs where breath inspiration has made oxygen readily available across a single cell margin. The waste-product, carbon-dioxide, is exchanged for the fresh supply of oxygen. The haemoglobin must be free to respond to the offer of oxygen in the alveoli of the lungs. The alveoli are the final tiny chambers to which air penetrates, and to which the blood in the capillaries comes to make contact with fresh air.

Normally, the existential involvement of the haemoglobin with the oxygen brings the red blood cells to the fullness of their potential. The power to respond to the source and convert what is offered into the product that can become part of the organization, and so be carried by it to the place of out-put, is essential, whether the cycle is biological or ontological. Thus, by the end of this phase the blood has arrived at the *bene-esse* of its power as a conveyor of certain vital supplies to the whole body. At full oxygen tension the blood leaves the resource point to move back to the many points of distribution.

Status. With its 'well-being' or 'status' fully restored, the arterial blood flows from the lungs to the left side of the heart where it is strongly pumped via the aorta and the arteries into the capillaries, its place of work in the tissues.

Achievement. Here there is more prolonged contact with the tissues to which the oxygen has to be imparted. The achievement of the purpose for which the circulatory system exists (so far as its oxygen-bearing and carbon-dioxide removing properties are concerned), is fulfilled here in the tissues. The illustration has a further dynamic aptness as analogy in that the blood does not give off all its oxygen, but only a limited amount (falling to about 70 per cent oxygen tension) before it returns by the veins to be recharged in the lungs. Its service is not unlimited, but within set bounds.[69]

Later developments

TIGHT CORNERS IN PASTORAL COUNSELLING (1981)

In its original form *Tight Corners in Pastoral Counselling* was a much longer book than the one eventually published. Some 400 pages of typed manuscript clearly needed to be reduced to more manageable proportions; an additional problem was the disorganized nature of the manuscript. A semblance of order was urgently required to give the material an intelligible form for the reader. This thankless task was undertaken by Michael Jacobs, of Leicester University, for whom the difficulties were compounded as the work got under way: 'Frank said I had carte blanche with it, and yet when it came to the final proofs, he still had to add some pages to the introduction, which spoiled the gentle shape I had given it, and he reinserted at that point (having previously accepted the draft for the printers) considerable footnotes to make other points which were still occurring to him. I was not sure he could really let go of the book to me as he had originally been happy to.'[70]

The volume's essential ideas and conclusions are set out in chapters 2 and 3, where he discusses what he calls the *Maternal–Foetal Distress Syndrome*. Dr Roger Moss is currently engaged in an in-depth study of the whole subject,[71] and no attempt at a full-scale analysis will be made here, but Frank Lake's main conclusions must, if only for the sake of balance, be referred to.

These conclusions may be enumerated as follows:

1 The foetus is vulnerable to all that is going on within the mother: 'Affliction in its worst forms strikes in the first three months of pregnancy after conception.'[72] This is more fundamental than merely whether she was pleased or not about being pregnant. In this respect Frank Lake was at variance with the then psychodynamic theory that there is 'no noticeable difference between spending nine months in the womb of an abundantly happy mother, or forty unloved weeks inside an anxious, distressed or suicidally despairing woman'.[73] In fact, he dismissed such a theory as 'ludicrous', and he reaffirmed:

> Before birth, the foetus may be seriously damaged if the mother is dependent on alcohol, nicotine or other drugs. It is also damaged by the less readily identifiable changes that transmit to the baby a mother's rejection of a particular pregnancy and of the life growing within her. Any severe maternal distress, whatever its cause, imprints itself on the foetus. These damaging experiences are now accessible to consciousness without undue difficulty.[74]

2 Perinatal experiences powerfully determine the whole of a person's background of feeling and attitude to transition and change: 'It is from these experiences that our perception of the cosmos derives. Our basic expectations of what it means to live outside in "God's world", and to depend on others for gentle handling, love and mercy, take their origin here.'[75] And this is how he describes the effect of 'Distress in the Womb':

> Although there was ample evidence in the work of Fodor, Peerbolte and F. J. Mott, we had not realized until 1976 how severely painful and how well remembered is the much earlier invasion of the foetus by maternal distress. Nor had we then collected enough 'evidence' to establish the correlation between the origins of this widespread and crippling syndrome of affliction, and the very early and overwhelming invasion of the foetus by maternal anxiety, depression, hatred, despair, coveting, envy, jealousy, and the whole gamut of [the woman's] bad feelings. Whether these are the consequences of her own bad life situation during the pregnancy, or of a difficult situation now made much worse by her own early conditioning, when she was in *her* mother's womb and in her subsequent childhood, they are, by some mechanism we do not understand, made vividly present to the foetus and become part, the earliest part, of the conditioning or learning process.[76]

The two key elements here are, first, the invasion of the foetus by the mother's often complex emotions:

> She may have loved the man by whom she became pregnant, while hating the resultant foetus, or loved the

> prospect of having a baby, while hating, fearing or feeling deeply disappointed and neglected by its father. The foetus receives all such messages, but has difficulty (in so far as primal work provides us with usable evidence on these matters) in distinguishing what relates specifically to it and what belongs to the mother's feelings about her own life in general.[77]

and, secondly, the foetal response: 'The tendency is to feel identified with all these invading maternal emotions in turn and to react to each. This produces, in some people, a life-long imprinting of distressful feelings that have nothing whatever to do with any of their own life situations. They prove to be a direct transcript, often in extraordinary and specific detail, of the pregnant mother's disturbance.'[78]

3 Post-natal dereliction is just one of the roots of affliction, the tap root, according to Frank Lake, being firmly placed in 'the first trimester, within three or so months of conception'.[79]

4 The significance of all this for pastoral understanding and counselling in terms of the 'Healing of the Memories' was obvious enough to Lake, who sought a therapeutic alliance in which the adult was able to identify with, and '*give recognition and acceptance to their own inner child of the past and foetus in the womb*'[80] (his italics).

This task of integration (re-birthing), or, to use Frank Lake's metaphor, the stitching-up of the torn garment of self so that it becomes whole again, was carried out in Primal Integration conferences or residential workshops. The procedure adopted at these sessions is described below from personal experience:

> The method that Frank Lake worked out can be called the simulation method. He works with small groups (5–7 persons) with a leader/therapist and a co-leader in each group. After a meal and a short introduction the participants tell what they choose about their lives, their problems, why they have come, what they want to work on and what they hope to achieve. There is always someone starting and others who continue with their stories. It is all very informal. Despite the differences between the participants regarding age, education and profession you never-

theless recognize yourself in the others' stories. Basically our problems are rather similar.

The first meeting usually takes place in the evening and in the morning after that the participants are divided into small groups and the real work starts. If there are participants who are well aware of what they want to work on and have a clear understanding of their problems they can very soon get down to birth experiences. Others, who feel their problems more vaguely or don't have a clear picture of their problems, might need other methods before they are 'ripe' for a birth experience. Frank Lake and his co-workers often use *gestalt* methods in such cases.

In the small groups you usually work with one person at a time. The important thing is that security is created within the small group – that is the prerequisite for deeper experiences. The person that the group works with lies normally down in a foetal position, where he/she is recommended to relax and breathe deeply. Sooner or later something happens – memories can emerge, you can go deeper into feelings and/or you can start moving forward in movements reminiscent of a foetus. The therapist usually holds his hands round the head of the 'patient'. The pressure on the head must be in accordance with the process. The other group members give support for the feet and form a 'uterus' with the help of big cushions placed around the 'patient'.

What happens then depends on the birth history of the individual, but common to most people are the convulsive, propelling movements, that often can get enormously strong, and the feeling to be shut in with no possibility to get out. The strong pressure on the head feels like the nourishing from the birth canal. Many experience difficulty in breathing, you are nearly suffocated, get nauseated, feel tensions in chest and stomach, spasms, crying, shouting. Some people can get detailed memories of their own birth and many come into a real confrontation with death.

The birth is over when the head pushes out from the birth canal and people often repeat the characteristic head-rotation that newborns do. After this, many people feel enormously abandoned and deserted and stay in that feeling for a while, but little by little you return to the surface again. You are now conscious of where you are, the people around and what you have experienced. That can give you an unimagined sense of liberation. A session like this takes normally between one and three hours. During a workshop for three days all participants can have a real session each; during five-day workshops there is more. Much of the value with the small groups, besides the security they give, lies in the fact that you are participating in the experiences of other group members. You assist them and feel with them in their pain.[81]

The same person chronicled what actually happened to her in two of her own primal sessions:

In my first primal I laughed when I finally after a hard but not this time hopeless struggle (I felt love from my mother and she let me rest between contractions this time), came out and I shouted 'I'm here, I'm here'. I have now asked my mother and she says that she was given no gas or anaesthetic whatsoever when I was born. Anyway, this feeling of exaltation after being born was quite new and unexpected for me. I had a long while of deep relaxation lying on my back with folded arms in this primal. I knew I was lonely but that didn't hurt, in fact I felt I was sufficient for myself and that I could stand a lot more. I felt immensely strong and knew somehow that nothing could hurt me. I felt like a king. It felt good just to be, and to be me. A lot of energy was streaming through me, coming into my feet, streaming upwards towards my spine, up to my head and down along the chest and abdomen to my genitals. A kind of soft and gentle orgasm. I got a vision of my family at that time and myself as the guru of the family giving them all (mother, father, and a five years older brother) lots of energy. I felt like after a storm, after the rain just before the sun comes back and the birds start singing. I got a vision of myself in a forest, hearing the grass and leaves growing, and the sound of an eternal waterfall in the background. I felt like a cat being out walking in the grass, stretching, my tail ending in a flower – a big dandelion. I then changed into a blackbird sitting on a tree watching the silly cat that can't fly, the simplest thing in the world. After these visions I got up on my feet and had a very strange body-feeling. My body felt very vast, definitely not confined to my muscular body and I had to sit down for a while to regain my ordinary body-feeling and orientation. The prevailing feeling after this primal was an exalted feeling of calm and strong pleasurable feeling of being me.

In my second primal, which started from my feeling of smallness and hopelessness towards Jim, I stayed mainly in the uterus feeling vulnerable and exposed to bad stuff coming in from outside – as well as moments of self-affirmation and love. Also several strong urges to vomit up bad stuff. This something coming into me was associated with the vision of this big, black bird, a kind of vulture being very threatening, waiting for me to die so he could eat me up. I had very strong feelings of fear in connection with this. Then there was a big, cold eye watching me and penetrating my brain, splitting it to pieces. After this fearful attack there was a strong feeling of exaltation and relaxation, when I saw music being brought by beautiful blue birds. I moved around a bit feeling weightless. It was nice again. I then got the feeling that this cold eye penetrating my brain in some way wanted to test me, if I was worthy to go on living. I stood the test. Could it have been an unintentional abortion attempt due to strong emotional stress on my mother? I don't know, and when I asked my mother, very carefully, how she experienced her pregnancy, she didn't remember any difficulties.

After a second attack of bad stuff, I saw a rainbow – and then rock-carvings of the kind you find in Sweden. There were carvings of ships and different animals. Our ship then was materialized. It was a Viking ship and I was on board. We were rowing – I don't know where. We were singing while rowing in a rhythmical way. Next vision was a huge battlefield where thousands of people were slaughtering each other, shouting in rage and fear. I was just an observer. The people were fighting with words and they wore clothes of a very ancient kind. I got the feeling that I was witnessing the struggle of the last days – in Nordic mythology that is called Ragnarok. Somehow the blood from the battlefield was flowing into one stream that was coming down my throat. It felt very life-giving.

In another vision following this one I was walking on the very green grass of Iceland. I felt somehow that this was the place where the huge battle had been fought. The grass and the black lava stones were cool. When walking I felt the cool water between my toes. After another attack of the bad stuff, trying to vomit and get rid of it, I got a strong sense that I am good. The bad stuff could not make me hate myself. 'They who pour this material into me are the bad ones,' I said. 'Who are they?' I was asked. 'Not only my mother. I see the black bird again. I want to bite it,' I said.

A cushion was then given me and I bit and bit, again and again, growling and hitting the cushion. Finally I threw it away, saying that I had killed it. I then felt strong vibrations of love coming from and through my mother. It was like being protected by a big purring cat. I knew she was happy. I then got a vision of the house that Jim was asked to build in the morning meditation that day. My house was just by the sea and I sat there rocking in the rocking-chair, just looking at the sea. I made rocking movements with my body and started singing a Swedish summer hymn which is always sung when school ends in the summer. It goes like this: 'The flower time is coming, with great delight and beauty. You are approaching sweet summer, when grass and crops are growing. With gentle and vivid warmth, to all that has been dead, the rays of the sun approach, and all is reborn.'

In fact, I was born on the 19th of May; according to my mother, a delightful early summer day. After singing the hymn it was dinner time and I got up feeling extremely well.[82]

The whole purpose and intention of this reliving was to verbalize the hitherto unexpressed foetal pain and, by reliving it, to use it in a creative way so that the end product is healing and growth. Frank Lake believed that, at this juncture, the Holy Spirit 'seems quite clearly to lead people into an actual reliving of the pain, *within the power of the Saviour who shares it*'[83] (my italics). In *Tight Corners in Pastoral Counselling*, he denies that he equated the reliving of birth as part of the healing of the memories with the experience of the new birth

(John 3), but goes on to say that he observes 'a close relationship between their physical birth and the ways in which people experience difficulty or ease when they come to consider whether they can accept the new birth by faith into Christ'. Then he adds this:

> All the fears, doubts and commitment anxieties that beset them at their physical birth tend to crowd round people at the proposal of a second birth. Indeed, to force oneself towards the experience of being born again into the family of God can evoke primal disturbances of psychotic intensity, if the actual gestation and birth were accompanied by pain of mind-splitting character. Just as Christ healed people physically but left them to decide later what they would do by way of faith and discipleship, so, if we can clear a way through the living debris of the first womb and the first birth, we do at least make it possible for a person to consider the second birth and the womb of the Spirit without the degree of panic and confusion, resistance and dread which accompanied the first.[84]

Frank Lake offered the 'Maternal–Foetal Distress Syndrome', therefore, as a model for understanding individual needs, with especial reference to anger, violence, fears, doubts and anxieties, but also, in other words, as 'the hermeneutic or interpretative principle for our understanding of the origins of disorders'. He also saw it as matching and correlating with the detail of the 'redemptive identification of Jesus Christ with our race in God's supreme act of love, justice and power. The Cross, of Christ, offered in depth at the point of primal impact, offers immense prophylactic possibilities.'[85]

'HEALING OF THE MEMORIES' AND THE CHARISMATIC RENEWAL MOVEMENT

Frank Lake's work with primal pain, leading to his convictions regarding the importance of perinatal experiences may, instructively, be compared with certain developments within the Charismatic Renewal Movement, to which he was increasingly drawn from the early 1970s onwards; in particular, to the expectation called the 'Healing of the Memories', and to which Lake refers in *Tight Concern in Pastoral Counselling*. Cognate terms for this are 'inner healing' and 'soul-healing'.

The earliest reference in charismatic literature to this form of healing (at least, as far as I am aware) occurs in Agnes Sanford's book, *Healing Gifts of the Spirit*, first published in 1949. Her use of the expression 'Healing of the Memories' thus pre-dates Frank Lake's use of it in *Tight Corners in Pastoral Counselling*, by about thirty years. What is more pertinent is the method and procedure she adopted when counselling people with deeply embedded psychological hurts. This is how she dealt with a person who had told her about some persistent temptation, or some old sin or an irrational fear:

> I ask him a little bit about his childhood. Then, as he talks, I listen. I concentrate my full attention on him, praying that the Spirit of Christ will bring up from his memories whatever needs to be brought up, will guide him to say the key words and will help me to recognize the key when I hear it. Having prayed thus, I forget myself entirely. I am not aware of thought or feeling. I do not 'pour out love' to this person, knowing that my human love is insufficient for his healing and might even become a trap to him. Moreover, to 'pour out love' would be to have my mind on myself rather than projecting my whole mind and soul into the other person. Nor do I listen with any attempt to preach or moralize.[86]

She would then adopt the following approach:

> I give myself to them only in the hope that whatever they have done may be forgiven through my sharing it with them, so that I can also share the life of Christ with them. Jesus had respect for their souls and died for them. Shall I not therefore accomplish the little death of laying aside my own life for a moment that I may enter into theirs? Certainly they should not fear. But unless the perfect love of Christ can be projected into them through me so as to cast out fear, they cannot help but fear.[87]

The third stage, based on the information given her, would be prayer:

> I simply pray, usually with the laying on of hands, for the love of Christ to come into this one and forgive the sins and heal the sorrows of the past as well as the present –

> the little child who used to be, as well as the grown person who is now. I begin at the present and go back through the memories, mentioning every sin and every grievous incident that has been told me. Indeed, I go further back than this, and pray for the healing of those impressions of fear or anger that came upon the infant far beyond the reach of memory. I carry this prayer back to the time of birth and even before birth and pray for the restoration of the soul, for the healing of the soul – the psyche – of the real, original person.[88]

Two aspects of her method are similar to Frank Lake's: identification with the distressed person, and the journey back to the birth or even the pre-birth stage.

Another leading exponent of this process of healing is Francis MacNutt. In his book, *Healing* (first published in 1974), he stipulates that a complete healing ministry comprises for basic prayer the methods (1) for repentance, (2) for inner healing, (3) for physical healing and (4) for deliverance. The first is for personal sin, the second for a wider range of emotional problems, the third for physical sickness and the last for demonic oppression.

What MacNutt found in his pastoral ministry (as a Roman Catholic priest in the United States) was that he seemed to have very little to offer the people who were hurting the most: a situation reminiscent of his Anglican counterparts in Britain. To the well-balanced person he could offer helpful suggestions, but if that person had a deep emotional wound, then MacNutt found that his resources were severely limited:

> I found, of course, that my concern and caring were in themselves a healing force. But I didn't have time to listen to all the disturbed people asking for appointments. The psychiatrists, too, were overbooked and unless a person had done something desperate, they had to wait a month for a first appointment. What could I tell the mentally depressed woman who could not believe that God loved her and whose whole experience of life simply demonstrated to her that no one really cared about her – especially if her husband had deserted her? The only one who would listen to her was a psychiatrist at $50 an hour. What could I say to the homosexual who simply was not attracted to women

> and whose tendency went all the way back as far as he could remember? What hope did he have for a change; what did the Church offer him as a real help?[89]

All of this caused him to reflect seriously on why, if Christ comes to bring liberation (salvation and freedom), was there not any realistic hope for those deeply wounded psychologically? At that point he heard of Agnes Sanford's phrase ('Healing of the Memories'), and the effect on MacNutt's thinking was, to say the least, startling and dramatic:

> It was as if the whole wall of an unfinished building suddenly went into place. It made sense not only because Christ came to free us from the evil that burdens us, but also because it was in accord with what psychologists have discovered about the nature of man: that we are deeply affected not only by what we do, but by what happens to us through the sins of others and the evil in the world (original sin). Our deepest need is for love, and if we are denied love as infants or as children, or anywhere else along the line, it may affect our lives at a later date and rob us of our peace, of our ability to love, and of our ability to trust man – or God.[90]

But what is inner healing? According to MacNutt, the essential idea is that 'Jesus who is the same, yesterday, today and forever, can take the memories of our past'. When this happens, those wounds that affect our present lives are healed, those places in a person's heart that have been empty or corroded for so long are filled with his love. For MacNutt this involves two related processes: bringing to light past hurts, and prayer for the healing of the traumatic incidents of the past. Significantly, too, he says this:

> Some of these hurts go way back into the past; others are quite recent. Our experience coincides with the findings of psychologists: that many of the deepest hurts go way back to the time when we were most vulnerable and least able to defend ourselves. There is a good deal of evidence that some hurts go back even before birth while the child was still being carried in the mother's womb. Just as John the Baptist leapt in Elizabeth's womb when she heard Mary's greeting, so every child seems sensitive to its mother's

> moods. If the mother does not really want the child or is suffering from anxiety or fear, the infant seems somehow to pick up the feelings of the mother and to respond to them. (In praying for inner healing I have seen an adult woman re-experience in an amazing way the time before birth and verbalize it during the prayer. 'I'm not going to come out; I'm not going to be born!') These earliest memories up to the time we are two or three years old seem to be the most important in setting the patterns of our future behaviour.[91]

A comparison between MacNutt's emphases and Lake's reveals the following picture. Both recognize that repentance – the Church's traditional remedy – is 'insufficient advice' (MacNutt's words) for those whose emotional problems had gone down deeply into a person's subconscious, and for whom the problems were largely involuntary and pre-verbal. Both pinpoint the inadequacy of recommending willpower and intelligence in such situations. Both state that the traditional methods of medicine and psychiatry do not always help either. Both accept the creative fusion of psychiatry (with its insights about the nature of man) and theology. Both place stress on the importance of prayer in applying Christ's redemptive, healing power to the afflicted and suffering. Both have confidence in God's transforming love to effect release from the most long-standing of inner emotional turmoils. Both favour an extended application of Scripture as it applies to a particular situation. Both indicate that the Church has to reflect Jesus's wish to heal and to bring a person to wholeness. MacNutt declares that man's most basic need is to 'know that he is loved – not for anything he can achieve or do, but simply because he is. If anyone does not know God's love in this way, Jesus eagerly desires to show us how much he cares for us by healing us of those ancient hurts that have withered or broken our hearts and spirits',[92] while Lake says: 'In the person of God the Father's fully human, reconciling Son, he speaks and acts into the clinical situation of cosmic pain suffering and pain.'[93]

Where, however, both Sanford and MacNutt diverge from Frank Lake is with regard to the techniques employed to get at the root of the emotional pain. Neither of them uses (or used) LSD, or Freudian therapeutic techniques, or deep breathing, but simply attentive listening and the application of Christ's healing power through prayer and the dynamic power of the Holy Spirit.

This latter method is also favoured by John Wimber, the founder of the Vineyard Fellowships in California. In *Power Healing*, he defines inner healing as 'a process in which the Holy Spirit brings forgiveness of sins and emotional renewal to people suffering from damaged minds, wills and emotions';[94] and he sees the damaging experiences that lead to a person's needing inner healing as falling into three categories: the damage that is part and parcel of being born into a sinful world; wounds inflicted by other people; and damage as a result of personal sin. Wimber makes little or no reference to the birth or pre-birth experiences.

Not all modern charismatics, however, agree with – and still less practise – inner healing. One such objector to this process is the Revd Colin Urquhart, founder of the Bethany Fellowship (now called Kingdom Faith Ministries) in Sussex. In *Receive Your Healing*, he makes this statement:

> You are not the person you were before you were born again. You have a new nature. Christ lives in you by the presence of His Spirit and you are being changed from one degree of glory to another – into His likeness. When you see Him face to face, you will be like Him. God's purpose of wholeness for you will then be completed.
>
> You are being healed and changed through the truth of what Jesus has done for you. If there is anything from your past that has caused emotional or physical sickness, the Spirit is willing to reveal that the cross of Jesus has covered that need. The Scriptures warn us against digging and delving into the past. *You do not need to keep going over the details of the old life in order to be able to live the new.*
>
> If you have a need which is the result of something in your past, this is a present problem. It may be an unresolved conflict or resentment that has been bottled up for years. But the problem is a present one and forgiveness will be the gateway to the healing, whether emotional, physical or both.
>
> The basis of *all* divine healing is what God has done for

us. Faith enables you to know that you do not have to be a victim of your past. *Christ has set you free to live His new life.*

Often people receive ministry that takes them back farther and farther, reliving the details of their past, because of the lack of faith to believe that Jesus has dealt with these things.

You do not have to relive your past sins before they can be forgiven. You believe that to confess the fact of them is enough to secure God's forgiveness. So why treat sickness any differently when both sin and sickness have been dealt with at the same time – on the cross? *God is equally able to free you from the fact of your emotional need without your having to relive those past experiences. It is His truth that sets you free.*[95]

This argument would not have impressed Frank Lake because he knew, as indeed modern discoveries in medicine have confirmed, that memories powerfully influence our attitudes and behaviour so that, as John Wimber says, 'even when we do not consciously remember painful events, we still feel the effects of them'.[96] And he adds: 'Through the power and grace of the Holy Spirit these memories may be consciously recalled, faced and prayed for, with the person experiencing peace and release from their hold.'

Lake knew, too, the vital importance of differentiating between surface and root memories. The former (surface) is defined by Michael Scanlon as 'memories that can be called forth into the consciousness of the person',[97] for example, guilt, memories of an embarrassing incident. He defines root memories as those 'embedded deeply in people's subconscious minds, below the level of awareness – these may include a recent memory of rejection, or a hidden repressed memory of early life, or even a pattern of life that continues almost independently of any memories'.[98]

Frank Lake also knew of the dichotomy, that so often afflicts evangelicals, between what is supposed to be true, on the one hand, and what is actually true, on the other hand. After all, it is merely an ostrich-like posture to declare what ought to be happening when the opposite is actually occurring. The fact is that Urquhart's view on this particular issue is unrealistic, whereas Lake preferred to approach people from where they were theologically, psychologically and emotionally. To ignore the evidence is to adopt a foolishly triumphalistic approach which can often ensnare people, giving them false expectations.

Lake received a great deal from his contacts with charismatics by way of reinforcement and encouragement. What he brought to them was a profound awareness and understanding of the human psyche, together with the insistence that some suffering can be creative. This insistence he based on the analogy of our Lord's experience in Passion Week, when he had to go through the 'dark night' of the soul (Good Friday) before emerging into the newness and beauty of resurrection life on the third day.

This theme is developed succinctly and powerfully in one of Lake's sermons entitled 'Christ the Therapist'. His argument is worth setting out in some detail:

> Christ can enter the empty room that is the heart of every afflicted person, though its doors stay shut for fear of exposure, because He can enter it, as He entered the Upper Room on the first Easter Day, behind closed doors. Like the disciples, the afflicted man is anxious to have Jesus closely visible inside the room of his life. But, like them, he cannot, because he dare not open the doors for fear of the inrush of hostile elements. He fears the shame of emptiness. Internal persecutors, or a dreadful nothingess would, he fears, burst into consciousness, overwhelming him like great waves.
>
> If understanding this, a man can desire it to be so, Christ, who has Himself done all the necessary rescue work of passing through dread, dereliction and infinite separation from God on our behalf in order to get to us, is invited to enter behind the defences, in spite of our compulsively closed doors. He is indeed already there with the afflicted child, within the private hell we are afraid of re-entering. So it can happen, that without, as yet, fully entering into his own personal experiences of dereliction or dread, a man becomes confident that Christ is no stranger to it. Though he cannot yet be related to his own abyss of non-being by direct introspection, he can be related to it, and in a sense, accept it, through faith in Christ who has entered, ploughed up and harrowed hell for all men.

> This 'faith existence' changed the effect of affliction on the sufferer. Christ enters by His Holy Spirit, in spite of all our rage against Him, in spite of our paradoxical love–hate feelings towards Him and our suspicion of His providence. Christ enters and enables the afflicted person to accept the closeness of others and some measure of intimacy and commitment. Loving movements are initiated, not passively and fearfully waited for. The degree to which pain is banished varies. It is often transformed into a kind of joy the world has no conception of, with firm hope and expectation. With the trial is now a 'way of escape' – not so that we do not bear it any longer, but that we may be able creatively and joyfully to bear it. Unbearable affliction, the annihilation of trust in persons, and with it despair of one's own selfhood, is transformed, by Christ's alongsideness in the dereliction, into that tribulation joyfully borne, out of which all the Saints have come.[99]

And in another sermon Frank Lake summarizes the significance of all this for the Christian who, undergirded by Jesus's strength, peace, joy and power, is able to face the 'dark night' of the soul with life-giving confidence:

> When our outward man is perishing, because we have been promoted to the level at which our incompetence, in the wildest human sense, is more and more in evidence, must we not look at our need for this second stage of the healing miracle of Jesus? Though painful, as the outward man perishes, an inward man, something perhaps we have never imagined before, will be renewed from day to day. At the end of the dark tunnel will be the light of re-birth. Passing through a dark baptism of overwhelming waters, we emerge on a new unimagined shore. And all this happens long before we take that final plunge we call death of the body.
>
> This is the victory that overcomes the world, not our struggling to retain the sense of competence, but our faith in the wounded physician, who conquered because he could bear defeat, who gives us eternal hope, because by his Cross he dared to become our neighbour in despair.[100]

T. S. Eliot encapsulated this beautifully when he wrote:

The wounded surgeon plies the steel
That questions the distempered part:
Beneath the bleeding hands we feel
The sharp compassion of the healer's art.*

The final vision

WITH RESPECT: A DOCTOR'S RESPONSE TO A HEALING POPE (1982)

This book was almost entirely written in June 1981 when Frank and Sylvia spent a three-week holiday in the West of Scotland. Its material is but a short step from *Tight Corners in Pastoral Counselling*. In that earlier volume Frank Lake had reiterated, time and time again, his high respect for life at its pre-natal and post-birth stages; and alongside this respect, and complementing it, was his conception of what became for him his life's work and justification:

> As pastoral counsellors, dealing with those who are emotionally sick, our work is somewhat like that of the mission hospital. Our work is to practise the works of love rather than to preach the Word of life. In fact we do both, and I find myself speaking the Word of life much more frequently than I did as a medical missionary commissioned to do the works of love.[101]

The core argument of *With Respect*, the question of abortion, must be viewed against the background of radical shifts in two crucial areas. First, the ethos of the medical profession itself. Over forty years earlier Frank Lake had assented to a revised form of the Hippocratic Oath in which 'Apollo' had been replaced by 'God'. By 1948 the Geneva Declaration, approved by the World Medical Association, left 'God' out altogether, but preserved this twofold promise:

> *I will maintain the utmost respect for human life, from the time of conception*; even under threats I will not use medical knowledge contrary to the laws of humanity.[102]

This honourable adherence to the protection of the human

*

foetus and regarded as a 'law of humanity', was under considerable pressure at the time Frank Lake wrote *With Respect*:

> This code of practice no longer has any official force in England or Scotland, though it does in Ireland. Laws are always bound to be, to some extent, sensitive to current public opinion expressed through the legislature. But a profession must at times be prepared to hold to its own ethical standards, with some rigour, against the demands of a political régime. World medical opinion expected doctors in Nazi Germany to have done this. More recently, psychiatrists in Soviet Russia are held to have been ethically at fault, since, when expected to certify political dissidents as insane, then forcibly to 'condition' them to a brain-washed compliance, they complied and supervised the procedure.
>
> Some Christian obstetricians and gynaecologists in Britain have held to the spirit and letter of the Hippocratic Oath. For refusing to perform abortions on demand they have lost consultant appointments for which they were otherwise well qualified. The bulk of the profession, however, 'moving with the times', has been caught up in the tide of modernity. To earlier generations this 'modern' outlook would have been regarded as a condition of moral laxity, of ethical corruption and collective irresponsibility. To itself it is now, without question, a 'progressive' measure.[103]

The second area was that of the liberation of women. Vociferous voices were demanding three 'freedoms' in particular for women: from the risk that sexual intercourse will lead to pregnancy; from the risk of having to carry, for full term and birth, an unwanted foetus; and from the risk of having to remain with an unwanted husband.

Frank Lake was not impressed and regarded abortion as unjust killing:

> Abortion on demand is in another moral category than contraception (where only the method can be reasonably in dispute, not the desirability of it in certain cases) or divorce (where Scripture itself envisages conditions under

which it may properly take place). In the matter of abortion, according to Bernard Häring's authoritative text on *Medical Ethics*, the prohibition is held to be an absolute which can call forth the august doctrine of the infallibility of the Church's teaching office and function: 'On questions of morality, the role of infallibility is limited to the enunciation of the most basic principles, to declaring, for instance, the fundamental right of man to life and prohibiting unjust killing.'

Those who advocate abortion for reasons of personal or social inconvenience are usually insistent that the foetus has no human sensibility, no self-awareness or knowledge that it has a life which, by the abortifacient agent, is being brought to a violent end. They state that in no sense could the foetus be regarded as a person or a human being. As their asphyxiated, surgically evacuated bodies are carried out of the operating theatre to the incinerator, along with tumours and amputated limbs, they are not to be regarded as premature infants looking for decent burial, but 'uterine products' no more to be respected than excised cancers.[104]

His objections were all the more strident and strongly-held because of the thousands of hours he had spent with adults who, with total conviction, were 'reliving their actual remembered experiences within the first three months after conception, and who, in consequence, have realized their acute awareness as the foetus of the mother's emotional states, both before and after she recognizes she is pregnant. I have no room left for doubting that the aborted foetus knows that its presence is unwanted and that the action taken to produce the abortion is meant to dislodge it from the womb and thus cut it off from life.'[105] He also makes this personal statement:

For me, as for all those who have taken part in this research, many of them in the caring professions, the Hippocratic Oath to 'maintain the utmost respect for human life, from the time of conception', which has been binding on doctors since before the time of Christ, is not in any sense a traditionalist, 'hard-line' attitude, insensitive to the needs of women to have 'full rights over their own bodies'. Nor are we insensitive to the distress of the mother that is transmitted to the unwanted foetus. We know all too well the

> often grim alternative to abortion, in the Maternal–Foetal Distress Syndrome.
>
> Indeed we have evidence that in many cases, in the first trimester, foetal distress at the overwhelming influx of black and bitter feelings from the mother is . . . horrible.[106]

'I could no more assist', says Frank Lake just a little later in the book, 'in the "euthanasia" of the afflicted foetus than in the euthanasia of the still-afflicted adult. "Mercy killing" of either kind is forbidden by the Hippocratic Oath.'[107]

On this issue, as on the social stress of contraception, Frank Lake is entirely at one with Pope John Paul II, whom he sees as wanting to be alongside people in their agony and suffering. Indeed, his respect for the present Pope is profound in *With Respect*, deriving principally from what Lake sees as his great sensitivity as a physician with regard to the whole range of human sickness:

> As a physician he knows that he cannot proceed until he has listened to his patient, individual or corporate. The disunity of the Church, for instance, is incompatible with its Catholic health. The churches into which it is fragmented have, until recently, added to their disease of disunity the chronic disability of being deliberately deaf to each other's positive witness to Christ. If there is to be any remedy, it requires, of those who set about the healing, that they be, first of all, listeners. John Paul II expressed this unequivocally in his address to the Secretariat for the Union of Christians, led by Cardinal Johannes Willebrands.
>
> > 'Unity calls for a fidelity that is constantly deepened through listening to one another. With brotherly freedom partners in a true dialogue challenge one another to a more and more exacting faithfulness to God's plan in its entirety.'[108]

And he concludes his study of the Pope as a person, speaker and writer, with these words:

> It is as a physician, a wounded physician, that we need him now. He can do much in the years to come to effect an even closer rapprochement between the Churches in

England which will heal our divisions sufficiently to enable us to engage in an even closer working and witnessing together.[109]

With Respect is by a remarkable man about another remarkable man. It clearly signals Frank Lake's interest in the question of ecclesiastical unity, something he brought to the work of the Clinical Theology Association as a whole. It also shows the width and extent of Lake's reading. What drew Frank Lake to this particular Pope was not essentially a theological matter, rather the question of the schizoid personality syndrome, to which he of course devoted the longest chapter in *Clinical Theology* (1966). It was precisely the issue which attracted him to such writers as Kierkegaard (with his copious references to 'dread' and 'double despair'), and to Simone Weil (with her repeated stress on '*malheur*' or '*affliction*'). And he is, of course, talking about himself when, in the Preface to *With Respect*, he refers to the most fundamental needs of those classifiable as schizoid personalities:

> The schizoid personality reaction indicates suffering beyond the limits of the capacity of the organism to oppose invasive evil from the environment. A reversal mechanism takes over which attempts to put an end to the pain by siding with the destructive force against oneself, intensifying self-destructive urges of every kind. The pastoral and therapeutic care of such persons is bedevilled by their actual experience of God's creation, during the most vulnerable and earliest months of life, as utterly untrustable, hostile and evil, so that death is preferable to that travesty of life. The usual pastoral approach, which proceeds from a conviction of culpable sin against a good God, who nevertheless, in Christ forgives the sinner, is as irrelevant to their basic dilemma as Job's friends' approach to him was irrelevant. They need to know Christ as the one who does not blame them, but apologizes, so to speak, on God's behalf, by suffering alongside and within them in their innocent affliction.[110]

This latter concept of Christ apologizing on God's behalf raised problems with some of the reviewers of *With Respect* as it had done when the same idea was touched upon in *Tight*

Corners in Pastoral Counselling. The relevant section in that book is the one (quoted below) in which Frank Lake discusses the role of the pastor in relation to the matter of foetal distress:

> On behalf of a creation that has miscarried and on behalf of a society and families that have passed on and perpetuated injustice to this hurt person, I am there to apologize. I invite their forgiveness by hearing the anger of their protest against injustices without reproach. The message of my being there is the one God gave so powerfully to the Lady Julian of Norwich, 'I saw no blame'.
>
> If the Cross of Christ says anything to the afflicted, who suffered first, and fatally for their trust, in the first trimester of life in the womb, about the forgiveness of their sins it is that *he is God, begging their forgiveness* for the hurts caused by the sins of the fathers, funnelled into them by the distress of the mothers. This theme, of Christ as the innocent, just man, as the Lamb taken from the flock to have the sins of others laid on his head, sharing the lot of all the innocent afflicted, this is the deepest and earliest level of meaning in the suffering of the Son of God.[111]

The difficulty here is that of the conflict between phrases which resonate emotionally, and undoubtedly contain valuable pastoral insights, but which are not in perfect accord with the theology of the New Testament. This is how the Revd David Atkinson saw it in his review[112] for *Third Way*: 'There is little in the book [*Tight Corners in Pastoral Counselling*] about the Pauline emphasis on God justifying us, and of Christ having acted to take hurt from us, in our stead. There seem to be places where Lake is tailoring his theology to fit his psychological and therapeutic assumptions.'

With Respect is an amalgam of many different subjects, not all of which are or can be integrated together. It is a slightly amorphous collection of essays, therefore, somewhat disorganized and in need of further pruning. But it is a valuable work in that it charts Frank Lake's thinking right up to the end of his life. That it did not attract the sort of critical scrutiny accorded *Clinical Theology* and *Tight Corners in Pastoral Counselling* must not be allowed to detract from its obvious importance for a full understanding of Frank Lake's work as a whole. This is so not least because it illustrates the inevitable tensions when a committed evangelical like him attempts to correlate psychoanalytical perceptions with biblical truth. The tensions remain, will always do so, but *With Respect* confirms memorably that the attempt was worth the making. Above all, perhaps, there is his portrayal of the extent to which our Lord identified himself with suffering humanity:

> Christ came to a few, to relatively few people, in the days of his ministry of power, in such a way as to raise them and heal them directly. Through his Body, the Church, he still enacts that messianic compassion. But the deeper mercy was in his readiness to be placed alongside us, the victim of mercilessness. In this he gives dignity to all humiliated persons by the manner of his bearing of his humiliation.[113]

6

In Retrospect

The purpose of this chapter is to bring together some of the dominating features of Frank Lake's life and work, and to peruse them in an objective and analytical manner.

Frank Lake: the man

He was undoubtedly a complex man. His forceful personality meant that people had a definite reaction to him: it was impossible to be neutral about him which, in turn, meant that it was, for most people, impossible to be neutral about his work either. He polarized opinions in a quite distinct way. Thus his views, ideas and theories, all held and discussed with dynamic conviction and zeal, tended to be received either with adulation or with strident opposition. This was a pity, because some rejected what he had to say more on the basis of personality than on calm objective judgement. But the responsibility for this was not entirely theirs.

Frank Lake's energy and productivity were alike prodigious. As Sylvia has said: 'His drive of energy was unbelievable, and people often feared for *him*. I think I feared for *them*.'[1] He frequently referred to himself as a 'workaholic', and he could get by on very few hours sleep each night; by eight in the morning he had often put in half a day's work. His work for the Clinical Theology Association continued unabated and relentlessly even on family holidays – he would be writing endlessly while the other members of the family would be swimming or playing on the beach. Many would consider this selfish behaviour, though his family accepted it with much good (though undoubtedly frustrated) grace.

There was within him a driving compulsion, a boundless enthusiasm, allied to which he was able to carry others along with him and inspire them with his vision and his passionate desire to heal people and to bring them to wholeness. The negative side of this enthusiasm was that he often got swept away on a wave of zealousness which detrimentally affected his judgement and critical faculties. This led to what some considered to be dubious techniques: for example, his use of LSD and 're-birthing'. Another negative effect was an inability to comprehend why others could not follow him all the way, either in terms of commitment or conceptually. This fact was well known and is, I believe, the significance of Professor Pond's letter (only one of many I could refer to) on the appearance of *Clinical Theology* and about which Pond had some reservations:

> You will shortly be seeing my review, in *Theology*, of your book. I know you will accept its somewhat critical tone with understanding. It is precisely because I feel the work is so important that I thought it necessary to say some hard things. I very much hope that you will be able to publish some of the work in other forms – perhaps in technical journals. I have in mind particularly your account of psychological disorders found in ministers.[2]

Frank Lake's extreme sensitivity to criticism was most notably, publicly and distressingly illustrated, of course, after the publication of *Tight Corners in Pastoral Counselling*.[3]

Excessive enthusiasm led to Frank's accepting too many commitments. It is also the reason why he seemed incapable of editing his own written material, both for books and journals, and he invariably produced an excess of the amount required for any given article. The most glaring example of this tendency that I know of is preserved among his correspondence in the Lingdale Archive. It consists of an article entitled 'Theological Issues in Mental Health in India', written for the Indian journal *Religion and Society*. The text runs to 178 pages, each with an average of almost 300 words: more a book than an article.

Another negative aspect to his enthusiasm was felt in his home. He was not a peaceful person to be with, and home was not a restful place precisely because of the tension he created around himself. Indeed, because of his obsessiveness, everything (family, social life, etc.) was sacrificed to the cause of CTA.

Frank Lake was a man of startling paradoxes. He was at times extremely sensitive, at others grossly insensitive. He listened attentively in counselling situations, but outside them he was frequently dismissive. In therapeutic sessions he would identify people's feelings with the utmost precision, whereas he frequently rode roughshod over family and colleagues. An interesting insight into this whole area was given me by Sylvia:

> On one occasion I got struck down with *polymyalga rheumatica*, a very painful stress illness which curtailed a lot for me.
>
> Eventually I went on to a steroid and was able to take a limited part in the work of CTA. Frank tried to sympathize, but never found other people's illness or weakness or inability easy to bear, unless they were 'on the other side of the fence', namely his clients, and for them it was quite a different story.
>
> I did find this very hard, but my Christian faith made sense of a great deal of the difficulties, and my own reading and search for meaning had continued from those early days and upheld me through this trial.
>
> It seemed that the nearer one got to Frank, the greater was the possibility of hurt, and the negative destructive force felt more keenly. Living out love for him through a lifetime was very hard work.
>
> Many people recognized his genius and were immensely helped by him, and some bore the injuries inflicted by his darker side.

He was an erudite man, with an extensive memory, able to recall matters and relate them to what was currently on his mind. He was gifted and musical, indeed knowledgeable about music, but he did not often find time to listen to music. He was a voracious reader, though he seldom read a book through from page one to the end; rather, he sought out all those things which were grist to his mill.

Frank Lake's earnestness precluded real humour. He made the odd clever or ironic or amusing remark,[4] but he was rarely observed laughing in company. There was clearly a stern side to him which, as one member of CTA explained to me, 'was quite daunting'; and while he showed warmth, there was never the warmth that flows naturally, for as he often explained to gatherings of CTA, he had his own schizoid nature to contend with.[5] The conclusion from all this is that he was not at peace with himself, and with few exceptions would not let others help him either.

But in spite of these conclusions, and the throes of life lived at a hundred miles an hour, he was very definitely a man of faith, with deep evangelical roots. His copy of *Daily Light* went with him everywhere. Frequently it was left behind at the places he visited, and frequently too it was returned, unsolicited, by British Rail; on one occasion it was even returned by aeroplane from Australia.

Frank Lake was a man of many parts: missionary doctor, scientist, psychiatrist, therapist, counsellor, a charismatic leader of CTA, father and husband, man of faith, and a preacher of mesmerizing eloquence. He was not a man who would have enjoyed retirement or the debilitation of old age, and in God's grace he was spared both.

Clinical Theology and the Clinical Theology Association

Purists within CTA might well object to this grouping together of Clinical Theology and what came to be its umbrella association, on the grounds that a clinical theology was part and parcel of the Church's life and witness long before the CTA came into existence. That, of course, is true. In fact, the only justification for doing so here is convenience.

Clinical Theology, viewed in terms of the twentieth century, was a pioneering movement within the Church. Like any other system, it was open to criticism and it attracted a great deal of it, not all of it fair, a considerable amount of it prejudiced and slanted. The problem is to identify, and differentiate between, its positive and negative aspects.

Positive features

At the most basic level of all, it raised, quite considerably, the level of self-awareness among the clergy and made them conscious of the need for psychiatric medicine.[6] It also helped pastors to regain 'confidence in their ability to give care and counsel, which had been greatly undermined by the emergence of professional carers like social workers, psychotherapists and counsellors'.[7]

Both these opinions highlight the distinctive contribution Clinical Theology and CTA made to the training in pastoral care, at a time when such resources for the clergy were extremely thin on the ground.

From the start, too, it had a specific conceptual framework. The Revd Lee Eliason, Dean of Studies at Bethel Theological Seminary, Minnesota, applauded, in his Masterate in Theology thesis, its offer of an 'unusually deep interpretation of a Christocentric model for the understanding of human dynamics in health and in emotional sickness. It seems to integrate a number of valid concepts for secular psychology so thoroughly, they have few contradictions with his theological affirmations'. In this way Clinical Theology was able to escape the charge, which could be levelled at the clinical pastoral movement in the United States at this time, that it was too dependent on the resources of secular counselling and psychiatry rather than on theology for its understanding of men and its resources in giving help. This whole matter was taken up by Frank Lake in February 1967:

> But this [that is, Clinical Theology's theological affirmations] has had its repercussions for us in that a genuinely theologically orientated pastoral counselling is therefore somewhat less comprehensible to the secular helping professions, and has a harder task to establish itself as a valid form of counselling and personal help. But this could hardly be otherwise and the gain in the long run will, we hope, be greater. Pastoral counselling, concerning itself with the ultimate God-given aims and meanings of human life, is one of the few disciplines which cannot properly begin to understand itself at a secular level, and then accept the necessity to import theology as a foreign body at a later stage when all the conceptual framework has been worked out on alien models, based not on Christ but on fallen man. The very ways in which we think about and understand clinical pastoral care must *derive from* Christian involvement

> and perception of what is involved for people in the 'strange victory' of Christ, for us and in us.[8]

A little over a month later, in an address to a local Rotary Club, Michael Hare-Duke had this to say about the link between theology, on the one hand, and psychological understanding, on the other hand:

> Arising out of this course of training which attempts to connect psychological understanding with the truths about the love of God, social workers have come to find a new meaning in the techniques which they learned in their own professional training. It has helped them enormously to persevere in the care of those whom, in the technical jargon, one calls 'socially inadequate', the people of whom one has very little hope of any sort of improvement in their way of living, that they should be able to see them, not merely as cases whose behaviour they can understand, but as children of God's love who are worth caring for through thick and thin.[9]

What Hare-Duke is pointing to here, of course, is the two-way flow between psychology and theology.

Institutionally, therefore, the Clinical Theology Association existed – and exists – at the boundary between the ministry of the Church and the discipline and practice of psychiatry and psychoanalysis; and with its clear Christian commitment, its purpose is to enable Christian ministers and laity to take up clinical insights and skills so as to exercise their ministry more effectively. And it certainly achieved this purpose, as letters to the CTA office, letters in theological journals and papers, and articles in general bear ample testimony.

ANGLICAN VICAR

> I have never wanted to be anything other than a parish priest. My only interest in Clinical Theology is in the hope that it may enable me to be a better parish priest, and also enable me to help my congregation to be a fellowship where there is understanding of, and a willingness to share, one another's burdens.
>
> The difficulty in the past has been my helplessness when faced with so many unhappy and disturbed persons who

looked to me for help. Of course, like any other priest, I could tell happy stories of people whom I have been able to help through the laying on of hands, Holy Unction, the gift of absolution and in other ways. But I have also been haunted by the thought of those whose needs I did not understand, and whose needs I was not able to meet from the resources of the Gospel.

I began to attend a Clinical Theology seminar and at the same time talked freely from the pulpit about what I was being taught about the origins of these burdens, and the resources in the Gospel designed by God to relieve them, or to enable us to bear them and also to share them with one another.

I cannot speak for other people, but as far as I am concerned I have not felt so helpless when confronted with these problems. We have not done anything very startling, but we have I am sure become an understanding, accepting, and burden-bearing community.[10]

ANGLICAN DEACONESS

I learnt the need for self-awareness and a perception of my relationships. The value of being aware of what is happening in parish and pastoral situations gives a feeling of being in control, of the right sense of power. Or, as I read recently, avoids the feeling of being 'kicked about like a football'. A few weeks ago I read a farewell letter of a vicar to his congregation after a relatively short ministry with them. It was evident that he had become trapped between two factions. As a counsellor there is immense benefit in being aware of the perils of collusion, manipulation, projection and transference, and in the parish situation too.

SCOTTISH EPISCOPALIAN

I appreciate the support and the identification with me in a bereavement which the community shared with me.

I wonder what other Association produces such care and concern as part of its life. Many people gave me the support of their prayers over that traumatic weekend, and because of that the task of leading a whole community in its mourning was made possible. All went well and I believe that we were able to help people to their own feelings and to feel that the crucified God was alongside them to give the promise of hope and purpose in their grief.

FEMALE LAY ELDER

My own experience of the seminars, assistant tutorship and a small amount of counselling has been invaluable in my fairly recent role as an elder in the United Reformed Church. In fact, without CTA I doubt whether I would have had any idea where to begin this task. The seminars were a unifying experience, where clergy, lay (and non-Christian at times) came to a better and more loving understanding acceptance of each other, and, by extension, of our world.

UNITED REFORMED MINISTER

The insights of Clinical Theology colour the exposition of the Bible in preaching and the preparation of congregational prayers, and so gradually people come to see the implications of the Gospel in a different kind of way, *living more easily with their past.* Of course there are implications for one-to-one counselling, and the effects can spread out as the healed become healers; those who have been heard at depth are themselves better able to hear others.

FREE CHURCHMAN

Perhaps I can best describe the CTA course by citing its effect on my own ministry. First, it has enabled me to become a far better listener. By enabling me to keep a finger on my own emotional pulse while the speaker is unburdening himself, I am able to learn a great deal about the true nature of the speaker's problem, of which he may have no conscious awareness at all.

Second, I have been equipped in some measure actually to treat minor emotional disturbances.

Third, I have been helped to recognize some of the very serious neurotic and psychotic disorders requiring specialist psychiatric treatment. This enables me to refer the sufferer and at the same time to give him the Christian support during his treatment so necessary to ensure him proper aftercare on his return to the community.

Fourth, and not least, I have come to know myself better. I can now correct far more easily my own prejudices and emotional reactions, not only in the pastoral care of individuals but in such routine matters as the chairing of church meetings and serving on committees. The Clinical Theology course has convinced me of the importance of the Church as the healing community *par excellence*. Salvation, wholeness, and healing are virtually synonymous in the Christian's vocabulary.[11]

A DOCTOR

Clinical Theology in my experience as a doctor is a particular understanding of the root causes of psychological (or emotional) human distress and suffering or maladjustment; *and is the ability to help manage or alleviate it.*

All these viewpoints suggest, most persuasively, that Clinical Theology works, and that the association that embodies its perceptions and skills came to be a supportive and encouraging body of advice for those at the grass roots of church life and its attendant pastoral care. But what of those who had responsibility for others (for example, ordinands in the Church of England)? This is how C. W. J. Bowles, former Bishop of Derby and Principal of Ridley Hall, Cambridge, reflected on his introduction to Clinical Theology:

My introduction to Clinical Theology came through the need to find ways of giving ordinands such equipment as courses of lectures could provide for pastoral ministry to the mentally and emotionally sick. Clinical Theology made clear, of course, as previous lectures had done, that much spiritual sickness is psychological in origin. From the early 1940s the college in which I worked had been well served by a succession of lecturers. What they said reflected different stages of development: an almost intellectual approach gave way to a more pastoral one, though the best of our visitors made plain that the two could not be separated. Something, however, seemed always to be missing and I suppose it could be described as a lack of integration. The time came when I heard something of what Dr Frank Lake was beginning to do and so I invited him to give a course of lectures. These, with lots of discussion and many personal interviews following them, were so good that I invited Dr Tony Bashford the following year and each has come in alternate years ever since.

The proof of the pudding was in the eating. The college membership would have been abnormal at the present day if it had not included a certain number of men who needed different degrees of psychiatric help. Talks with the lecturers prepared the way for visits to Nottingham and it is beyond doubt that many men, along with, in consequence, their wives and their parishes, have been saved from the burden of later breakdowns. I do not know of any other means of treatment which has had such lasting and consistently good effects. Alongside this went the clear insight that nearly all students gained into the dynamic forces at work in themselves. The teaching was directly relevant.

It was the relevance partly of the healing effect of deep self-knowledge and of understanding what had previously been inexplicable, frightening or embarrassing. It was the relevance, even more, of teaching which in its wholeness stabbed the mind awake with its self-authenticating truthfulness. It related psychology and theology, psychiatry and pastoral care, spirituality and dealings with other people. The world only works in one way and that is the way of God's truth, which is consistent with itself in every part of man's life – this came home to numbers of men as divine illumination.

There were practical consequences of this. Ordinands were given a preliminary equipment to recognize people who need psychiatric help and to understand why some people, both the devout and the not-so-devout, are difficult. They also came to see not only the limitation of any psychiatric work they themselves could undertake, but also much more of their distinctive work as clergymen. At the same time this distinctive work was humanized. It was not to be directed to souls merely, but to persons – souls, minds and bodies – in their wholeness. This would mean lots of listening so that through a gracious human relationship God might do his work of salvation.

> Such an approach is bound to break up fixed patterns of evangelistic counselling and spiritual direction. Much that is thought to be sinful needs to be reassessed so that a true sense of sin may grow. Much devotional advice provides no deep healing of the spirit and only aggravates disturbing mental and physical symptoms. To be put in the way of gaining fuller understanding of God's dealings with human lives, which is what Clinical Theology has done for many clergymen, is to be set on the road of a deeper compassion for people and a more effective love.
>
> This road includes the acceptance of people. The dry bones of the doctrine of justification by faith come to life. It is the article of faith by which the Church stands or falls, because it affects all the time every part of our relationship to God and should control all our dealings with our fellow-men inside the Church and outside it. It is the way of life for psychiatrist, priest and layman. It ceases to be an arid bit of controversy between Protestant and Catholic and becomes rather the means of laying hold on the resources of God's grace.[12]

What the Clinical Theology Association achieved, according to Canon Hugh Melinsky,[13] was nothing less than 'a signal contribution to the life of the Church', not least by 'clearly signposting some of the pitfalls in a no-man's land'. And in surveying the initial decade of the movement, he suggested that five lessons had been learned: first that, academically speaking, 'it has been a brave attempt to marry the diverse disciplines of theology and psychology', but he felt that it had tried to do this over 'too selective an area and on too uniform a levels; second, that Clinical Theology has shed light on 'the manner of learning', thus exposing the deep things of the human personality 'for inspection'; third, that it had raised such fundamental questions as 'what is pastoral counselling?' etc.; fourth, that it had identified the need for some 'resource-point' or 'resource-person' in the community: 'He (or they) would be known as someone to whom a person in trouble can go'; fifth, that it illustrated the need for some sort of 'standing organization to review methods and procedures' in the whole area of pastoral care and counselling.

Clinical Theology, then, offers a means of understanding

those disturbances which normally require in-depth analysis, and brings them within the scope of pastoral care and into an ambit in which the resources of the Christian Church are readily available to the client.

Some negative aspects

In its early days the Clinical Theology Association aroused suspicion, and encountered opposition from several different directions. It was in a sense inevitable, because theology and psychology are, in many ways, widely divergent, and their practitioners invariably react from their defended positions. Indeed, many maintained, on theological grounds, that it was inappropriate for a clergyman to plunge into areas of deep psychological concern. They were, for example, deeply against the suggestion that a phobic problem in a parishioner might be the proper matter for inquiry by a pastor. Such people saw the clergy's role in terms of maintaining the community as a healthy organism, and not in devoting a great deal of time in the therapy of the specifically sick.

The movement's theological standpoint, too, came in for thoroughgoing criticism. Some objected to the fact that its 'methods of understanding' seemed to stem more from a 'satisfaction' theory of the atonement than from anything else.[14] To others the continual emphasis on 'brokenness' seemed to 'be another phase in the old theological argument about total depravity and a blow in favour of the twice born over against the once born'.[15] CTA's theological teaching all too often became a party issue: 'Its theological adherents did not necessarily belong to any particular alignment in the old sense of being "high" or "low" church. There were various people for whom its formulations had attractions. It appealed to all those who wanted to give the biblical imagery a new vitality. Those who were happy with a more radical, demythologizing approach did not find it so helpful to see new, psychological slants in psalms or crucifixion narratives. In this was involved a whole theology of the interpretation of Scripture which was extraneous to the subject in question but which influenced both adherents and opponents in their respective attitudes. On another side were those who felt that the approach gave too little weight to the doctrine of Creation and hence saw little use in the Church's involvement in its more traditional work among structures of society. Since the original teaching was devised out of medical rather than parochial experience the pattern of a doctor's way of working tended to emphasize the theological bias and to lay great stress on personal counselling at length. If this were to be the outcome of the course then many students would find that they had no time for much else that the parish priest had normally expected to be part of his ministry in the community.'[16]

Another danger of the CTA method was observed in some disillusioned priests and ministers who felt themselves 'irrelevant in a changing society and turned to the idea of counselling with alacrity. Where this was an uncritical approach one found that some people had abandoned their parishes in favour of a few *patients*.'[17] It must be said, however, that for many others the insights which their clinical theology understanding gave them set them free both to see their own previously defensive patterns (which might include the joining of a seminar), and also to look critically at some of the unconscious patterns displayed in Frank Lake's formulations.

Other critics viewed CTA as a monolithic type of indoctrination which excluded people from appreciating other points of view. It is true that some of its followers gave the impression that it was the one way, the Christian way, of dealing with emotional disturbances and traumas, in other words *the truth* – which it was not, and is not.

On the medical side, a number of doubts were expressed in general about the dynamic approach to the understanding of personality, which though acceptable, sometimes leads to the suggestion of a hard and fast relation of causality between certain symptoms and certain causes.[18] On the psychological side, critics saw that Clinical Theology offered an easily memorable scheme for understanding personality patterns but wished only to use it as a useful starting point rather than in a fundamentalist sort of way, which can only lead to the rejection of additional insights from a wider experience.

A further problem for many people was the relationship between secular skills and the question of redemption. David Atkinson in a review of *Tight Corners in Pastoral Counselling*[19] raised the point about the eclecticism of Clinical Theology and the use it makes of secular therapies, and then said this:

'I believe that all truth is God's truth, but I also believe that there must be criteria of discrimination in using what are simply techniques.' He went on to ask a series of questions: 'By what criteria do CT practitioners discriminate between therapeutic techniques? Is CT alert to the dangers of "baptizing" secular therapies on the basis of pragmatic criteria? What are CT's criteria for use? Are there even those who are taking Dr Lake's methods outside the context of Christian discipline, care and love within a supportive eucharistic fellowship, and using them in a possibly harmful way?' David Atkinson is perfectly right to raise these cautionary questions. Put more directly, the implication of what he is asking is just this: if the values of the counsellor do not stem from religious (that is, Christian) suppositions, what is the source from which they are drawn? Or put another way: what has a counsellor's Christian calling to contribute which is not available from a skilled humanist working in this field? Such issues, questions, problems and queries were voiced in the formative years of the Clinical Theology Association, and properly so, and they remain pertinent for those whose responsibility it is to organize and develop the work of the association as the 1990s approach. There was never any doubt about Frank Lake's commitment to the Christian Gospel, but the same could not always be said about some of his fellow-workers who were more heavily into secular therapeutic techniques than they were into the sustenance that comes from the spiritual life. There was never any doubt either that the conceptual framework of Clinical Theology was firmly wedded in the Christian tradition, but the real danger was the balance between that and some of the techniques which Frank Lake himself seemed to adopt so readily and enthusiastically. This whole area was even more controversial because of his obsession with primal therapy, etc.

To summarize: it is undoubtedly the case that, whatever its deficiencies, the Clinical Theology Association *acted as a catalyst within the Church.* One observer accurately summed up its effect like this:

> When Dr Lake first began his work, he was a pioneer in the field. It was a measure both of his ceaseless energy and the enormous need that the Association mushroomed

> between the years 1958 and 1964 to run seminars in almost every English diocese and over the border into Scotland and Wales. Whether they had taken the course or not, there was hardly a clergyman who was unaware of the movement. The very fact of the presence of a clinical theology aroused many others into activity. Just because they felt that it presented a one-sided picture they were determined that it should not hold the field alone. As a result theological colleges and directors of post-ordination training began to be at pains to enlist the services of psychiatrists and caseworkers to help in giving the clergy some understanding of the new disciplines.[20]

What is vitally important here is that the example of CTA motivated others not only to think but to act, in a practical way, as well.

It is also true that CTA through its national network of seminars and workshops disseminated Frank Lake's ideas to countless thousands of people who had hitherto regarded the behavioural sciences, counselling and psychotherapy as deeply suspect. In addition, the work of CTA was a genuine attempt to bring theology and the behavioural sciences together in a creative fusion. But, as Dr Irene Bloomfield says in *Manna* (No. 14, Winter 1987), 'Pioneers in every field have to struggle hard for acceptance of their ideas, but without them there would be no growth or development.' In this sense alone, we owe CTA and Frank Lake a very great debt.

Primal integration therapy

This was without question the most controversial aspect of Frank Lake's work. Related terms include primal pain or primal trauma, the Maternal–Foetal Distress Syndrome and, by extension, inner healing or healing of the memories.

The psychological basis can briefly be re-stated as follows: (1) all events in a person's past are stored, including memories of the event, the feelings associated with it, and also the thoughts connected with it; (2) memories are not available for conscious recall because they are simply uneventful, are painful, or totally locked away, or because they are in early childhood or before; (3) these memories, although not available for conscious recall, heavily influence and shape the individual's perception of life. This essentially psychoanalytical hypothesis is contentious because it cannot be proved by controllable experiment, while the assertion that pre-natal experience can be remembered is a highly disputed area. Primal therapy works on the basis that access to the early and repressed memories can be gained through deep breathing and the work of the Holy Spirit leading, opening up and bringing the memories to be relived in terms of bodily and emotional thoughts and feelings.

These ideas, to which Frank Lake devoted so much of his time during the last four or five years of his life, have been subjected to close scrutiny, and I wish to refer to two main lines of inquiry as far as this whole matter is concerned. I shall deal with them under these headings: (*a*) The view of the evangelical world in general, and (*b*) the specific views of those within the Charismatic Renewal Movement in Britain.

THE GENERAL ARGUMENTS WITHIN EVANGELICALISM

The sharpest riposte against inner healing and its link with some of the ideas perpetrated by Frank Lake – though he is not mentioned by name – is found in *The Seduction of Christianity: Spiritual Discernment in the Last Days*, by Dave Hunt and T. A. McMahon (first published in 1985).[21] Its authors, while not naming Frank Lake, refer to some of the practices he followed, and name some of those who influenced him: Freud, Grof, and Janov. This is sufficient justification for utilizing their arguments in a general perceptual sense. Their assertions may be categorized under four central assertions:

First, they *reject* as a 'common delusion' that salvation or healing 'comes through uprooting memories of "hurts" from early childhood and even the womb that are supposedly deeply buried in the subconscious from where they dictate our present behaviour without our knowing it'. In this respect they consider that the blame is far too often placed on the past and upon other people rather than the individual himself.

Second, they *object* strongly and directly to what is called 'fantasized regression' as practised by Stanislav Grof and Arthur Janov, because such a process, in their view, merely confirms through use of LSD what Freud and Jung discovered through hypnosis. Put another way, Hunt and McMahon dismiss as theories and as unscientific the basis for psychotherapy and Christian inner healing.

Third, they *denounce* 're-birthing' as a 'pop' psychology, and as a westernized form of ancient mythology that is closely related to the fertility cults: 'It attributes mystical significance and godlike powers to the birth process.'

Fourth, they *view* the primary foundation of inner healing as a misinformed acceptance of Freud's 'discredited theory of psychic determinism'. Psychic determinism is the belief that human behaviour occurs in accordance with intrapsychic causes, and is controlled by impulses, many of which are buried below the level of awareness.

Hunt and McMahon do admit that there may indeed be something in the past that needs to be dealt with, for example, something causing bitterness against those who have wronged us, or guilt, etc., and that the Christian person should not continue, 'for one more moment', with something like this on his conscience. How then should a Christian deal with such problems? They say this:

> All that we need for dealing with such problems is found in the fact that Christ died for our sins and has risen from the dead to live His life in us. No one who has truly received God's love and forgiveness as a sinful rebel can possibly withhold that same love and forgiveness from those who have wronged him. We love and forgive others because of God's love and forgiveness to us. It is that simple. This is the 'fruit of the Spirit' that results from Christ living in us. If we are willing to face this truth, then He will give us the strength to carry it out. Inner healing is based upon a denial that this is all we need; 'something more' must be involved, and that 'something' is borrowed from a variety of psychotherapies, most of which are related to shamanism.[22]

This is the *classic* evangelical position, thoroughly Pauline in its theology, and one with which other approaches heavily utilizing secular therapies can have little or no common ground or place of meeting. With this in mind, it is not difficult to see why Frank Lake's approach, and his teaching on primal integration therapy caused disaffection among many evangelicals in general.

THE RESPONSE OF THE BRITISH CHARISMATIC RENEWAL MOVEMENT

In the second half of the 1970s concern about the psychological and theological presuppositions involved in primal therapy were particularly keenly felt within the Renewal Movement in Britain. Several prominent leaders of renewal, including David Watson, David MacInnes and Tom Smail, met Frank Lake. They described themselves as 'considerably reassured' by much of what he said, but felt that some very important questions still needed to be pursued, because they had not been 'satisfactorily answered'. This disquiet was communicated to Frank Lake by the Revd Tom Smail, then Director of the Fountain Trust, in a letter dated 22 December 1976. The disquieting questions fell into three main areas:

> 1 *Psychological.* I have spoken recently to several professionally qualified Christian psychiatrists who have expressed the strongest reservations about the psychological soundness of primal theory and therapy, and especially about the powerful and permanent dependencies that it can create. I think it needs to be made clear to people that this is a highly controversial matter where it is dangerous to be too dogmatic or committed.
>
> 2 *Theological.* The questions about the relationship of primal therapy to the Christian doctrine of man, sin and salvation remain. Is it God that needs justifying, or man? What needs to be expressed and what repented? How is liberation by reliving this trauma related to salvation in Christ? Does healing require this kind of exposure and technique?
>
> 3 *Structural.* Does Clinical Theology really set people free for Christ or draw them into a network of ministering and being ministered to, so that they become evangelists for its techniques rather than for the Gospel, and are joined to its courses rather than the Church? There is a good deal of widespread disquiet about these sort of questions.[23]

The same letter contained a request for an article from Frank Lake 'of around 4,500 words on the theological presuppositions of Clinical Theology'. Tom Smail recognized that there were considerable risks in bringing the issues out into the open in this way, but he explained: 'Whether we like it or not, this matter is now on the agenda and being discussed, and it seems to me that we have a common interest in seeing that it is talked about in the right way with the real issues in the forefront.'

Frank Lake's response

The upshot of this ferment was that Frank Lake wrote an article, for *Renewal*, entitled 'The Work of Christ in the Healing of Primal Pain'.[24] Its length makes it unwieldy to be reproduced in its entirety here, so it is published as Appendix A at the end of this book. Readers will thus be able to refer to it as the arguments and counter-arguments in this chapter proceed.

This article did not convince the doubters, who came back at him with sharply honed and developed arguments and comments. The Revd Peter Hutchinson, of Bradford, wrote:

> Readers of *Theological Renewal* who have not undertaken any academic study of psychological theory should perhaps be advised that this new area of knowledge has the crippling disadvantage of being an entirely self-authenticating system. Those who believe in it, believe in it; those who do not, do not. Clinical Theology, unlike a school of psychology, has no sets of theories based on hypotheses that have been tested and evaluated in the normal way of scientific theory, but is more of a movement, centred on its founder, which seeks followers. It effectively isolates its adherents from any outside criticism by using the classic Freudian device of categorizing critics as sick people resisting the healing offered them. Thus Dr Lake writes of many, 'particularly among the members of the helping professions, (who) do experience deep, emotionally charged resistances even to considering (primal pain) as a possibility, for themselves or others'. Later in the article Dr Lake uses theological vocabulary for a further smear when writing, albeit somewhat obscurely, of those 'who tend to triumphalism and cannot stay with the afflicted', who need 'Christ's strength to go what might be called the hard way'. Were this an adolescent game on the school playing field you

would observe that young Lake has invented a new game of whose rules he is the sole judge, has picked both the teams and erected notices declaring that all who refuse to play thereby show themselves to be spoilsports.[25]

Dr J. N. Isbister, of the Psychological Laboratory, Cambridge, commented: 'The main point that needs stressing is that it is by no means proven that "primal pain" exists. The work of the "primal therapists" is still disputable, and certainly the little that I know of it (in particular, the work of Dr A. Janov) does not inspire confidence.' And he concluded: 'Examination of the doctrine of the "primal therapists" reveals little that we as Christians, committed to the truth of Christ, can support.'[26] The Revd David MacInnes's reply was equally astringent. He asked four main questions, as follows:

1 *The theological analogy – is this misleading?*

Dr Lake begins with an intriguing interpretation of the cross as a sharing of the two basic 'pre-natal catastrophes'. But the moving description of the crushing and desertion of our Lord is liable to obscure the issue, because it is at this point that we are being introduced to part of the theory which he is expounding, i.e. that birth is frequently an experience of two catastrophes. But this is *theory*. Certainly many people have described their own early fears of swallowing up and abandonment, and deduced from very primitive but currently experienced panics that these derive from instinctual anxiety, and relate to very early experience. But whether these *actually* are related to early experience is open to question. Therefore the correlation with Christ on the cross can be used only tentatively. Obviously there is much in the passion of Christ which will speak to our experience and be used in our healing. But Dr Lake comes perilously near to establishing his psychology as a theology, e.g. 'the crown of thorns (so like the crushing of the baby's head into the hard bony circle of the pelvis – as several patients undergoing it have remarked)'.

In psychology, as in many other disciplines, distinctions have to be made between (a) those theories which are capable of experimental testing, and (b) those which attempt to make *sense* of the data so produced, taking into account other phenomena (including clinical experience) which *cannot* be tested, and then building up a grand theory, such as psychoanalysis.

The trouble with such 'grand theories' is that they can easily become a kind of religion or metaphysic which positively inhibits the practitioner's openness to re-examine them. Hence the rivalry between schools of psychological thought. It is therefore dangerous to base any definitive theological explanation on a particular psychological theory, in case the former should be discredited, if the latter should prove inadequate.

2 *The theodicy – is this imbalanced?*

Following from this, the whole matter of innocent suffering must be a theological question rather than a psychological one. To try to make primal pain necessitate a certain theological position is very doubtful. The author comes near to saying that God is *actually* responsible for the pain and suffering in the world, and therefore in all justice *had* to provide a way of redemption. This is undermining to the whole emphasis on the cross as sheer grace. Surely, too, it is nowhere suggested that Job was right in his protests, however much we can identify with them? The paper comes dangerously close to saying that redemption discharged a debt to mankind, as though God's credibility demanded it. Is this really compatible with the thought of the epistle to the Romans, and is there not also a fundamental misunderstanding of the 'ought' in Luke 24? Is not the biblical emphasis squarely placed on God justifying the sinner rather than justifying himself? And is this not a very important emphasis to retain when dealing pastorally or clinically with the Job-like cries and protests from the depths? I wonder whether Dr Lake has followed the Freudian rather than the biblical stress at this point.

3 *The trauma of the pre-natal events – is this a new problem?*

Although there is cause for concern over some present practices in childbirth, more evidence is needed about the *actual* damage to later development. And it is difficult to see how it can be demonstrated that there are so many more of this type of sufferer today than in the past. A condition called 'moriarmur' was described of which understimulated infants died, but not all unwanted babies perished in this fashion. Are we really being flooded with a new type of sufferer, or is the experience of primal pain just one of the many perennial manifestations of the human dilemma and anger against God?

4 *The importance of early experience – is this really a new psychology?*

Few would doubt the importance of early experience upon the adult but the correlation between traumatic birth experiences and later manifestations of problems seems to rest on fairly flimsy evidence, as so much in the way of later experience has intervened. Much of Dr Lake's theory (as with Janov and others) appears to rest on the assumption that infant or childhood memories, though concealed from consciousness by repression, can be *accurately* recovered through abreaction or re-living in primal therapy. That memories can be uncovered through a spontaneous work of the Holy Spirit or induced by LSD or techniques is well known. But how accurate are the data so produced? A host of questions arise. Given that the foetus has some form of recording mechanism, and given too that the 'tape can be re-played', how pure are the data so produced? An immense amount of interpretation has to be done by the therapist. Is the sense of pressure on the head really due to the pelvic bone? Is the long dark tunnel actually the birth channel? To what extent is the material being reinterpreted by the patient himself? How many other factors are colouring the data? Is it really possible to draw anything but the most tentative conclusions? If the birth memories are valid, what about the memories of previous lives which are also sometimes 'recovered' in abreaction, and 'verified' as including information which the patient could not have known? This seems an area where any kind of dogmatic assertions are out of place.[27]

David MacInnes also pointed to the difficulty of distinguishing between therapeutic results and the theories erected on them as a consequence: 'Success in therapy is a doubtful justification of the theories used'; accepted that Frank Lake avoids the excesses of Janov's claims[28] that primal therapy is the 'only effective treatment' for neurosis, psychosis, sexual problems, and various other disorders including drug addiction, colitis and asthma; indicated the possibility (tragic, in his opinion) that primal therapy would form 'round itself a gathered community who looked mainly to it for help and freedom'.

From the more detached and impartial vantage-point of a decade later, it is instructive to attempt to unravel some of the strands in the debate, as outlined in Tom Smail's letter of December 1976.

Psychological

Four aspects of Frank Lake's approach call for attention.[29] In the first place, he quite obviously believes that a key (that is, controlling) in determining psychological health is perinatal experience; additionally, that therapy is the indispensable pathway to psychological healing. He is, secondly, eager to establish the validity of his methods, and for them to gain large-scale acceptance, but particularly to the satisfaction of psychiatrists, especially the Christians in their ranks. Thirdly, he sees psychiatry as being in confusion and disarray. Fourthly, he appeals for casework evidence to support him in his attempt to achieve the second of his objectives referred to above.

But even if the validity of his first contention is granted, and the second is achieved, there remains a considerable tension between the second and third features, the second and fourth, and the third and the fourth. Even if Frank Lake is right in his claim in point 3 above, to speak in these terms will be counterproductive with regard to establishing the validity of his methods. On the other hand, if acceptance of his methods is to be achieved, it could only be on the basis that psychiatrists are no less reasonable than Frank himself. Put another way, psychiatrists could equally fairly respond to his assertions by postulating another interpretation of the situation: that it is Frank Lake who is the maverick, out on a limb, and who is desperately projecting his problems as he psychologizes on others. This kind of argument is fruitless. Similarly, if we are to assume that Frank Lake's contentions regarding contemporary psychiatry are true, no amount of evidence derived from casework study will make any essential difference.

What Frank Lake's critics were asking for was nothing less than a controlled, scientific study of birth trauma and its effects. Until that could happen, and its results be presented to the profession, and made available for public debate and analysis, psychiatrists or psychologists would not be convinced by the evidence he was asking for. What existed, in their view, was merely casework evidence.

Theological

The underlying fear in the theological debate was that Frank Lake's emphasis on people's needs rather than their responsibilities was rather too closely in keeping with the spirit of the age in the 1970s. It was not that such people would lapse into legalism (that fear had passed), but into antinomianism: the implication being that his emphases would encourage moral solipsism, which was prevalent in any case. His detractors also pointed (perfectly correctly) to the biblical assertion that both the sins of the fathers are visited on their children and that these same children are sinners responsible to God for their sin and invited to repentance and faith.

Structural

Frank Lake seems to admit the validity of these observations, while regarding Clinical Theology functioning as a church as something quite unintentional.

The debate was not resolved either way. How could it possibly be, with the opposing sides taking such committed positions? What is certainly without doubt is that the reservations expressed by those who differed from Frank Lake on the question of primal therapy and primal integration therapy remain so to this day.

Additional doubts centred, for some, on the place of prayer for divine healing within the whole context of primal work. John Webster reports[30] as follows, on what was happening at Lingdale as late as April 1981, just about a year before Frank Lake died:

While there was generally some prayer for Christ to be present and to guide there was generally little specific prayer that God would heal the hurt parts of the personality. In Frank Lake's work this lack seems to stem from his view of the Clinical Theology Association work as like the last parts of Christ's ministry – from Tabor to Golgotha – a 'making available the power of the Holy Spirit, who sustains Christ in the crushing terrors of Gethsemane and the agonizing loneliness of Golgotha'. This he contrasts with the sort of ministry exercised by Francis MacNutt which he likens to Christ's ministry in Galilee – that is, a straightforward cure. However, I am inclined to say that prayer for healing should be included after exploring and contextualizing the pain.

Whatever the merits and demerits of the arguments which circulated about the time of Frank Lake's article – both before and after – his obsession with primal therapy had several detrimental effects. In some people's eyes, primal therapy and the Clinical Theology Association were synonymous, being lumped together as 'controversial', and thereby attracting a great deal of opprobrium. Then again, even those who viewed primal therapy as having a real potential for understanding causative factors in neurotic and psychotic developments felt that these theories regarding Primal Therapy and the Maternal–Foetal Distress Syndrome were 'highly speculative and not able to bear the interpretation weight Frank Lake attached to them; that they caused him increasingly to underestimate a wider developmental picture; to produce an evangelical once-for-all conversion expectation; and to virtually ignore the analysis of the transference'. This is the considered opinion of the Revd John Gravelle, who was a close colleague of Frank Lake for many years. Thirdly, the primal work tended to obscure the primary work for which the Clinical Theology Association came into existence:

> Clinical Theology arose out of my concern as a doctor who had worked first of all in India as a parasitologist, and then came to England and changed over into psychiatry, to have something relevant to say to men and women who came to me because I was a Christian, and they were Christians. Naturally at first one used all the ordinary resources of

> psychological medicine, drugs, physical treatment, group therapy, hospital work and so on, but then there were some for whom our psychiatric resources just ran out. They had to bear affliction and go on bearing it. The question was this: was there any helpful meaning or resource of meaning that I could offer them in this circumstance? And out of this thought together arose what we call Clinical Theology.[31]

At the time of Frank Lake's death, therefore, the Clinical Theology Association operated on two main fronts: first, as a movement within pastoral counselling,[32] the theological basis of which assumed that 'parents, especially the mother, express on an emotional level the infant's experience of God, and secondly that Christ's creative encountering of the personal pain of humanity is both a resource we need to claim, and an example of both spiritual and personal growth';[33] and secondly, as dealt with above, primal therapy. How the association would cope in the post-Frank Lake era was a matter of speculation and discussion in the months before he died, and this will be the subject of the next chapter.

7

The History of CTA: the Post-Frank Lake Era

Frank Lake's death was a devastating blow to CTA. This was true in at least two crucial areas. First, *conceptually*, because he had always bubbled over with new insights, fresh ideas and new material, including his ever-present charts and diagrams. Secondly, *financially*: he had been CTA's principal fund-raiser for twenty years, generating thereby a substantial amount of income through his seminars, therapeutic sessions, and importantly through a range of contacts, both in Britain and abroad. In organizational and accounting terms, CTA was bankrupt, with an overdraft of £19,000 (after receiving the sale proceeds of Bentinck Road), as well as further interest-free loans of £10,000 outstanding. Neither could CTA's members (approximately 1,000), not all of whom were paying the subscription of £5 per annum (a hopelessly inadequate amount), nor the income that might accrue from seminars, possibly provide realistic funding to deal with the financial emergency. A time of crisis had arrived with a vengeance, though in fact many people closely linked with the association had seen it coming for several years.

What Frank Lake's death did was to brings matters to a head in a quite dramatic way. Emotionally people felt shocked, bereft and uncertain about the future. Indeed there were those who considered CTA to be in imminent danger of demise. The perfectly understandable thinking behind this viewpoint was that the association had been a particular vehicle for the work of a particular man, after whose death the vehicle itself was not really necessary. Certainly this was the initial opinion of CTA's Council in the period immediately following Frank's death.

The 1982 Annual Conference was therefore one of the most momentous occasions since CTA was first founded.

Conceived as a bereavement exercise, with John Foskett, Chaplain of the Maudsley Hospital, brought in to facilitate this, many people responded angrily. A particular source of annoyance was the fact that the Council could decree what happened in the association's affairs, leaving the professional associates and other associated members without any voice at all. The conference also strongly resisted the suggestion of closure, arguing that a supportive network for people within pastoral counselling was highly necessary, and not at all redundant in the wake of Frank Lake's death. Importantly, too, a constructive byproduct of the intense mourning was that, with reflection, came an awareness of the need to reconsider CTA's priorities, aims and future intentions.

Four pertinent questions were asked: (1) was Clinical Theology a bigger movement than its founder, Frank Lake? (2) what style of leadership was appropriate for the future? (3) how could resurrection out of the old structures be effected? (4) how could the continuing (and, hopefully, developing) work of CTA be financed? The response to these and other related inquiries was, inevitably, painful, and different opinions and suggestions were proposed on how the work could best be carried forward. Three definitive responses to the issues raised may be referred to.

1 *Draft proposals at the 1982 Annual Conference*

These proposals,[1] formulated by a working party following the 1982 Conference but in time for the October General Meeting, attempted to clarify future aims and methods of operation. In the first place, the document pointed to the advisability of *a federal system with a centre*. The various regions could thus offer seminars, supervision, and promote personal growth. A three-tier model of training was thus the intention: (1) people helpers, to enable people-in-the-pews to be effective carers; (2) professional skills: this would operate at a deeper level for clergy, social workers, teachers; (3) developing specific counselling skills, for example for those wishing to work full time in the area of pastoral counselling. In this model the centre would act as a co-ordinating resource centre, but significantly as a place to develop growth in skills by way of annual conferences, specialized workshops, for consultations with experts from other counselling disciplines, together with the development of theological input and critique of Clinical Theology. Secondly, the document suggested the *formation of a new Council*. Paddy Marsh, a London solicitor, was asked to draft a new constitution set in legally sound terms. Thirdly, the proposals suggested the *appointment of an interim executive*. The Bishop of Sherwood, Bishop Richard (Dick) Darby, was asked to continue as Chairman, together with three members of the 'old' Council and six members from the Annual Conference. Lastly, *funding and staff*. To deal with this fundamentally important matter, it was suggested that funding should be drawn from a revised membership list (known as 'Friends of CTA'), a realistic revision of subscription fees, and from interest on capital from the sale of Lingdale.

2 *The Revd D. J. Bick's Report (September 1982)*

As to the nature of Clinical Theology, David Bick endorsed the view of the 1982 Annual Conference:

> 'Clinical Theology' is bigger than Frank Lake and therefore must continue. Frank Lake was seen as the initiator of a movement whose main genius was that of putting together the insights of many others, seeing how these insights relate to the Christian Gospel, and their relevance to Pastoral Care in the modern world. His energy started 'Clinical Theology' moving, but he could not be seen as an originator of new ideas, or indeed of the 'Clinical Theology Movement'. Much of the material used in seminars was produced by a number of 'Clinical Theology' Tutors and it used the work and insights of a wide variety of people. Those outside and on the fringe of the 'Clinical Theology Association' tend to be confused about the relationship between 'Clinical Theology' and its first leader, mainly due to Frank Lake's own interest in 'Primal Therapy' and 'Intrauterine Experience' work during the last few years of his life. The controversies surrounding this and allied subjects took the attention of many away from the wider work of the 'Clinical Theology Association'. There is, therefore, a widely held view that if the things which the 'Clinical Theology Association' stand for are of God and represent something

bigger than Frank Lake, then it will go on in some form or other.

David Bick's report also stated quite categorically that there *had* to be a change in CTA's style of leadership, in order to meet and adapt to the changed – and changing – circumstances. He was perfectly correct in claiming that the old-style leadership exercised by Frank Lake had inhibited growth in and development in others who could not mature within such a leadership structure; all of which had been happening within CTA for a number of years before May 1982.

As to the third matter, that of death and resurrection, Bick said this:

> The death of one organization can only lead to the resurrection of another if there is something in the dying one that is more than the organization itself. This something must be bigger than the organization and able to survive in spirit without the organization. Its need of an organization is to enable it to fulfil its purpose in the present world. The death in the 'Clinical Theology Association' must be seen as the death of an organization only. Its spirit, aims and purpose live on in many ways. The resurrection is of a new body or structure as a vehicle for its spirit, aims and purpose. What then is this essential spirit of 'Clinical Theology' for which a new resurrection structure is required? Is it not a commitment to Jesus Christ and his kingdom together with an openness towards where the Holy Spirit is leading, especially in relationship to the new therapies, and other insights from the many approaches to counselling in our present needy world? The new structures must enshrine these ideals and also have an input channel. The input needs to be provided by people who can research and reflect upon all developments in the counselling world in the light of the Christian Gospel, and keep good relationships with such bodies as the Association of Pastoral Care and Counselling and the British Association of Counselling. The output side should be a wide variety of training courses and workshops for personal growth that can be offered by the Association's tutors.

The ferment after Frank Lake's death was positive and

constructive in a number of different ways. It was vital, for example, for the association to reaffirm, as it did in the 1982 Annual Conference, its aims and future intentions:

i To train highly competent professional counsellors and provide means of accreditation that will be recognized by the British Association of Counselling. Also to provide supervision for those engaged in counselling.

ii To help professional people in any of the helping professions to have an extra Christian/theological dimension to their work by running seminars in which they are able to look at issues that arise out of their day-to-day work in the light of the Gospel.

iii To offer training in the basics of counselling to non-professional 'people in the pews' so that they can be more effective in helping their neighbours and letting the Church become the Body of Christ.

iv To run workshops for personal growth and development and train people as group facilitators.

3 Memo from the Bishop of Sherwood

Dated 8 September 1982,[2] it said this:

> Ever since our last meeting when we decided after much careful debate to close CTA I have been considering the implications of this decision, and have been much concerned.
>
> As a result of all this thinking a possible way forward has emerged which would not simply be a perpetuation of the name and organization for the sake of perpetuating it but which I believe has as its basis a mission of what we should be doing, a positive next stage forward for CTA.
>
> Our contribution to the Church and to Christian thinking over the last few years has been largely in the field of Frank's research and the practice of primal theories. However important, this has contributed little to the work of enabling the Churches' ministers in their leadership and pastoral roles to become more sensitive and competent in their work.
>
> One of our consultants, Brian Hawker, since the time that we ceased to employ full-time consultants, has

continued his ministry as a CT consultant independently. He has recently set up a Community in Somerset which is the centre of his work and he is shortly to be joined there by another of our consultants, Basil Hobbs. I went to have a look at the work which they were doing, and which they propose to do, and was very impressed. I put before them an idea which I asked them to think and pray about and it is that which I want to put before you for consideration on the 24th September.

As the Community is already working on a CT basis, running seminars and conferences, growth groups and doing personal consultations, why not continue CTA based upon the Community – which would consist mainly of two of our longest serving and knowledgeable consultants, where there are possibilities, including residential facilities, for developing the outreach of CTA, where the leading members of the Community are well known to the Church at large and from where we could start again the work of passing on to ministers and leaders in the Church the insights which CTA has in its spiritual storehouse.

A major hindrance to our ministry over the last 4 or 5 years has been finance. We have been acting big without thinking big and consequently as our life-style has bloomed and our costs have soared we have been touching fewer and fewer people (e.g. seminars have dropped from over 100 per year to just over 10 a year). Basing CTA on the Community in Somerset would free us from our wretched financial fetters as the Community is entirely self-supporting, through its seminars and conferences, etc. and would be able to take on CTA administration, which is now much slimmed down, and what monies come in from subscriptions, literature, etc. would not be immediately soaked up in salaries and bills for keeping Lingdale going.

A great deal of thought still has to go into this. I stress that this was an idea of mine which came as a complete surprise to Brian and Basil and about which they were initially very hesitant. However, I asked them to write me a note about their thoughts and how they might see this working out, and here they are:

Brian Hawker to the Bishop of Sherwood (30.8.82):

The situation as I see it revolves around the purpose of CTA and how it can best serve the Church as a whole and not just a few who like the close encounters of much so-called modern therapy. I believe the task of the Association is to be of use to the clergy (i) in helping them to deal with their parishioners, (ii) by providing theological reflections on the nature and task of the pastoral ministry which would be of practical use within the parish situation, (iii) to be a resource place where the life of the priest himself could be helped. I am concerned in (iii) with helping the helper when he/she is in difficulty.

I feel that the proposed community at Huntham Cottage would be able to deal with all of these aspects of the Association's work.

It would further be able to deal with the Pastoral Care and Counselling seminars on a residential conference basis and be able to act as a resource centre for those in the regions who would still wish to continue running seminars on the old model.

I believe the accreditation scheme for counsellors should be handed to the APCC section of BAC of which most of us are in any case already members.

Should *Contact* magazine continue then we could be responsible for its mailing to members of the Association together with a twice-yearly newsletter of happenings/conferences, etc. at the Huntham Centre.

I feel that the administrative paraphernalia of Council, etc. would need to be disbanded and in its place a Board of Trustees (of which I hope you would be chairman) would meet possibly once a year to receive reports of work undertaken in the name of CTA.

We would welcome the continued support of members through their annual subscription to the Association and this would be used to finance the publications and pay for specific works done solely for the Association. Fees for seminars/conferences would accrue in the normal way to the Huntham Community.

The possibility of continuing the annual conference would need to be reviewed in the light of how the members related to the new-look association during its first year.

> I am aware that in the light of this week's Conference of the Association other moves are afoot for setting up a continuing CTA and only want you to have this letter as a résumé of our own discussions on the 10th and 11th August. In the end my only concern is that the Association be of service to the Church and not an embarrassment by indulging in far-out unproven therapies.

The need for decisions

But if CTA's recovery was to be more than a matter of talk and discussion, hard logistic and financial decisions had not only to be faced, but also implemented. Foremost among these was the decision to sell Lingdale, which closed on 31 December 1982. It had been, as the Bishop of Sherwood explained in *Newsletter 42* (1 February 1983), 'a hopeless drain' on CTA's finances, and no case could possibly be made out for its retention.

This decision was perhaps even more important on a symbolic level: it represented a break with a past that had been so dominated by Frank Lake. And there was a further consideration, as the Bishop of Sherwood (Richard Darby) said in *Newsletter 42*: 'What we are seeking to do is to prepare ourselves for a ministry in the regions, that CT as a Centre should be in a position to facilitate the work being done in the regions, and to keep all those who are involved in our work fully informed and up to date with what is happening'. He added: 'The membership of the association must remain our lifeblood, and with the slimming down of the central organization it is essential that the membership all over the country be kept in touch with what is happening in all the regions. To this end a publications working party has been set up to see that the necessary literature is available, to edit and publish articles, pamphlets and teaching materials. A conference working party has been set up to organize an Annual Conference that will be relevant, cogent and exciting.'

Someone was also needed to co-ordinate the work and the Revd Peter van de Kasteele was appointed Administrative Secretary.

A fresh start

A new era had begun for CTA. New patterns of working had to be adopted, and St Mary's House, Church Westcote, Oxford OX7 6SF (near Oxford, but in Gloucestershire) became the association's new headquarters. By 1983 members began to feel – albeit tentatively – that CTA would survive. Indeed, for many the 1983 conference was a most valuable experience, not least for those attending a Clinical Theology conference for the first time. Valerie Bryant, from Scotland, wrote: 'First, let me say how much I enjoyed it. The group work amazed me . . . the necessity to be utterly honest I welcome with relief. The conference was so positive an experience.'[3] A similar note was struck by Peter Louis, of Coventry: 'I can't recall four days in which I have learnt so much, or at least had so much new data and so many new situations upon which to reflect . . . On the whole a valuable experience, sensitively managed.'[4] Marc Seccombe, a Doncaster clergyman, wrote encouragingly, even enthusiastically: 'CT lives. That was the message of the conference . . . a new sense of optimism and renewed purpose. The workshops and probably the more personal growth groups had a positive feel about them, with an emphasis on healing and wholeness, rather than a preoccupation with primal pain.'[5] Others, like John Rowan, a humanistic psychology therapist, author of *Ordinary Ecstasy* (Routledge and Kegan Paul 1976), felt that Frank Lake's work as an original and exciting contribution to the theory of Primal Integration ought to be given its due and proper recognition by CTA and in its ongoing programme: 'To me Frank Lake is a daring pioneer, an astronaut of inner space, an intrepid diver into the deepest trenches and fissures of the human spirit. And the theory of Primal Integration . . . seems to me one of the most fundamental in all psychotherapy, and essential to the education of any therapist who is going to be effective in transforming deep crisis.'[6]

Another important development was the decision to hold, each year, a Frank Lake Memorial Lecture. The first one, in July 1986, was, appropriately enough, given by Frank's brother, Brian Lake, who took as his subject 'The Cultivation of Competence'. During this period, too, the number of people attending CTA seminars gradually increased, with 500 in the year 1985/86, rising to 700 in 1987/88. In 1986, an abridged version of *Clinical Theology* was published, skilfully edited by Martin Yeomans; it remains in considerable demand, so much so that a reprint was ordered before the end of 1986. The following year saw the republication of *Tight Corners in Pastoral Counselling* which had not been available for three or four years.

Significant recovery

CTA's position has certainly been stabilized: a significant recovery in the post-Frank Lake era has been made. This recovery has been most apparent in two ways. First, in the realm of *ideas*. Clinical Theology, a previously highly individualistic model, is now recognized as only a model. No one appreciates this more keenly than Peter van de Kasteele who, in a lecture in 1987, pinpointed the weaknesses of Clinical Theology in the following way:

> First, the normative model tends to be hidden by the pathology of the personality reaction patterns; for example, my schizoid personality (when I recognize it) may cause me to withdraw from other people when I am stressed, but it also enables me to apply myself to intellectual tasks.
>
> Secondly, the normative model *may* have imposed onto the dynamics of the adult life of our Lord more than exists; the evidence of John's Gospel needs to be supplemented from the other Gospels, and also a complete Christian doctrine of persons derived from the Old and New Testaments.
>
> Thirdly, the mental pain of early trauma cannot be likened (without any qualification) to the suffering of the Cross; Frank Lake's theology of the Cross becomes too subjective, and loses an objective element in the work of Atonement. Frank Lake seems to have read Lutheran theology, but it may be that James Atkinson's Foreword to the recent *The Enigma of the Cross* is relevant. 'Moses (on Sinai) begs to be made *certain* of God's presence . . . God tells Moses that he shall never see his face, only his back . . . Luther interprets "the back parts of God" to mean the despair and anguish of the absence of God, of being for-

saken by God, of the contradictions of life: in short, the Cross. But it is of decisive importance to see what Luther taught was not that God is somehow there, *in spite of* defeat, sorrow, pain, humiliation, anguish, failure, sin and death. Not at all! He taught that God himself confronts us in person and makes his presence near *in and through* defeat, sorrow, pain, humiliation, anguish, failure, sin and death . . . It is the back of God which is revealed – but it *is* God, and not another.'

Fourthly, the validity of extrapolation of the model needs to be tested; the model is extrapolated 'forward' into adult life, here-and-now relationships, and the spiritual life; Frank Lake also extrapolated the model 'backward' into foetal life, including the first trimester. The assumption of pre- and peri-natal psychology has yet to be adequately validated, though there is enough evidence for it not to be dismissed.[7]

Fifthly, the model is used individualistically without regard for the social context, networks and systems in which the individual is involved.

Sixthly, the normative model is made to imply that the mental pain of early trauma may be retrieved and re-experienced and thereby relieved, whereas Christian tradition teaches that pain and suffering may sometimes have to be borne with the help of the sufficiency of God's grace. 'A thorn was given me in the flesh . . . Three times I besought the Lord about this, that it should leave me; but he said to me, "My grace is sufficient . . ." ' (2 Corinthians 12:7–9).

In addition, the association is keenly aware of the need to provide theological bases for its work. Towards the end of his life Frank Lake lost the sense of the 'objective validity' of the cross and became more dependent on secular therapies; currently CTA has reversed the trend, placing less emphasis on the importance of secular therapies.

Secondly, in the realm of its *structures*. In his review of the year 1986/87, CTA's administrative secretary was able to announce the names of seven people who had consented to be publicly associated with CTA as a *panel of reference*: Richard Darby, Bishop of Sherwood; the Revd Donald Eadie, currently Chairman of the Birmingham District of the Methodist Church, and Tutor at Wesley College, Bristol; Dr George Giarchi, Head of Social Work, Health and Community Studies, at Plymouth Polytechnic; the Right Revd David Konstant, Bishop of Leeds; Mr Paddy Marsh, a London solicitor and formerly Warden of Scargill House; the Right Revd David Sheppard, Bishop of Liverpool; and Dr David Toms, Nottingham's consultant psychiatrist.

In the same review Peter van de Kasteele reported that the Council of CTA was in the process of forming a *consultative panel* which would have three advisory functions: to monitor the work of the association; alert it to trends and developments in counselling and pastoral care and associated disciplines; and to advise in particulars, normally through the administrative secretary.

Yet another demonstration of CTA's concern for public credibility, and the highest standards of its ministry, is the procedure for the authorization of tutors, the panel's first external assessor being the Revd John Foskett, Chaplain of the Maudsley Hospital. The purpose of this whole procedure has been carefully laid down, as follows: 'In order to maintain and raise standards of practice and to ensure an awareness of accountability, the Council of the Association has adopted this procedure for the recognition of a minimum of self-awareness, and of pastoral counselling and of teaching competence, required of those Professional Associates who conduct the Seminars.'

The Clinical Theology Association *has* recovered after the trauma of Frank Lake's death. It will only develop as it remains alive and alert to the possibilities presented by an ever-changing world, with all its problems psychologically, emotionally, theologically. How this alertness may demonstrate itself will be the subject of the closing chapter.

8

Conclusions

The overall purpose of this final chapter is to assess – albeit briefly – some of the cardinal features of Frank Lake's achievements, and to indicate some pointers for the future direction and development of the Clinical Theology Association.

Frank Lake and CTA

The first twenty-five years of CTA's history were dominated by Dr Frank Lake, whose achievements were, by any objective criteria, considerable. He initiated a movement and overcame the obstacles that, inevitably, stood in the way of a pioneering movement of the sort he had set in motion. He brought to this task what can only be described as 'missionary zeal'. This particular strength was highlighted by Bishop Michael Hare-Duke in his obituary notice in the *Church Times*: '[Frank Lake] was indefatigable in his promotion of the cause to which he was passionately committed, lobbying church authorities, offering courses wherever there seemed a likely or unlikely opening, and driving immense distances to attend seminar after seminar. His personal charisma was undeniable, and he was in constant demand as a compelling speaker even though people did not always agree with him.'[1] He was also armed with the rich resources of an incisive intellect, boundless determination, and a deeply-rooted faith that expressed itself in a caring, compassionate regard for his fellow human beings, especially those suffering the ills of humanity. This caring responsiveness was particularly in evidence in his 're-birthing' workshops: 'Watching Frank at work in them was something of a revelation. He gave so much of himself and was certainly very impressive,' said Dr Irene Bloomfield.[2] Whether the observed symptoms in such sessions could be explained in other ways – and certainly they needed to be considered and evaluated – does not detract at all from his willingness to listen avidly and follow the process through with an extensive interpretation, both psychological and spiritual. And there is plenty of testimony to the profound help he gave to countless numbers of people and to the importance of such encounters in their lives.

A valuable extension of the personal help he gave to people was to be found in his letters. Here is but one example of scores of similar letters that could be quoted to show the seriousness and the detailed understanding with which he approached the emotional dilemmas of others:

> Thank you for your letter which must have involved a good deal of costly self-disclosure, and deserved an immediate answer.
>
> Although there sometimes is a paradoxical kick-back when those of us who in one sense would much prefer never to make any disclosures about ourselves, do so, and find an immediate benefit, as though we had thereby become in a new sense 'human', the kick-back is I think to be explained by our fear of having let a part of ourselves, and our enclosed inwardness is a part of ourselves, go out, unprotected, into the world in which we find it hard to trust; yet for all that, our initial impulse to communicate was a right one.
>
> In everything you write, there is a sense of the hand of God upon you. Conversion does not reach down at once into the roots of basic personality difficulties, but it does give us Christ's guarantee that in His own good time He *will* confront all our inner dreads and overcome them. No one is in greater need of patience than the afflicted person, because, as with St Thomas, the evidences of the truth of Christian faith in his life always seemed to come rather later than they do in other people's. Yet in the long run, he has the greater cause to praise his Saviour. In His redemption the Saviour had to enter a like affliction and a greater affliction.
>
> I was delighted to hear of your response to the work-people and their more direct and readily accepting sense of relationships. That was a tremendous move forward.

The kind of job you have at present, with its changing targets and a basis of friendly relationships, couldn't be bettered in view of the task you have ahead.

In regard to your relationships with women: I would say this. The person who has your kind of affliction, and it is common enough among us, always does find it insuperably difficult to discover in himself, by introspection, the sense of personal identity which would encourage him to think of himself as of the marrying sort. The idea of taking on responsibility for another woman, when one's own mother did not really take responsibility for oneself, seems a quite intolerable prospect.

As you go on living as a Christian, discovering your valuation of yourself, not by looking into those internal eyes which rather despise you and tell you that you are no good, but by looking into the eyes of Christ and discovering in His countenance the glory of God and His kind of love for those of us whose natures are 'fast bound in misery and iron', you will yourself be transformed in your valuation of yourself.

Moreover, you will be able to expect that the love of God has provided all things that are best for you. With the greatest of ease, the Holy Spirit could put into the heart of a girl whose life had been transfixed by the Cross and transfigured by the Resurrection, an *agape*-type love for you. She might herself be a full-blooded person, or herself one who has suffered in like manner, and by nature could only feel as unloved as you do. That is to say, when a relationship of great intimacy like marriage comes near to you, avoid like the plague introspection, because that will only lead you to devalue yourself. The natural self is a devalued one anyway. That is the moment to live by faith and be engaged by faith, and be married by faith. The source of all love is the God Who, if this is His purpose, will draw you and the woman of His choice irresistibly together in the power of His love. This I have seen happen often enough to know its absolute validity. It has come very near to my own experience.[3]

This letter has a number of notable qualities: a definite interest in the plight of his correspondent, personal warmth and identification with the person undergoing stress and tension, and a committed faith in Jesus Christ as Healer. The arguments are developed carefully and comprehensively without taking the responsibility for action off the shoulders of the person being advised, but above all with sympathy and a high regard for personal identity and dignity. In many ways, Frank Lake's letter is a classic in terms of counselling.

But Frank Lake not only gave CTA its initial impulse and thrust: he also set up the whole network of seminars throughout the dioceses of the Church of England. This was, undoubtedly, an immense administrative undertaking; and he too produced the back-up material of charts and booklets, and maintained a flow of new material which acted as a stimulus for CTA members.

Put briefly, Frank Lake was responsible for bringing theology and psychiatry together in a wide-ranging and comprehensive way. Writing to him in 1978, Professor Tom F. Torrance said: 'It is good to hear from you, and to learn through your own inquiries, with the remarkable blend of the psychiatric and the theological . . . I do not know anyone who has been delving into these connections in the way you have.'[4] This approach was appreciated not only by academics like Professor Torrance but by clergymen like the Revd Marc Seccombe who found their perceptions enlarged in crucial ways: 'I was one of several "green" curates who first came across Frank Lake via post-ordination training at Nottingham in the early 1960s. As someone with a strong evangelical background, I had my eyes opened by his approach, which emphasized the human experience and the "hidden agendas" in life. Later I attended Clinical Theology seminars and conferences, including a Primal Workshop held at Lingdale. This I found personally very disturbing. But I always valued Frank Lake's courage in examining the frontiers between theology, psychiatry and peri-natal pathology. It was his widening of horizons that I found appealing and challenging.'[5]

Frank Lake never ceased to quest into, explore and redefine this relationship between theology and psychiatry, and as the Right Revd Richard Darby claimed in a newspaper article towards the end of Frank's life, 'Today his methods are used not only by clergymen but by teachers and social workers all over the world. People who help people in need have to be trained to listen and understand their problems and to help them come to their own conclusions. Dr Lake recognized this and offered his services for training when he established the association.'[6] It is also the case that he went 'more deeply' (Dr Roger Moss's words) than others into the application of psychology to pastoral care; and his seminars probably gave more information and practical skills than any others in a comparable framework of time and energy. These seminars also taught professionals (for example, general practitioners and paramedicals) other than psychiatrists much that was not available to them via their own professional training. In addition, Frank Lake kept the CTA in touch with other pastoral movements at home and abroad, notably the United States: in other words, he did much more than merely provide a framework which thereafter stagnated. This aspect of his work was strengthened by his worldwide travels, which enabled him to assess and qualify his own perceptions in the light of other cultures and other counselling and pastoral practices.

Frank Lake's work with CTA was clearly a relief to Christians: here was a thoroughly knowledgeable professional doing more than merely giving justice to theological considerations.

Frank Lake and primal integration therapy

Frank Lake is considered to be one of the founding fathers of primal therapy, and Dr Roger Moss, who is currently engaged in writing up this aspect of Frank Lake's work, considers his contribution to be unique in two ways.[7] First, that he stressed the importance in the formation of personality of the first trimester of pregnancy, 'a perspective now becoming acknowledged but still not worked out in such detail by anyone else'. Secondly, his insistence that the link between foetus and mother, particularly hormonally, 'was the thesis to concentrate upon from the point of view of scientific training'.

Frank Lake's absorption with primal therapy raised problems on levels other than the theological. There were some within CTA who regarded it as a divergence from the 'real work' of the association, and some members of the Council left out of frustration at the impossibility of getting Frank to separate himself from research into primal therapy and to concentrate on the more routine work of counselling and seminar work. There were others within the association who viewed his work with primal therapy as the formation of a movement within a movement, essentially divisive, because it appeared to be perceived by Frank as a panacea for all ills, thus discounting much of his earlier work: quite rightly, such people insisted that in psychotherapy no 'mythology' can explain everything.

It is also a fact that his obsession with primal work, and related psychological theories, blinded him to physical and medical realities, both in himself and in other people. As far as other people were concerned, one CTA member wrote: 'At a time when Frank was seeming somewhat god-like to many of his faithful followers, I had a glimpse of clay feet when he was in the "Birth Trauma"/"Primal Scream" stage. He was preaching the need for re-living the birth stage experience as a "cure-all". I happened to have a severe attack of asthma and his insistence upon pressing my head and getting the group to surround me closely when what I urgently needed was oxygen nearly killed me in "status asthmaticus".'[8] On another occasion, this time in March 1978, 'Frank began complaining (in a Primal Workshop) of a headache and at one time became convinced that it must be due to his own birth material being re-stimulated. However, after some time another member in the group began to notice that Frank had physical signs as well: slight paralysis of one side of the face, and unsteadiness in walking. Only with some difficulty was he persuaded to leave the group, go to bed, and call a doctor.'[9] The physical reality that Frank tried to ignore was later diagnosed as a brainstem haemhorrage.

The net result of Frank Lake's involvement with this type of work was that in some not-well-informed circles CTA became synonymous with primal integration therapy, which was, after all, a late development in its history.

A brief critique

CTA's history up until 1982 was very largely identified with the personality, abilities and gifts of one man: Frank Lake. Its failings, therefore, were closely related to his failings and his own idiosyncratic behaviour. This was inevitable. He signally failed to make the association self-perpetuating, simply because he could not resist interfering with the controls at *all* levels of its operations. Even when he had apparently given free rein to someone to run seminars and arrange other CTA events, there was the feeling that he had to have the last word. Some did not object to this rather constricting attitude, whereas those who did, disagreed openly with him and left CTA. To that extent he would stand his ground, would not easily compromise, and when others left in frustration he would pick up the threads and, without rancour, would continue on his chosen course. Maybe it was something of the messianic spirit referred to earlier that caused him to press relentlessly on.

Administratively, this led to very serious difficulties and, eventually, impaired the organization of the seminars which were the jewel in the crown of CTA. According to the Revd David Bick, Frank Lake's main failing was that he could not delegate or choose the right people to develop his work: 'He did choose some very able people but they soon gave up and left him when they discovered this weakness. He seemed to resent the initiative in those who worked closely with him and therefore CTA never had a good administrative system during his time. He lacked the overall vision and political awareness that a movement with the potential of CTA needs. He also had the strength of character and manipulative prowess to frustrate anyone who did and who made suggestions that would seem in his eyes to threaten to wrest control of his baby out of his hands.'[10] Eventually, it seems, the Council attempted to take away from him the seminars (which because of his absorption with primal work from the mid-1970s onwards had begun to decay) and put him in charge of the Research Department. This initiative did not work because Frank was able to manipulate all the resources his way, and there was no one willing or able to push the seminar issue to a major confrontation.

Another problem area concerned CTA's interaction with the universities and the academic community in general. Dr Alastair Campbell, of the Department of Christian Ethics and Practical Theology in the University of Edinburgh, put it like this: 'As regards failings or disadvantages related to Frank's approach and to the CTA, I would say that the interaction with the universities was and continues to be always a difficult one. Perhaps there has been misunderstanding on both sides from time to time and I have certainly seen it appropriate to keep very much in touch with CTA and to use the material coming from that source whenever possible. On the other hand, universities tend to be less committed to a particular point of view than was the case with the Clinical Theology Association in various aspects of its development. Looking from the outside it frequently seemed that CTA was going to be in danger of taking on the latest fad rather than using the kind of rigorous methods of conceptual analysis that a university is concerned about.'[11]

There was disquiet, too, about other features of the association's work. One related to its tendency to use too much jargon, and to labelling people according to Frank's types, about which Canon Hugh Melinsky has this to say: 'To identify Mary Magdalene as a hysteric because at the end she wishes to cling to the Master is to go some way beyond the evidence; so also with the Syro-Phoenician woman as "hysterical in her need and clinging; afflicted and ready to shrink away like a beaten cur into a cringing schizoid detachment"; so also is identifying the hypocrisy of the Pharisees with a generous use of dissociative personality mechanisms.'[12] Canon Alan Wilkinson feels that Clinical Theology sessions were overloaded with heavily written and indigestible didactic material much of which was produced by Frank Lake, and he asks this pertinent question: 'How could anyone offer, for example, the following title for a section: "The Substitution of the Fixated Infantile Identifications with the Loss of Well-Being, Inadequacy, Inferiority, Emptiness, Tiredness, Weakness, Fatigue, Exhaustion, Meaninglessness, Persecution, Suspicions, Fear and Cruelty, by Overweening Attention and Concern given to an Unconsciously Selected Limited Part of the Total Fixated Infantile Experience".'[13] It is difficult to escape the conclusion that while Frank Lake's material was often daringly original, it was, as Canon Wilkinson claims, 'too individual and eccentric, theologically and psychologically, for a basic training course'. Another charge was linked to the intensity of CT sessions: that they dug deeper into people's personalities than was necessary.

None of these issues, however, can obscure the nature and

extent of CTA's achievement. Today departments of psychotherapy operate in NHS hospitals in all of Britain's major's towns. They are served by one and not infrequently two consultant psychiatrist-psychotherapists, a senior and sometimes junior psychiatric registrar, and frequently by psychotherapy-trained nurses, social workers and occupational therapists. Alongside them are departments of psychology with psychologists who also specialize in a variety of psychotherapies. In the 1960s there were virtually no such departments outside London (and few there) apart from a small presence in Leeds, Birmingham, Edinburgh and Aberdeen. The rest of the country was virtually destitute of professional psychotherapeutic support. In an encouraging number of dioceses, too, an adviser in pastoral care or counselling is appointed and the training of clergy, and counselling, is increasingly available: a situation directly related to CTA's impetus and influence. 'Everyone in CTA', says Dr Brian Lake, 'played some part in educating and encouraging people at the grass roots and at the highest level to recognize the need for, and the possibility of, this extraordinary achievement.'

CTA's abiding value

An important aspect of the association's value is that it is one of the few (only?) bodies to provide seminars in pastoral care and counselling in *local areas* throughout the country. Consequently it can respond, with flexibility, to areas of need without being overdependent (now) on a central resource. CTA also provides a specifically *Christian* resource within the labyrinths of the counselling world, and is committed to looking at the theological concepts which lie behind human growth and development. Hamish Montgomery, who has developed the Tom Allan Centre in Glasgow into one of Scotland's leading pastoral care and counselling centres, made this qualitative comment to me: 'It seems to me to be an important part of the message of Clinical Theology that, while providing sound psychodynamic, human growth and development training, it allows for an eclectic approach to therapy. And while it is clearly Christocentric, believers, nonbelievers and those of other faiths seem to feel at home in the groups. I think that this is largely because of the emphasis on integrating material into one's own Christian, or other, experience.'[14] The result of all these influences is that CTA has helped to widen the concept of pastoral care.

What of the future?

An association like CTA has constantly to be assessing its priorities, practices and motivations to ensure growth and development. Reliance on past achievements would lead only to a moribund state of affairs, with decreasing vision and decreasing influence. As an outsider with no axe to grind but absolutely convinced of the importance of CTA's work, I would suggest that the following issues need to be carefully and regularly monitored if future growth is to be a *sustained* reality.

Leadership style(s). Memories of Frank Lake have been very largely shaken off, but CTA, which was birthed as a pioneering movement, must guard against settling for the middle ground in an attempt to be 'safe'. It must also attempt to regain those contacts with Nonconformists and Roman Catholics which seem to have declined in recent years. The increasingly complex demands of society will require as much stimulus and vision on the part of CTA's leaders as they did when the association first came into existence.

The attitude to primal integration therapy. The continuing uncertainty towards this form of therapy must be ended, preferably with a clear, unequivocal statement from CTA's Council. If these workshops are to continue, three safeguards must be insisted on. The first is that the consequences of an action must be followed up and carried through *after* the workshop itself. In Frank Lake's day the participants were allowed to return to their home milieu without appropriate support being given in the ensuing days and weeks. Frank himself gave lip-service to the need for supportive back-up, but not much action. To leave threads undone in this was, undoubtedly, irresponsible. The second is that the primal 'freak' (who makes primal integration therapy a way of life when more orthodox cognitive therapy might be valid) must be severely discouraged. The third is that a medical man, and someone preferably with psychiatric training, ought to be in overall charge of such work.

The seminar programme. This programme, which imparts a fair degree of reality by allowing people to bring insights from their own experience, must be closely related to the *thorough training* of men and women in its pastoral and counselling methods. Dealing with emotional pain and trauma which involves dealing with and counselling vulnerable people is, at best, delicate, and, at worst, hazardous: moreover, it is an area in which a little knowledge can be dangerous. In this context it is all too easy for seminar members with limited expertise to get out of their depth. To look under the surface of people's behaviour (in a caring environment) in order to understand their difficulties is valid and praiseworthy, but it *has* to be approached with humility, sensitivity, and a considerable degree of skill: bungling amateurs, however well intentioned, can cause mayhem.

CTA's administration. Quite considerable improvements have been made in recent years, and indeed they had to be, because careful, systematic, day-to-day administration was not Frank Lake's forte. Practical issues such as the collection of fees from seminars and sending capitations to headquarters were neglected. It was not a question of wilful neglect, rather of muddled, incompetent administration. Energetic efforts have been made to put this right, but it needs constantly to be worked at, honed and sharpened, which with all the resources of computers ought to be a fairly routine matter.

Finance. Overall directive vision has to be applied to CTA's finances, which were in a state of chaos and near-collapse when Frank Lake died. Undoubtedly the association's financial position has been stabilized, a situation greatly helped by the paring down of costs at CTA headquarters near Oxford. The financial drain of Lingdale is a thing of the past but, like its general administration, CTA's finances must continue to be a matter of high priority.

Theology. It is vital for the association to insist on its strong theological bases. It is unique in that it is the only institution that pays equal regard to theology and psychology in its teaching on human relations, pastoral care and counselling.

It not only wants people to grow in personal insight and to be free from self-defeating obstacles (just like any other secular counselling institution), but also to utilize the *full* breadth of Christian revelation and Christian resources: this means primarily justification by faith, by grace and the perpetual presence and succour of the living Christ. Unless CTA remains theologically strong and vibrant, it could degenerate into a neo-Gnostic sect. For this reason its members, and especially seminar leaders, need to have a clear, unambiguous perceptual awareness of the key doctrines: Creation, Sin, The Fall, and Redemption.

Denominational structures. CTA began in the Anglican stable, and even though the seminars are ecumenical, the good news needs to be carried through into structures of the Church other than merely the Church of England. 'Church' in CTA terms is still mainly Church of England, a situation requiring urgent attention and imaginative action.

The nature of CTA gatherings. It was suggested to me in the course of my research that the typical CTA gathering today, be it seminar or conference, is more female than male, more elderly than young, more 'southern' than 'northern', still primarily Anglican, and with almost no one from the black or coloured communities. The implication of such observations is obvious enough: that CTA is, at present, confined to a relatively narrow grouping of individuals, the preserve of what someone has called the 'neurotic well'.

Is this fair and accurate? Not entirely, for although in some ways the association's gatherings reflect the Church as a whole, yet in comparison to both the Church and the present British pastoral counselling scene, it is managing to embrace a wider selection of men and women. Nor are such gatherings all that 'elderly'; the northern versus southern divide is false; and CTA has very special links with Scotland, and has had since the early days.

Research. In a lengthy report to the Council towards the end of the 1970s Frank Lake suggested[15] three possible areas of research for CTA. In terms of *clinical theological research*, one possibility was to assist pastors, doctors and others to 'discriminate' between the 'brokenness' of spirituality patterns which accompany profound spiritual changes, such as the 'dark nights' of ascetical theology or the manifestations of revival in evangelical experience, and the 'breakdowns' which may simulate them. As far as research on a *more specifically psychiatric front* was concerned, Frank Lake urged the collection of data suggesting that a prima determinant of migraine is birth-injury, and that the migraine attack under situations of emotional pressure from all sides, represents a partial abreaction of a phase in the second stage of labour. Thirdly, there was what he called *cross-disciplinary research*, including theological, philosophical and psychoanalytical evaluation of the states of 'being' and 'non-being', anxiety and dread, and also research into the relationship between pastoral and medical care and bereavement. The limited resources of CTA, both in terms of finance and manpower, rule out much of Frank Lake's projected research topics, but it is surely of the utmost importance, as he said in his report, 'that clinical training be informed by and keep itself informed about the training and practice and on-going reflections of the social casework professions'. Perhaps a research officer could be appointed to keep the association in touch with those trends and publications which have a direct or indirect bearing on clinical pastoral education.

It is encouraging to report that the association has begun to develop the 'federal system' as proposed in 1982), that new technology (in the form of computers) is being used, that a professional survey of CTA training and its effectiveness is being embarked upon, that the theology of the Church in relation to CTA is being seriously re-examined, that careful consideration of leadership style(s) appropriate to the future CTA is being given and that an Assistant Director (Training) is to be appointed. Alongside these important developments is the realization that the issue of primal integration must take account of international interest and research within and outside orthodox medicine, while the whole question of training versus therapy is being teased out: having fulfilled the objectives of the 1982 working party in the five years since then, the association is to engage in a full review of the choices currently before it.

The need for courage

The initiatives referred to above will go a long way towards ensuring CTA's continuation as a viable institution in the field of 'human relations, pastoral care and counselling', and could, additionally, lead to as signal a contribution in its second quarter of a century as it did in its first twenty-five years. Inventiveness, vigour and creative ability will all be needed in abundance in order to achieve this, but so will courage, and that of a very special sort.

It is the courage, as Frank Lake showed so movingly in chapter 6 of *Tight Corners in Pastoral Counselling* to put up with the tension of conflict, resistance and even controversy:

> 'Standing out' is a factor that commonly puts people under such pressure that they feel abnormal. They are under duress to comply with the weight of social opinion, even at the expense of their own integrity. If something in the individual rebels against the weight of group opinion, the person with a strong, independent, confident ego or self will maintain his or her own stance. Quite appropriately, he asserts his right to be different. The 'leader', for this is what he has become, may or may not be conscious that he is appealing away from the customs and morals of the community around him to an 'ethical absolute'. There is an inescapable ethical preference which has grasped him. He becomes the bearer of a better expression of man's duty to man and a challenge to the group to accept their need for ethical development towards caring and responsibility. All our great social reformers, so many of whom have been 'outstanding' men and women, have done this. They have been attacked for doing it, often for many years, before the advance which began with their lonely stand was recognized.[16]

It is the courage of prudence:

> Pastoral counselling is pre-eminently concerned with enabling people to do the right thing at the right time. It makes the actively active task possible. It is equally important to facilitate the actively passive task which is, when the occasion is favourable, to make it possible to assimilate into consciousness those experiences of early infantile and

childhood pain which, until this favourable moment, have necessarily and prudently been shut away. The inherent wisdom of the psyche has insisted on its dissociation and defence by repression. Abundant health, both within the person and in the environment and occasion provided by the group, creates a favourable possibility for a deliberate breakthrough, dissolving those defences so that integration can take place. To help people to do, or to bear (a kind of not doing), whatever constitutes the probable next stage of growth and development, at the most favourable, or the least unfavourable time, is a focal task of pastoral counselling.[17]

Perhaps, above all, it is the courage to be 'real to people and real to the living Christ, our contemporary' and Frank Lake saw this process as occurring in the following way:

> The Holy Spirit proceeds from one Person of the Trinity to the other, from God to us, and from us to God, and between ourselves. He is the daily renewing co-inherent enabler of this core task of every theologian (in the sense that all God's people are theologians) conveying God's word back and forth effectively, where time and eternity are conjoined.[18]

Dr Frank Lake achieved so much precisely because he had vision, determination, faith and immense courage. Provided CTA's leaders and members similarly possess such qualities, the last decade of the twentieth century and beyond will be years of solid and lasting achievement.

Notes

CHAPTER 1 – INTRODUCTION

1 Frank Lake's own description in correspondence in the Lingdale Archive, no. 525.

2 Part of Dr Roberts's paper, 'A Review of Clinical Theology', dated April 1970.

3 *Institute of Religion and Medicine Newsletter* (October–December 1981), no. 53.

4 The article is preserved in the Lingdale Archive, no. 014.

5 *Clinical Theology* (1966), p. 84.

6 Lingdale Archive, no. 810.

7 See Lingdale Archive, no. 038: a radio talk (December 1966) entitled 'What is Clinical Theology?'

8 The article is headed 'Are We Really the Body of Christ?'

9 Roberts, ibid.

10 Lake, Lingdale Archive, no. 014.

11 Lake, Lingdale Archive, no. 014.

12 I am indebted to the Revd John Gravelle for these emphases.

13 Communicated to me by letter.

14 Sent to me in a letter dated 16 February 1988.

CHAPTER 2 – THE HISTORY OF THE CLINICAL THEOLOGY ASSOCIATION (1962–82)

1 *Newsletter 19*, p. 1.

2 *Newsletter 1*, p. 4.

3 *Newsletter 2*, p. 4.

4 *Newsletter 2*, p. 4.

5 *Newsletter 10*, pp. 14–15.

6 *Newsletter 6*, pp. 4–5.

7 Communicated to me in a letter dated 15 December 1987.

8 *Newsletter 10*, pp. 16–17.

9 The full review was published in *Contact 19* (January 1967).

10 Part of a letter to me dated 12 December 1987.

11 Part of a letter to me dated 24 December 1987.

12 Full details are found in *Newsletter 9*, pp. 10ff.

13 Letter dated 31 May 1973, now in Lingdale Archive, no. 543.
14 Submission dated 6 November 1988.
15 *Contact* (1985:3), p. 9.

CHAPTER 3 – A SKETCH OF FRANK LAKE'S LIFE

1 Brian Lake became unhappy about his own role within CTA and its general direction in 1969. He felt that its original dynamic was being impaired in a number of ways and so he returned to private practice.
2 *Contact 81* (1983/84).
3 *Contact 81*, p. 3.
4 *Contact 81*, p. 4.
5 Held on 7 July 1982 at All Souls', Langham Place, London.
6 Preserved in Lingdale Archive, no. 202.
7 His brother Ralph feels similarly about her.
8 Lingdale Archive, no. 064.
9 *Tight Corners in Pastoral Counselling*. (Darton, Longman and Todd, 1981), p. 68.
10 *Tight Corners in Pastoral Counselling* pp. 68–9.
11 Based on information supplied by Sylvia Lake and Ralph Lake.
12 Coming from an Army background, she had been a missionary right up to the time of her retirement, when her strength of character and uprightness were as impressive as ever. Later, when David Lake was three months old, Frank and Sylvia took him to the hills of Gulmerg where, against a background of distant snow-capped hills, Miss Eger was delighted to see Frank (her 'godson') and his family again. Another influence on Frank's thinking regarding missionary work was the Revd J. C. Hart.
13 *Contact 81*, referred to earlier.
14 *Contact 81*.
15 When I interviewed him in April 1988 in Yorkshire.
16 A statement found in an article headed 'The Bearing of Our Knowledge of the Unconscious on the Theology of Evangelism and Pastoral Care' (now Lingdale Archive, no. 009).
17 Based on a submission by Sylvia Lake herself, and also from conversations with the Lake family.
18 Information about her career is contained in Brother Kenneth's book, *Saints of the Twentieth Century* (Lutterworth Press 1976), pp. 172–7.
19 Here is a typical example from Frank Lake's correspondence, this time describing the events of February 1943:

My dearest home folks,

The month of February has been very full indeed. I told you in my last that on hospital Sunday I was preaching for the Revd R.

P. Desh Paude in the central C of S Church in Poona City. It was a most inspiring service in which all the Hospital Staffs of St Margaret's and the Wadia Hospital took part, and all the children of the Sunday School brought gifts. It is rather new to me (coming from Bengal) to see a congregation of 600–700, all fairly well dressed – and mark you, about 60 per cent able to understand English. That seems to me very remarkable. In the week following I spoke to the Poona Toc H branch on the Medical Mission problems in India. Some of the leading officers are keen on Toc H and they do a lot of good work in the hospitals.

Then on the Sunday following I had a difficult task indeed. Mahatma Gandhi was in the second week of his fast, and very ill. The Poona SCM had most surprisingly asked me – an Englishman in the uniform of the ruling raj – to give the address and lead the devotions at their annual meeting. It was a strange position – in that I know perfectly well how they feel for Mr Gandhi – an intense love and loyalty stronger even than their loyalty to truth and reason, and on the other hand the Viceroy's case seems to me to be clear and logical, though most unimaginative.

My only message had to be fundamental and Christian. We who are Christians are one Body in Christ, are in fact more closely brothers and sisters than we are to even our own family, if they are not also members of His Body. In Christ we *are* one. God sees us as one organism – the Body of His Son – and if God regards us as such, that is what we are. Our aim is as Luther said, 'To become what we are', and indeed we who are so divided by race and national interest, do enjoy this supernatural fellowship. It is a great thing to belong to the Universal Church.

20 *Clinical Theology* (1966), Introduction, pp. xv–xxx.
21 *Clinical Theology* (1966), Introduction, pp. xv–xxx.
22 *Clinical Theology* (1966), Introduction, pp. xv–xxx.
23 *British Weekly* (9 October 1969), p. 9.
24 Letter dated 20 March 1945; now in Lingdale Archive (unnumbered correspondence).
25 Interview in January 1988.
26 She made a written submission, April 1988.
27 Written submission and personal interviews in London, February 1988.
28 This title is taken from Bob Lambourne's review in *The Christian*.
29 *Theology* (November 1966), p. 515.
30 In *Catholic Herald*.
31 *Regina* (Trinity 1970), pp. 27ff.
32 In *Church of England Newspaper*.

33 In *Church of England Newspaper.*
34 Lingdale Archive, no. 201.
35 Lingdale Archive, no. 066.
36 Lingdale Archive, no. 031.
37 Dated 17 March 1978, now in Lingdale Archive, no. 540.
38 Lingdale Archive, no. 547.
39 Lingdale Archive, no. 211.
40 29 September 1981, now Lingdale Archive, no. 209.
41 19 October 1981, now Lingdale Archive, no. 220.
42 21 November 1981, now Lingdale Archive, no. 233.
43 *Contact 74*: review also preserved in Lingdale Archive, no. 094.
44 *Contact 75* (1982:2), pp. 27ff.
45 Circular, dated 3 March 1982, to John Gravelle, Brian Hawker, Basil Hobbs, Oliver Horrocks, Dennis Hyde, Roy Ward and Martin Yeomans.
46 *Mutual Caring*, Introduction, p. 1.
47 *Mutual Caring*. This manuscript remains unpublished.
48 *Contact 81*.

CHAPTER 4 – SOME PERSONAL VIEWPOINTS

1 The view of the Bishop of Sherwood (the Right Revd Richard Darby) in the *Nottingham Evening Post* (6 May 1982).
2 The opinion of the Revd Dr Tony Gough in a letter dated 10 February 1988.
3 See also by the same man, 'Sciences of God and Sciences of Man', in *New Blackfriars* (1969), pp. 411–18.
4 See David Bick, 'The Place of Small Groups for Promoting Scriptural and Emotional Growth, with guidelines for their leadership' (1987), and 'A Guide to the Counsellor's Relationship with God' (undated)
5 In the New International Version it reads: 'Dear friends, now we are the children of God, and what we will be has not yet been made known. But we know that when he appears, we shall be like him, for we shall see him as he is.'

CHAPTER 5 – LISTENING AND HELPING – A GUIDE TO FRANK LAKE'S SEMINAL IDEAS

1 *To Kill a Mockingbird*, by Harper Lee (first published 1960; 1974 reprint used here, p. 35).
2 *Clinical Theology* (1966), Preface, p. xii.
3 *Clinical Theology* (1966), Introduction, pp. xv–xxx.
4 *Clinical Theology* (1966), Introduction, pp. xv–xxx.
5 *With Respect* (1982), pp. xv–xxiii.
6 *With Respect* (1982), pp. xv–xxiii.

7 Lingdale Archive, number 074.
8 *Clinical Theology* (1966), Introduction, p. xv.
9 *Clinical Theology* (1966), p. 2.
10 *Clinical Theology* (1966), p. 2.
11 *Clinical Theology* (1966), p. 11.
12 *Clinical Theology* (1966), p. 11.
13 *Clinical Theology* (1966), p. 14.
14 *Clinical Theology* (1966), p. 15.
15 *Clinical Theology* (1966), p. 2.
16 *Clinical Theology* (1966), p. 4.
17 *Clinical Theology* (1966), p. 5.
18 Ezekiel 3:10–15.
19 Isaiah 53.
20 Lingdale Archive, number 048.
21 *Clinical Theology* (1966), pp. 15–16.
22 *Clinical Theology* (1966), p. 9.
23 *Clinical Theology* (1966), p. 17.
24 *Clinical Theology* (1966), p. 10.
25 *Clinical Theology* (1966), pp. 19 and 29.
26 *Clinical Theology* (1966), p. 28.
27 *Clinical Theology* (1966), pp. 35–7.
28 *Clinical Theology* (1966), p. 11.
29 *Clinical Theology* (1966), p. 11.
30 *Clinical Theology* (1966), p. 21.
31 *Clinical Theology* (1966), p. 21.
32 *Clinical Theology* (1986), p. 19.
33 *Clinical Theology* (1986), p. 19.
34 *Clinical Theology* (1986), pp. 19–20.
35 *Clinical Theology* (1986), p. 20.
36 *Clinical Theology* (1986), p. 22.
37 *Clinical Theology* (1986), p. 23.
38 *Clinical Theology* (1986), pp. 22–3.
39 *Clinical Theology* (1986), p. 25.
40 *Clinical Theology* (1986), p. 26.
41 *Clinical Theology* (1986), p. 26.
42 *Clinical Theology* (1986), p. 28.
43 Diagram appearing in *Clinical Theology* (1966), p. 133.
44 Lingdale Papers 2, p. 3.
45 *Clinical Theology* (1966), p. 135.
46 *Clinical Theology* (1966), p. 135.
47 See H. D. Macdonald, *Jesus Human and Divine* (Pickering and Inglis 1968), p. 41–3.
48 *Clinical Theology* (1966), pp. 37–51.
49 *Tight Corners in Pastoral Counselling* (1986), p. 17.

50 *Clinical Theology* (1966), p. 699.
51 *Journal of Psychiatric Research* (vol. 22, 1978), pp. 227–38.
52 *Journal of Psychiatric Research* (vol. 22, 1978), p. 228.
53 *The Trauma of Birth* (New York and London, Harper and Row), pp. 202–7.
54 *Clinical Theology* (1966), p. 1059.
55 *Clinical Theology* (1966), p. 1059.
56 Quoted in *Clinical Theology* (1966), pp. 1060–61.
57 *Journal of Psychiatric Research* (vol. 22, 1978), pp. 231–2.
58 CTA *Newsletter 9*, pp. 10ff.
59 CTA *Newsletter 9*, pp. 10ff.
60 CTA paper dated 7 December 1979.
61 *Clinical Theology* (1966), pp. 133–4.
62 *Clinical Theology* (1966), p. 135.
63 Leon Morris, *The Atonement: Its Meaning and Significance* (IVP 1983), p. 196.
64 For example, 2 Timothy 2:21; 3:17.
65 Peter van de Kasteele, January 1986, lecture, p. 38.
66 *Clinical Theology* (1986), pp. 4–5.
67 *Clinical Theology* (1966), pp. 28–9.
68 Lingdale Paper 2, p. 6.
69 Lingdale Paper 2, p. 6.
70 Letter to me dated 6 January 1988.
71 See *Primal Integration: a First Report from the Workshops* (May 1983); *Frank Lake's Maternal–Foetal Distress Syndrome* (December 1983); 'Review of Research, Frank Lake's Primal Integration Workshops', a private paper presented to CTA's Council, 25 March 1984).
72 *Clinical Theology* (1986), p. 15.
73 *Clinical Theology* (1986), p. 16.
74 *Clinical Theology* (1986), p. 16.
75 *Clinical Theology* (1986), p. 19.
76 *Clinical Theology* (1986), p. 21.
77 *Clinical Theology* (1986), p. 21.
78 *Clinical Theology* (1986), pp. 21–2.
79 *Clinical Theology* (1986), p. 23.
80 *Clinical Theology* (1986), p. 24.
81 Lingdale Archive, no. 811.
82 Lingdale Archive, no. 812.
83 See Chapters 2 and 12 particularly, in *Clinical Theology* (1986).
84 *Clinical Theology* (1986), p. 55.
85 See *Clinical Theology* (1986), Chapters 2 and 3.
86 Sanford, *Healing Gifts of the Spirit* (Arthur Jones 1949), p. 105.
87 Sanford, ibid, p. 106.

88 Sanford, ibid., p. 107.
89 MacNutt, *Healing* (Ave Maria Press, Notre Dame, Indiana 1974), p. 79.
90 MacNutt, ibid., p. 181.
91 MacNutt, ibid., pp. 183–4.
92 MacNutt, ibid., p. 191.
93 *Tight Corners in Pastoral Counselling*, p. 46.
94 *Power Healing* (Hodder and Stoughton 1986), pp. 161–2.
95 *Receive Your Healing* (Hodder and Stoughton 1986), pp. 161–2.
96 *Power Healing*, p. 103.
97 Quoted in *Power Healing*, p. 104.
98 See *Power Healing*, p. 104.
99 'Christ the Therapist', Lingdale Archive, no. 35.
100 Fragment preserved in Lingdale Archive (unnumbered).
101 *Tight Corners in Pastoral Counselling*, p. 55.
102 *With Respect*, p. 49.
103 *With Respect*, p. 49.
104 *With Respect*, p. 50.
105 *With Respect*, p. 51.
106 *With Respect*, pp. 51–2.
107 *With Respect*, p. 53.
108 *With Respect*, p. 302.
109 *With Respect*, p. 309.
110 *With Respect*, Preface, pp. xv–xxiii.
111 *Tight Corners in Pastoral Counselling*, p. 175.
112 Dated September 1982.
113 *With Respect*, p. 47.

CHAPTER 6 – IN RETROSPECT

1 In a letter to me from Sylvia Lake, February 1988.
2 Part of Pond's letter to Frank Lake, dated 2 October 1966.
3 For the details, see Chapter 3.
4 The Revd E. G. Symonds wrote to me as follows: 'Frank Lake was lecturing to deacons in a post-ordination course in Leicester in about 1959. As he spoke of various mental states we felt that all of us had traces (at least) of all of them. One student asked, "Have you ever known a fully balanced person?" Dr Lake replied, "No, but I have heard that there was one once".'
5 The Revd Derek Atkinson, in a letter to me dated 18 January 1988, said this: 'It was a personal reminiscence from Frank that when he was getting tired he would sometimes become aware of "the little frightened child within". That phrase immediately "rang bells" for me and provided at once an explanation, and the comforting thought that it was not only me, but great ones like Frank, who

still suffered "the little frightened child within".' A fuller version of the Revd Atkinson's recollections is given in Chapter 4.

6 See Dr Irene Bloomfield's review of *Clinical Theology* (1986) in *Manna* (no. 14, Winter 1987), pp. 17ff.

7 Irene Bloomfield, *Manna* (no. 14, Winter 1987), p. 18.

8 See Lingdale Archive, no. 531.

9 The address is dated March 1967, and is now preserved in Lingdale Archive, no. 802. Compare, by the same author, 'Science of God and Science of Man', in *New Blackfriars* (1969), pp. 411–18.

10 Charles Iball, in *New Christian* (26 January 1967).

11 Part of Gordon Harris's review of *Clinical Theology* (1966) in *Free Church Letter.*

12 CTA *Newsletter 10.*

13 Canon Hugh Melinsky, *Religion and Medicine* (SCM Press 1970).

14–19 See Lingdale Archive, no. 504.

20 Compare Hugh Melinsky's views in *Religion and Medicine.*

21 *Seduction of Christianity* was published by Harvest House Publishers, Eugene, Oregon, USA.

22 *Seduction of Christianity*, p. 180.

23 Letter preserved in Lingdale Archive, no. 078.

24 See Appendix A.

25 See Lingdale Archive, no. 113.

26 See Lingdale Archive, no. 113.

27 See Lingdale Archive, no. 113.

28 See Lingdale Archive, no. 113.

29 Based on a paper, by an unnamed author, in the Lingdale Archive, no. 079.

30 Counselling Placement Report (April 1980), Lingdale Archive, no. 807.

31 Preserved in Lingdale Archive, no. 038.

32 See Alastair Campbell (ed.), *Dictionary of Pastoral Care* (SPCK 1987). The article on Clinical Theology is by the Revd John Gravelle, p. 38.

33 See Alastair Campbell (ed.), *Dictionary of Pastoral Care*, p. 38.

CHAPTER 7 – THE HISTORY OF CTA: THE POST-FRANK LAKE ERA

1 Dated 26 August 1982, the notes were distributed by Martin Yeomans, together with a covering letter.

2 Document sent to me by the Revd Peter van de Kasteele.

3 *Newsletter 45* (January 1984).

4 *Newsletter 45* (January 1984).

5 *Newsletter 45* (January 1984).

6 *Newsletter 46* (November 1984).

7 Alistair McGrath, *The Enigma of the Cross* (Hodder and Stoughton 1987), p. 8.

CHAPTER 8 – CONCLUSIONS

1 The notice was published on 14 May 1982.

2 Part of Dr Bloomfield's written submission, dated 9 November 1987.

3 This letter was sent to me by a correspondent who wishes to remain anonymous.

4 The full letter is preserved in the Lingdale Archive, no. 203.

5 Part of the Revd Marc Seccombe's letter of 11 April 1988.

6 Part of an article published in a local Nottingham newspaper, the *Nottingham Evening Post*, on 6 May 1982.

7 Part of Dr Roger Moss's written submission to me in October 1987.

8 Part of Elizabeth Paine's letter, dated 30 January 1987.

9 A recollection communicated to me by Mrs Libby Wattis, Leeds, on 15 March 1988. The person in the group who noticed that Frank had something physically wrong with him was Mrs Wattis's husband, John.

10 Part of his written submission in January 1988.

11 Letter dated 17 December 1987.

12 *Religion and Medicine* (SCM Press 1970), p. 128.

13 Letter dated 26 January 1988.

14 Part of his submission, dated 13 January 1988.

15 Lingdale Archive, no. 535.

16 *Tight Corners in Pastoral Counselling* (1987 reprint, Darton, Longman and Todd), p. 88.

17 *Tight Corners in Pastoral Counselling* (1987), pp. 92–3.

18 *Tight Corners in Pastoral Counselling* (1987), p. 92.

Appendix A

Frank Lake's 'The Work of Christ in the Healing of Primal Pain'

Introduction

Two aspects of what Luther called the *theologia crucis* have recently become confluent. One derives from experience and theological reflection embodied in the discipline of 'Clinical Theology'. This has recently been expanded and (from the psychiatric standpoint) laicized in short conferences of the CTA under such titles as 'Primal Integrative Work in a Christian Context' and 'The Renewal Prayer Group and the Healing of Forgotten Pain'. Working in small groups, in the context of Christ's word, sacrament and fellowship, people desiring to be freed from distorted perceptions, emotions and relationships, concerning themselves intra-personally, and their interpersonal reactions, and from difficulties in accepting God the Father as Christ revealed him, discover the need for what could be called a retrospective evangelization of the dark continent of a forgotten babyhood and childhood. Remarkably simple methods render these very early traumatic experiences memorable in consciousness. What the infant could not assimilate at the time because of the catastrophic pain of it, and dared not accept because of the implication that the physical and human structures of its world were mercilessly destructive and hostile, can now be integrated into consciousness by the adult. By some adults, it would be truer to say, since many, particularly among the members of the helping professions, do experience deep, emotionally charged resistances even to considering this as a possibility, for themselves or others.

A theology of correlation

Working mainly, but by no means exclusively, among Christians, the staff and associates of CTA have been led to recognize close and significant correspondences between the two basic, and commonest peri-natal catastrophes, (1) a terrible, asphyxiating crushing affliction during the birth process, and (2) a separation anxiety which pushes the new-born to the limits of solitary panic – and beyond, over the edge of the abyss into dereliction and a falling apart of the self in dread and non-being, on the one hand and the two most terrible terminal experiences in the Passion of Our Saviour Jesus Christ on the other. He undergoes (1) the crushing affliction of Gethsemane, the lonely agony, the bloody sweat, the struggle in the human will to go on into the horror or to draw back, the flogging, the mockery and humiliation as all human rights are infringed, the crown of thorns (so like the crushing of the baby's head into the hard bony circle of the pelvis – as several patients undergoing it have remarked) and finally the long exhausting trudge under the crushing weight of the wood across the neck and shoulders. Then, so closely paralleling the primal dereliction of human infants as to be a marvel of appropriateness, he bears (2) the loss of all friendly faces, the pinioned anguish which cannot in any way find relief for the mounting pain, the sense of social alienation and shame, the 'concatenation of confusion' as to who in this hell he is, the totally condemned, cast out by a righteous God because of the sin with which he is identified, or the perfectly righteous and obedient Son, and finally the rising sense of awful dereliction, which ended with the great cry from the cross, 'My God, my God, why hast Thou forsaken me?'

Here I can only point to the correspondence. If I ever again write a book it will be to fill out the marvel of this theology of correlation as it is actually experienced by those who are undergoing the reintegration of primal, peri-natal injuries and dreads.

The dereliction is in essence worse and more unnatural than the crushing. No blame can attach to the parents for most abnormal deliveries. It is not so, to the new-born, denied an early opportunity to experience the mother's tender nearness. The failure of any human being to answer the urgent appeal for a presence gives rise to a deep inner horror of a *deus absconditus*, a 'god' who is dead, perhaps killed. The reproach re-echoes in the mind and still reverberates as a pervasive heart-break. A basic question of theodicy is avoided only by the infant's attributing the badness of the unbearable situation to some inexplicable but indelible badness in its own very being. This is the usual outcome. It is unthinkable that 'the gods' are bad. Far better take the blame and leave their righteousness intact. Parents are too powerful to dispute their handling. But we Christians have a God who 'is so near to us' (Dt 4.7) he is both *deus crucifixus* and the God who absconds from himself, the *deus absconditus*, in the hidden mystery of Golgotha. This, says Luther, is the *deus theologicus*, and the principle of our knowledge of him crucified is shot through with paradox and contradiction.

The charismatic phenomenon: 'the inner healing of the memories'

This, then, is the first aspect of experience which relates to a *theologia crucis* about which some further theological reflection is desirable. The second derives (a) from the experience of 'the healing of the memories', as practised over many years by the American Anglicans, Agnes Sanford and Anne White, and their associates in Prayer Counselling and Victorious Ministry and (b) from the growing movement for 'the ministry of inner healing' as practised by many American Catholic charismatic prayer groups and written about by Michael Scanlon, Francis MacNutt, George Montague, the Linn Brothers, and others.

These then are the two main streams of confluent experience which demand some theological reflection. I have referred on the psychological side to the writings of Arthur Janov and his neurologist colleague Dr Michael Holden, but our own entry into 'primal therapy' was based on therapy conducted, largely with clergymen and ministers, from 1954 to the present day. I have been illuminated more by Søren Kierkegaard's and P. T. Forsyth's reflections on men and God rather than by psychiatric studies, though Otto Rank's *Trauma of Birth* was a landmark for peri-natal studies.

On the practical side I have been helped by discussions with leaders of 'renewal communities' who have studied and practised 'primal reintegration' work with me, and who now use this approach, together with a 'deliverance ministry' in their communities.

I have now sketched the two main sources of data about primal healing and God's reintegration. Human need expressed in a sharing group has opened up God's word. Response to him here has led many into a new freedom to love and be loved. It has brought 'freedom from undue constraint', 'spaciousness', 'feet set in a large room' (which the Hebrew *yasha* for 'salvation' denotes). I want to preface my attempts at theological reflection with a few general points.

A clinical theology is inductive

My task is to approach 'the work of Christ' from the limited aspect of an inductive, strictly 'clinical' theology. I am not, as I understand my task, required to give a full and rounded account of the whole body of soteriological doctrine as such. I am not here a teacher of theology, responsible to leave nothing of importance out, responsible to stress this or that aspect in direct proportion to the stress it receives in the scriptures, and argue deductively that what must follow is such and such.

Approaching the theological task inductively my concern must be (as Bruce Kaye's introduction to the third NEAC 77 preparatory volume states), to take up 'an issue in the present situation' . . . and then to analyse it in depth, to see what is at stake in it and how Christian truth may be related to it. We might call this, he writes, 'the inductive approach to doing theology'. In keeping close to individual or family situations of need, in a joint search for God's specific remedy in Christ for these persons, in this crisis, we believe, as Kaye and his co-authors do, that we are being 'more scriptural and not less'.

A clinical theology, depending on the sense in which you intend to use the word 'clinical', means *either* the theology of the pastoral care of a person in trouble, sorrow, weakness, confusion, affliction, anxiety, depression and the like *or* the theology that informs a 'clinical meeting' where actual cases and concrete problems are being presented, analysed and discussed with a view to 'treatment' or the 'conduct of the case'. These overlap. So, while my colleagues and I as clinical theologians have the duty of understanding thoroughly what we do, and advising where advice is appropriate, we do not declare the whole soteriological counsel of God on each occasion. The whole pharmacopoeia of the gospel medicine is open to us to use. Our task is to move with the other person to the place where it becomes clear to one of us, or it is shown by the Spirit, what particular word, or insight or meaning clinches the matter in hand and makes the next task clear. If we visit our doctor, deaf in one ear, and he cures us by syringing it, it is inappropriate to blame him because he did not prescribe an antibiotic, chiding him that he had missed an opportunity for exhibiting one of pharmacology's most potent agents. Some criticism is levelled at our kind of work because at times we 'do not go deep enough into sin and salvation'. Other critics say that we look too deeply into what lies behind an apparently surface symptom and bring to bear the whole weight of the *theologia crucis*. ('Weight' is a right word there if you remember Samuel Rutherford's simile 'The cross is such a burden as wings are to a bird or sails to a ship'.)

What we do stands or falls by its faithfulness to the juncture between the particular human need and a particular God-given resource at whatever level.

Medical science ensures survival of the birth-damaged

Until this century, those whose births were so traumatic that they wished to die, would probably do just that, at birth. Or if they survived, they could easily slip away into the oblivion of death from some infection or other in childhood. It is no longer possible to do that. Medicated survival prevents it. But it does not prevent the persistence of a profound difficulty in speaking well about God if that is what his universe primarily did to you. Baby battering, child abuse, and broken homes increase. They do not abate in our culture at this time.

Must not pastoral care reflect this *preponderance of a new type of sufferer*? Is it not possible to beam in the bright light which shines from the cross from the less familiar angle of the cross as a theodicy, the angle that primarily makes sense to sufferers?

The history of pastoral care shows that, through the centuries, there have been changes of emphasis. At times, guidance has been the main form of shepherding, at others, reconciling those who had fallen away in persecution, at other times, sustaining the bereaved and sufferers in time of war, at other times the speciality has been healing. Now it is a particular combination of guidance, healing and reconciling that seems to be called for, based on Christ's identification with innocent afflicted persons.

The point we in Clinical Theology wish to make in discussion with academic theologians is not a debating point within the flux of theological fashions. It is a vital issue for pastoral care in the last quarter of the twentieth century. We must take account of observable historical changes in the human scene into which the word of God has all along been speaking, but which seem to have escaped the notice of theologians.

Fifty years ago, few indeed were those who followed Freud in his insistence that the sufferings of infants were still vividly present in their memories, though concealed from consciousness by repression. Nowadays, few people of intelligence could be found to dispute the overwhelming evidence that this early material is profoundly influential in the later life of adults. In every human being therefore, a new 'dark continent' has opened up, ripe for missionary evangelism. This continent was simply not imagined or known about at the turn of the century. In one sense, Kierkegaard understood it well. Because of his understanding he had already begun to highlight those aspects of theology. But his influence on mainline Anglican and Catholic theology was almost nil until a hundred years after his death. If these 'dark continents' are allowed to remain unevangelised, we are warned that from these human jungles, dark forces will emerge, often in 'psychic epidemics', to invade and disrupt cultures based on that precarious epiphenomenon, consciousness.

The corollary is that, since the further back you go to find the sources of later trouble and conflict in babyhood and infancy (*infans*, literally not yet speaking), the more the responsibility for introducing the evil must fall, not on the very young themselves, but on the older, adult members of the species. Responsibility and culpability, to which the gospel as at present preached addresses itself, so that conviction of sin may take hold, are minimal in these relatively innocent, because helpless, sufferers.

If there are 'other benefits of his passion' relevant to 'the release of captives', the recovery of sight as insight, the untying of the tongues of those who are struck dumb in the face of shameful parental cruelty, the healing by tears of those who are too terrified to weep at the time when the terror struck, these resources must now be brought out of the treasure house of grace.

In the presence of my sin, high handed and culpable, I need to know that the cross of Christ is the ground on which my justification, God's gift of right relationship, depends. In the presence, however, of unmerited cruelties, catastrophic in their destructive impact on the growing person right at the beginning, which lie like a heavy black cloud across the sky from horizon to horizon from birth to death, for ever afterwards the constant source of intense mental pain, irremediable guilt and inescapable social badness, the cross speaks another message also, that of a theodicy. This theodicy reinstates the goodness of God, and is in this sense, his justification of himself, when the innocent afflicted, like Job, accuse him of bungling his creation, loading the world with cosmic evil before man arrived on the scene. This theodicy proclaims the Lamb slain from the foundation of the world. The remedy is more than co-eval with the ruin.

Can the baby feel at birth? Can it remember?

Some may object that whereas it can be demonstrated objectively that births can be traumatic and infants be neglected, isolated and battered in the earliest months, it surely cannot be possible for them to experience pain during their births, or if they do, surely they cannot remember it later on in life. So we step back a while before proceeding to the theology to look at the history of scientific work on the trauma of birth.

W. D. Winnicott

There is sufficient evidence for the relevance of peri-natal injuries as lying at the roots of personality disorders and neuroses to make it a reputable psychodynamic development. W. D. Winnicott, one of the most highly regarded British pediatricians and psychoanalysts, held the same view about birth and the relevance of birth trauma as I do. Psychiatrists who value his work in all other respects tend to overlook his papers on birth.

Otto Rank

Otto Rank, one of the original group of psychoanalysts, wrote about it fully in 1923. Freud wrote of Rank's book *Trauma of Birth* on 24 March 1924: 'It is the most important progress since the discovery of psychoanalysis.' Ernest Jones protested to Freud 'lest the whole of his life's work be dissolved by the importance attached to the trauma of birth'. As we know, Freud had twice collapsed in a dead faint, once when Jung spoke of his being displaced as father of the movement. Freud was bombarded with protests from Jones, Abraham and others of the core group. At first he saw only the strength of Rank's position. But by 4 May 1924 he had yielded to the entreaties of those who could not bear to see father displaced. He wrote to Abraham 'I am getting further and further away from the birth trauma. I believe it will "fall flat" if one doesn't criticise it too sharply, and then Rank, who I valued for his gifts and the great service he has rendered, will have learned a useful lesson.' In MRA terms, the lesson would appear to have been 'not what's right' but 'who's right' is what matters in the Freudian household.

Nandor Fodor

Following Rank, Nandor Fodor, a psychoanalyst of repute, wrote a book on the birth trauma and a second on 'Freud, Jung and Occultism' in which he speaks of the personal reasons why neither Freud or Jung could accept it. Numerous psychiatrists in the days when LSD was used in psycholytic therapy reported on the reliving of birth traumata and of its value. I myself have been working on it for twenty-three years, although, for the first three of these, I resisted my patients' conviction that this was an actual reliving of their births.

Arthur Janov

Since then a large number of primal therapists have arisen. The best known and most prolific of them is Arthur Janov. His latest book, *The Primal Man*, written in collaboration with Michael Horden, a neurophysiologist, gives extensive information about the reliving of birth trauma.

Stanislav Grof
This Czech psychiatrist began to work with LSD-25 in 1956, two years after I did myself. We both recorded relivings of birth and peri-natal events from the earliest days, and have experienced this often several times a day, over twenty years.

Primal therapy and the Christian doctrine of man

The finding, common to those who work in the charismatic 'healing of the memories' and to Christian peri-natal therapy as we practise it, is that birth can still be 'hell' and 'death'. In both it is discovered that some parents have been cruel, others have been ignorant. The biblical doctrine of the solidarity of the race and the family in sin is underlined. The sins of the fathers and the mothers do descend upon innocent children. This can affect them for life. Fathers who overcorrect, as St Paul said they should not, do profoundly discourage some of their children. All this is to say that some suffering in later life takes it origin, not in the culpable sin of the sufferer, but from his involvement, while in a state of total dependency, in the sin of others.

It is easy to underestimate the severity of this suffering. Moreover, most adults find it hard to recognize how closely the afflictions of later life which drive people to despair or suicide are faithful reproductions of crises first encountered in the earliest weeks of life.

Before birth, the foetus may be seriously damaged if the mother is dependent on alcohol drugs or nicotine. It is also damaged by the more subtle changes that transmit to the baby a mother's rejection of the pregnancy and of the life growing within her. These damaging experiences are now fairly readily accessible to consciousness.

The process of birth itself can be tough but tolerable, or, on the other hand, devastating in its destructiveness. Cataclysmic muscular convulsions turn a peaceful haven into a crushing hell. This 'no-exit' phase, before the cervix begins to open, can last for hours or days.

The next phase, of travel through the pelvis, is at best an

energetic struggle, at worst a brain-destroying, suffocating, twisting, tearing, crushing torture, in which the will to live may be extinguished and a longing to die take its place. The hazards of obstruction, impaction, prolonged delays due to uterine inertia, or sudden violent extrusion when induction puts the uterine muscle into spasm, the hazards of forceps delivery, abnormal presentations, asphyxia due to the cord being round the neck, breech births or emergency Caesarean sections, all these possibilities of profound discouragement and catastrophe may occur during this phase. The will to live has often turned into a profound desire to die. The arrival under brilliant lights and loud noise, to be gripped by hands which suspend you by the feet, slap you and cut the still pulsating cord, and then, omitting the whole agenda of tension-relieving touch of the mother, neither establishing bondedness nor reassuring the infant that both it and the mother have survived the perilous process, omitting all this they put the baby at some distance away to be cot nursed among others of its unhappy kind, also screaming their protest. Here he may suffer alone the dreadful, unfamiliar enormities of space, unbounded by the expected human hands and face. The newborn may be left alone long enough to be nudged to the edge of the abyss of non-being, trembling through the phase of separation anxiety, eventually to fall, in a moment of horror, over the edge into the nothingness which is the abandonment of hope, love, desire for life, and expectation of access to humanity. And then within a few months, the infant may experience intense hunger, severe cold and hypothermia, love starvation, and even baby battering and child abuse.

Traumatic peri-natal events increase

These are not theories, they are facts. All available statistics show that many of these factors are on the increase, even that due to the obnoxious obstetrical practice of induction for no other reason than to bring all births within working hours. It is also a fact that these experiences are powerfully determinative of the whole of a person's background of feeling and attitude to the universe. It is from these experiences that the basic knowledge of what it is like to live in 'God's world', and to depend upon God for love and mercy come. Those who are most faithful to their origins encounter the most severe problems of theodicy. The more they are faithful to the truth within them the more they will cry out as Job did, 'Why was I not taken from the womb to the tomb?' 'Why had there not been any lap to lie on?' 'I don't want life.' 'God come and be kind, cut it off.' 'My experience of your world is such that your only mercy is to take me out of it into oblivion.'

The word of God to the innocent afflicted

This, in principle and in brief is a situation into which the word of God must speak if God is to make himself understood by the innocent afflicted. Their memories, the more impressive for not being accurately remembered in full connection with their original context, rise up in indignant protest whenever Christian apologists propose the step of faith and trust, or talk about commitment or a conversion which involves the acceptance of something called 'being born again'.

The question I have to ask myself as a Christian therapist and counsellor is this. Where, in current acceptable evangelical or charismatic theology, do we find this theodicy? Does the glorious and gracious gospel of Christ's justifying grace to culpable sinners, who, by the Holy Spirit, have been brought under conviction of sin, meet the requirements of the innocent afflicted to be reconciled to God? Of course in one sense they are sinners and they know it. But that is not the problem of their suffering but of what they do with their health. It is not the problem of their bondage but of their misuse of freedom. If it is appropriate to subsume them and their sufferings under the heading of culpable sin, as Job's counsellors attempted to subsume his suffering under the heading of culpable sin, then the biblical character of Job and his stance is invalidated along with theirs. They cannot affirm, as Job does (27:5,6) 'I will never, never agree that you are right. Until I die I will vow my innocence. I am *not* a sinner – I repeat it again and again.' The authentic awareness of primal suffering always carries with it this Job-like protest of innocence, or, since infants are much more likely to take the total blame upon themselves, to chronic unconditional and insoluble guilt, which does not yield to the offer of forgiveness. This persistent guilt is nothing other than the transformation of resentment and accusation in the presence of fear. As soon as the fear is removed, the accusation can emerge as a problem which can only be faced by a faithful theodicy.

Among contemporary theologians of weight and biblical profundity who have addressed themselves to a 'theology for the innocent afflicted', Jürgen Moltmann, in his *The Crucified God*, does this most convincingly. True, he has in mind the innocent afflicted of Belsen and Auschwitz rather than those of the 'delivery rooms'. Moltmann writes (p. 175), 'If the question of theodicy can be understood as a question of the righteousness of God in the history of the suffering of the world, then all understanding and presentation of world history must be seen within the horizon of the question of theodicy. (This must include, in the microcosm, the innocent sufferers' personal history.) . . . Only in the question of righteousness in suffering the evil and misery of the world of one man does one . . . come up against . . . the answer of Jesus and his history, the scandal of which cannot be set aside.' The hermeneutic point for the understanding of Christian faith in the resurrection must therefore be sought in the question of righteousness in the history of the suffering of the world.

Moltmann clearly interprets *the death and resurrection of Christ as both a theodicy, and a justification. It is a theodicy because it enables innocent sufferers to experience God's presence with them in their suffering, and by that act to reverse its impact on them*, from Job-like accusations against the horrors of God's providence, to Paul-like praise at the divine 'paraklesis'. Under a like 'thlipsis' or intolerable pressure the Lamb of God, who is the Lord of Life, suffers alongside his creatures. This makes a joyful bearing possible (hypomone), a 'sticking it out under' the affliction in the power of the one who is alongside. It is upon Jesus that the greater weight lies. This is the glorious possibility open to the interpretation of the cross as theodicy. As justification it speaks also to culpable sinners of the unmerited mercy of God in imputing righteousness, that is, the gift of rightly-related sonship to them. The innocent afflicted do not feel themselves to be sinners while they are merely automata, dust, weeping stone, worms and lower forms of life. It is the theodicy that makes their suffering human and turns them, for the first time, into sinners. Only human beings can be sinners, worms and dust cannot be guilty of sin, and such they feel themselves to be.

Moltmann writes: 'The horizon of universal history makes clear the breadth of the question of righteousness in the form of the question of theodicy, whereas the existential makes clear the depth of this question of righteousness in the question of justification.' Somewhat obscure, except perhaps to those for whom it is usual theological language, but its drift is clear.

The first approach to a sense of justice

Charles Williams in a Symposium, *What the Cross means to me,* wrote, in 1943, in the midst of the war, about Christ discharging his debt to the Holy Innocents whom Herod slew, 'by himself perishing innocently'. He develops this theme with an almost terrifying boldness. But I cannot quarrel with these strong affirmations as appropriate responses of an inductive theology for a war situation in which Jews were exterminated and infants bombed.

'If, obscurely, he would not cease to preserve us in the full horror of existence, at least he shared it. He became as helpless as we under the will which is he. This is the first approach to a sense of justice in the whole situation. Whatever he chose, he chose fully, for himself as for us. This is, I think, unique in the theistic religions of the world. I do not remember any other in which the Creator so accepted his own terms – at least in the limited sense of existence upon this earth. It is true that his life was short. His pains (humanly speaking) comparatively brief. But at least, alone among the gods, he deigned to endure the justice he decreed.

'This then has seemed to me now for long perhaps the most flagrant significance of the cross; it does enable us to use the word "justice" without shame – which otherwise we could not. God therefore becomes tolerable as well as credible. Our justice condemned the innocent, but the innocent it condemned was one who was fundamentally responsible for the existence of all injustice – its existence in the mere, but necessary, sense of time, which his will created and prolonged.

'I say then that the idea of the Cross does, on the one hand, make the idea of justice in God credible; and on the other certifies to us that we are not fools in being conscious of the twisting of all goodness to ignominy. We may (if it may be put so) approach God with that at least cleared up. We are not being unjust to his creation in the distaste we feel for it, nor even in the regret we feel that he allows it to continue. There would be other things to be said were we now discussing the Incarnation as such, but these are the things to be said peculiarly about the Cross. This is what Almighty God, as well as we, found human life to be. We willed it so, perhaps, but then certainly he willed that we should will.

'He submitted in our stead to the full results of the Law which is he. We may believe he was generous if we know that he was just. By that central substitution, which was the thing added by the Cross to the Incarnation, he became everywhere the centre of, and everywhere he energized and reaffirmed, all our substitutions and exchanges. He took what remained, after the Fall, of the torn web of humanity in all times and places, *and not so much by a miracle of healing as by a growth within it made it whole.*

'We are relieved – may one say? – from the burden of being naturally optimistic. "The whole creation groaneth and travaileth together." If we are to rejoice always then it must be a joy consonant with that; we need not – infinite relief! – force ourselves to deny the mere burden of breathing. Life (experience suggests) is a good thing, and somehow unendurable; at least the Christian faith has denied neither side of the paradox. Life found itself unendurable.

'It may seem that little has been here said about our salvation through his sacrifice. That would not be quite true, for all that has been said concerns our salvation. Our salvation is precisely our reconciliation, to nature and to the Church – not that they are so separate; our reconciliation both to him and to our present state, both at once and both in one. We are, by that august sacrifice, compelled to concede to him the propriety of our creation.

' "O fools and slow of heart, *ought* not Christ to have suffered these things, and entered into his glory?" Yes; he ought. He said so: "The Son of Man *must* . . ." But then also he did.

'Not the least gift of the gospel is that our experiences of good need not be separated from our experiences of evil, need not and must not be.'

Answering depths

Should we not expect to know more about the relevance of the cross of Christ as we get to know more about man, depth calling to depth, a new depth theology correlating with a new depth psychology. The Holy Spirit's work is to draw out truths about Christ we have not recognized. The apostle who peered into the mystery and spoke of what he saw of 'the unsearchable riches of Christ' would be, I think, astonished to learn that nearly 2,000 years after his day, Christians were afraid of discovering treasures of wisdom and foreknowledge in the cross for lack of clear precedent in his own writings.

In John 16:12 Jesus said: 'I have yet many things to say to you, but you cannot bear them now. When the Spirit of truth comes he will guide you into all truth. He will glorify me, for he will take what is mine and declare it unto you.'

'He will take what is mine.' The Holy Spirit did take and still does take the name of Jesus and declare it to us as the Saviour of sinners. The Holy Spirit took the Old Testament scriptures that 'are mine', that apply in depth and detail to Jesus, and declared them. Isaiah 53 particularly 'belongs' to Jesus Christ. He himself, speaking in the Spirit, used these verses of himself in the synagogue at Nazareth. Matthew's Gospel (8:16–17) declares the work of Christ to be a fulfilment of Isaiah 53. 'And he (Jesus) cast out the spirits with his word, and healed all that were sick: that it might be fulfilled which was spoken by Isaiah the Prophet, saying, "Himself took our infirmities and bore our sicknesses".'

'Infirmities' and 'sicknesses' are not sins. Admittedly, the Hebrew thought of sicknesses as consequent upon sins. But we must insist that Job breaks this sequence, and demands that infirmities and sicknesses be considered apart from sin. We would expect that, in taking the things of Christ and declaring them to us, the Holy Spirit would have as much to say about Christ's sickness-bearing as about his sin-bearing. 'He is despised and rejected by men, a man of pain and acquainted with sickness . . . Despised, we did not esteem him,

Surely he has borne our sicknesses,
He has carried our pains (sorrows)
And we – have esteemed him plagued,
Smitten by God, and afflicted . . . By his bruisedness, his stripes, there is healing to us.
Jehovah delighted to bruise him.
He had made him sick.'

Where this aspect of Christ's mediatorial work is allowed to take place, in establishing justice of a new and costly kind by his presence alongside the sufferer, indeed penetrating every tortured cell of the sufferer with the once and for all time agonized cells of his own divine–human body, then *the work of theodicy is over. Then the more familiar work of justifying grace takes over.* A sufferer, whose suffering had made him inhuman, alienated from the community of men, is drawn back by love into the group and discovers himself to be a human being. *All along he has also been a sinner.* He is now free to turn and acknowledge this sinfulness, indeed he is liberated in order to turn from confrontation of the other to self-confrontation.

Liberation and salvation

How is liberation by reliving this trauma related to salvation in Christ? It depends what we mean by salvation. In many people, this trauma is repressed and does not emerge into consciousness again until late adolescence, early adult life or even middle life. It emerges as a component in some dark night of the sense or of the spirit. It may emerge at a time of illness as a factor in breakdown. It may emerge at a time of abundant health, or indeed of the reception of baptism in the Holy Spirit, as the result of abundant health that sweeps the cellars of the deep self clean. In this sense, *a person may respond to the offer of the grace of Christ and enter salvation as a forgiven sinner while all unconscious of this depth dimension of innocent suffering.*

In those who have always been afflicted from their youth up this element of the saving work of Christ as theodicy will probably need to come in earlier. Earlier or later, I would consider it to be *part of the saving work of Christ*, and therefore and aspect of salvation. We do not have difficulty in experiencing both justification and sanctification as parts of salvation. It is perhaps in the area of sanctification that this work of Christ for innocent sufferers comes most into play. Sanctification means that the work of grace goes deep into the character structure, transforming and changing it. This is primarily to be received by faith as the life of Christ imparted to the human spirit. However, it is a common experience that *this time of sanctifying is one of a profound shaking of the foundations*. Human personality has its own rigid defences which do not readily give way.

The work of Michael Scanlon reported in his book *Inner Healing* indicates that when a person comes time and again with the same besetting sin, his practice is not simply to hear the confession of the same sin over and over again. He now calls upon the Holy Spirit to point up the area in the depth of the memory that is the source of this besetting sin. There is then a healing of the memories. Sometimes this is painless, sometimes it is exceedingly painful. In the one case the ego is not strong enough to bear the pain and Christ bears it all. In the second case, where the ego is strong enough and the context favourable, the Spirit seems quite clearly to lead people into an actual reliving of the pain that was caused, in the power of the Saviour who shares it. It is my experience and the experience of many others, particularly of those who have worked both in the Victorious Ministry movement and in Clinical Theology, that the second, in which the pain is fully brought to consciousness and contextualized, is the deeper, final and more finished work. But both give glory to God in Christ, the one simply, as in the Galilean ministry, the other paradoxically as in the ministry of Christ from Tabor to Golgotha.

Healing and salvation

There seems to be an anxiety here lest healing should be equated with the work of salvation. As an association of pastoral counsellors, dealing with those who are emotionally sick, our work is somewhat like that of the mission hospital. Our work is to practise *the works of love* rather than to preach *the word of life*. In fact we do both, and indeed I find myself speaking the word of life much more frequently than I did as a medical missionary commissioned to do the works of love.

And we recognize how closely these are put together in the Gospels and the Acts, much closer than they are in the church life which theologians express and write about without protest. We remember that Peter could summarize the work of Christ in the Acts in these words: 'How God appointed Jesus of Nazareth with the Holy Spirit and with power: how he went about doing good and healing all that were oppressed by the Devil, for God was with him.' Somehow he seems to have forgotten the preaching. And yet surely this was all about salvation.

There has been some suspicion that we have equated the reliving of birth as part of this healing of the memories with the experience of the new birth into the family of God by faith in Christ. It is of course not the case and would be ridiculous were it so. There is, however, a very close relationship between the ways in which people encounter difficulty or ease when they come to considering whether they can accept the new birth by faith into Christ or not, since all the fears, doubts and commitment anxieties that beset them at their physical birth tend to crowd round them at the proposal of a second birth. Indeed to force oneself towards the experience of being born again into the family of God through faith in Christ, can evoke such disturbances as schizophrenia, if the actual human birth was accompanied by pain of a mind-splitting character, if indeed, as Stanislau Grof has shown the birth was itself the first experience of that schizophrenia. Just as Christ healed people physically and left them to decide later what they would do with him by way of faith and discipleship, so, if we can clear the battlefield of the first birth of its living debris, we do at least make it possible for a person to consider the second birth without the degree of panic and confusion, resistance and dread, that accompanied his first birth.

The final theological question is 'Does healing require this kind of exposure and technique?' Obviously not. The charismatic movement is very well familiar with the healing of the memories as practised by Agnes Sanford and her followers, Anne White and hers, and more recently by the Catholic charismatic groups in the United States. This healing does go back to the birth, on frequent occasions people are led back to all kinds of emotional injuries, including, in the case of a distinguished Dutch charismatic woman, to leading people back to rejections that happened in the earliest days and weeks of the pregnancy when the mother was trying to abort the child. It was not by primal therapy but by healing within the prayer group that this discovery was made and a healing took place.

The extent to which the healing of the memories in prayer groups does or does not give people a full opportunity to relive the original pain that caused the problem, and fully to enter into the original context of life as it was then, seems to vary. For Francis MacNutt, the healing ministry is a glorious thing like the Galilean ministry of Jesus, with very little that seems to speak of his cross and the bearing of pain. This is the ministry entrusted to him. The ministry entrusted to us glorifies Christ in making available to the sufferer the power of the Holy Spirit who sustains Christ in the crushing terrors of Gethsemane and the agonizing loneliness of Golgotha, enabling him to become reconciled to what had hitherto been totally unbearable. Christ is glorified either way, in joy in the one, in joyful suffering in the other. Those who are moving deep into the road of spiritual maturity seem to require, even when they have been through the first kind, a later entry into the second. Those who had been taught when healed to be impatient of the suffering involved, tend to be impatient towards the suffering of others. They tend to a triumphalism which cannot stay with the afflicted. It is particularly important, therefore, for those who are called to be pastoral counsellors that they should have Christ's strength to go what might be called the hard way. It is none the less a very joyful way.

The above article was published in *Theological Renewal* no. 6, which was published with *Renewal* no. 69 (June/July 1977).

Appendix B

A Bibliography of Frank Lake's Writings

This bibliography details all those writings by Frank Lake read by me while preparing my study of Frank Lake and the Clinical Theology Association. It does not list his articles/notes in the association's *Newsletter*, all of which may obtained from St Mary's House, Church Westcote, Oxford OX7 6SF.

BOOKS (ARRANGED ALPHABETICALLY)

1 *Clinical Theology* (Darton, Longman and Todd 1966).

2 *Clinical Theology* (Darton, Longman and Todd 1986). An abridged version edited by the Revd Martin H. Yeomans.

3 *Studies in Constricted Confusion* (published by CTA and still in print).

4 *Tight Corners in Pastoral Counselling* (Darton, Longman and Todd 1981).

5 *Tight Corners in Pastoral Counselling* (Darton, Longman and Todd 1987). A reprint of number 4 above.

6 *With Respect: A Doctor's Response to a Healing Pope* (Darton, Longman and Todd 1982).

BOOK(S) IN MANUSCRIPT

7 *Mutual Caring* (unpublished).

SECONDARY WRITINGS IN THE LINGDALE ARCHIVE

These items are arranged numerically, following the numerical system in the archive itself.

8 'The Role of the Counsellor': Lingdale Archive 003. An incomplete version of a talk delivered at University College, Cardiff (1970).

9 'LSD-25, Birth Trauma and Claustrophobia': Lingdale Archive 004. A paper prepared for the Second International Congress of Social Psychiatry (4–8 August 1969).

10 An untitled talk describing his (Frank Lake's) work: Lingdale Archive 006 (1964).

11 'The Bearing of Our Knowledge of the Unconscious on the Theology of Evangelism and Pastoral Care': Lingdale Archive 009 (pre-1970).
12 'First Aid in Counselling', 17: 'The Threatened Nervous Breakdown: Part 1. Requiring Referral Aid, and The Pastoral Care of Impending Reactive Depressive Breakdowns'. Published in *The Expository Times* (June 1967). Now kept as Lingdale Archive 010.
13 'First Aid in Counselling', 17: 'The Threatened Nervous Breakdown: Part 2. Anxiety Threatens rather than Depression'. Published in *The Expository Times* (July 1967). Now Lingdale Archive 011.
14 'First Aid in Counselling', 19: 'The Homosexual Man'. Published in *The Expository Times* (September 1967). Now preserved as Lingdale Archive 012.
15 'Theology and Personality'. Published in *Epworth Review* (January 1981). Now Lingdale Archive 017, 018 and 019.
16 'Theological Issues in Mental Health in India'. Published in *Religion and Society* (1978). Now Lingdale Archive 021.
17 'Arthur Janov and Primal Therapy'. Unpublished. Now Lingdale Archive 027.
18 'The Violence of Love'. Published in *The British Weekly* (9 October 1969). Preserved as Lingdale Archive 030.
19 'The Health of the Clergy'. Published in the *Epworth Review* (1974). Now Lingdale Archive 033, which is a reworked version of Lingdale Archive 023.
20 'Too Much in Touch'. Possibly published in the *Church of England Newspaper* (1973). Now Lingdale Archive 034.
21 'Christ the Therapist'. Sermon originally preached at Great St Mary's Church, Cambridge (1963). Possibly published in the *Burswood Herald* (1973–4). Incomplete. Now Lingdale Archive 035.
22 'Priest or Psychiatrist?'. BBC broadcast, 18 July (28 June 1964). Lingdale Archive 037.
23 'Images of God'. BBC broadcast (18 July 1967). Now Lingdale Archive 039.
24 'The Neurological Basis of Primal Integration Theory'. Date not known. Now Lingdale Archive 041.
25 'The Significance of Perinatal Experience'. Published in *Self and Society* (1978). Now Lingdale Archive 042.
26 'Clinical Pastoral Counselling'. Undated. Lingdale Archive 045.
27 'Six Factors in the Counselling Situation'. No date. Now Lingdale Archive 045. See also Lingdale Archive 046 and 047.
28 'Treating Psychomatic Disorders Related to Birth Trauma'. Published in *The Journal of Psychomatic Research*, pp. 227–38 (1978). Preserved as Lingdale Archive 049.

29 'St Luke's Tide Sermon', delivered at the parish church, Hoddesdon, Herts. Date not known. Lingdale Archive 050.
30 'Sermon: Personality, Sexuality and Morals', delivered at St John's College, Cambridge (2 November 1969). Based on John 3:2, it is now Lingdale Archive 051.
31 'LSD: towards a solution of these problems'. Date not known. Lingdale Archive 052.
32 'The New Spirituality and Society'. Date unknown. Now Lingdale Archive 053.
33 'The Significance of Pre-natal, Birth and Intrauterine Development Events in Individuals, Family and Social Life'. Date uncertain. Lingdale Archive 057.
34 'The Concept of Health and Healing as Wholeness, illustrated from the Dynamics of Depressive Illness'. Date not known. Now Lingdale Archive 059.
35 'THEOLOGY: A Cognitive Exercise in System-Building, or the Result of Reflection on the Saving Acts of God in Christ'. Date not known. Now Lingdale Archive 060.
36 'The Sexual Aspects of Personality'. An address given at Great St Mary's Church, Cambridge (24 February 1965). Lingdale Archive 061.
37 'Counselling Others'. Date uncertain. Now Lingdale Archive 062.
38 'Frank Lake replies: Same Sex Loving, part 1'. Published in *Renewal 62* (April/May 1976). Now Lingdale Archive 067.
39 'Frank Lake replies: Same Sex Loving, part 2'. Published in *Renewal 63* (June/July 1976). Lingdale Archive 109.
40 'Frank Lake replies: I Don't Want To Feel Angry But I Do'. Published in *Renewal 59* (October/November 1975). Now Lingdale Archive 069.
41 'Frank Lake Replies: Praise God For Everything?'. Published in *Renewal 58* (August/September 1975). Lingdale Archive 071.
42 'Frank Lake Replies: Power to Throw Away'. Published in *Renewal 60* (December 1975/January 1976). Now Lingdale Archive 073.
43 'Frank Lake Replies: I Just Feel Worthless'. Published in *Renewal 67* (February/March 1977) and *Renewal 68* (April/May 1977). Lingdale Archive 074.
44 'Frank Lake Replies: Parasitic Parents'. Published in *Renewal 64* (August/September 1976). Lingdale Archive 075.
45 'Frank Lake Replies: The Realities of Living with People'. Published in *Renewal 57* (June/July 1975).
46 'Frank Lake Replies: More about Anger: Is It or Isn't It Sin?'.

Published in *Renewal 61* (February/March 1976). Lingdale Archive 110.
47 'Frank Lake Replies: Healing the Memories'. Published in *Renewal 65* (October/November 1976). Now Lingdale Archive 111.
48 'As I See It': No. 1: 'Mothers and Babies: The Spring of Trust'. Talk for ATV Midlands (date uncertain). Lingdale Archive 085.

OTHER SECONDARY WRITINGS
49 *Contact (1980:3)*: 'The Theology of Pastoral Counselling'.
50 *Contact (1978:1)*: 'The New Therapies – Introduction, Transactional Analysis, Primal Integration'.
51 *Lingdale Paper 1*: 'The Dynamic Cycle – Introduction to the Model'.
52 *Lingdale Paper 6*: 'Personal Identity – Its Origins'.
53 *Lingdale Paper 7*: 'Personal Identity – Its Development'.
54 *British Medical Association News Review*, vol. 7, no. 4: 'Foetal Memory: Fact or Fiction?'. (April 1981).
55 *Theological Renewal*, no. 6: 'The Work of Christ in the Healing of Primal Pain'. This article was published with *Renewal 69* (June/July 1977).

Appendix C

Select Bibliography

Surprisingly few people have taken up either Frank Lake or his work in print. During his lifetime he was particularly disappointed with the reluctance of the medical establishment to take his work seriously by way of rigorous attention and critical assessment. With hindsight, it is clear that the fault was partly his: he did not write up his work, with very few exceptions, for the scientific or medical journals. The following works, however, are useful:

M. G. Barker, 'Models of Pastoral Care', an article in M. A. Jeeves (ed.), *Behavioural Sciences* (Leicester 1984).
M. G. Barker, 'Clinical Theology', an article in *New Dictionary of Theology*, edited by Sinclair Ferguson and David F. Wright (IVP 1988).
A. V. Campbell (ed.), *Dictionary of Pastoral Care* (SCM Press 1986).
H. Faber, *Psychology of Religion* (SCM Press 1976). It only mentions Frank Lake in passing.
Leslie Feher, *The Psychology of Birth: Roots of Human Personality* (Continuum, New York 1981).
M. Hare-Duke, 'Science of God and Science of Man', in *New Blackfriars* (1969).
R. F. Hurding, *Roots and Shoots: A Guide to Counselling and Psychotherapy* (London 1986).
Hugh Melinsky, *Religion and Medicine* (SCM Press 1970). He is critical of certain aspects of CTA's work, but is fair and balanced. In reality, this work is little more than an extended review of *Clinical Theology* (1966). Published as it was in 1970, it makes no reference to the later developments in Frank Lake's thinking.

R. Ridgeway, *The Unborn Child: How to recognize and overcome pre-natal trauma*. He quotes Frank Lake extensively, having met him at the primal integration workshops. This work is a valuable summary of the work and evidence to date; and he shows Frank Lake's work as being in line or parallel with other workers in the field.

In addition to the above, and in support of what Frank Lake was doing, it is possible to cite the following:

David B. Chamberlain, 'The Cognitive Newborn: A Scientific Update', an article in the *British Journal of Psychotherapy*, vol. 4, no. 1 (Autumn 1987). This extensive paper, by an American psychotherapist who chaired the 1985 International Congress of the Pre- and Peri-natal Psychology Association of North America, contains many, many relevant research papers on the subject. Subsequent issues of this journal will show how the British psychotherapy establishment responds to all this.

Arthur Janov, Imprints. *The Lifelong Effects of the Birth Experience* (Coward-McCann 1983). This paperback gives evidence of clients reliving birth and pre-birth trauma similar to those in Frank Lake's workshops.

Index

Atkinson, David 173–4
Atkinson, Derek 90–1

Background to Clinical Theology 1–9
Background to the Clinical Theology Association 1–9
Bashford, Tony 11
Bick, David 88–9, 189–91, 205
Bloomfield, Irene 175
Bowles, Canon 169–71
Brunner, Emil 123

Campbell, Alastair 67–70, 205
Church Missionary Society 41, 43, 49
Clinical Theology 1–11, 106–8, 164–75
Clinical Theology Association 10–34, 164–75, 187–98, 199–203, 207–13
Coggan, Donald 10
Cotter, James 90

Darby, Richard 76–7, 189, 191–3
Dynamic cycle 121–38

Eger, Miss 41
Eliason, Lee 165
Evangelicalism and primal integration therapy 176–86

Gravelle, John 40

Halliday, Evelyn 89–90
Hare-Duke, Michael 14–16, 18–19, 79–82, 165, 189
Hawker, Brian 194
Healing of the memories and charismatic renewal 145–54
Hobbs, Basil 192
Huxley, Francis 19–20

Jacobs, Michael 86–7
James, Eric 5

Kasteele, Peter van de 107–8, 135–6, 194, 198
Keeley, Mrs Patrick 94
Kierkegaard, Søren 112, 225

Lake, Brian (brother), 23–4, 36, 95–100, 195
Lake, David (son), 49–51, 75–6
Lake, Frank, images of 8–9, 161–4
  life 32–4, 35–78, 187
  Clinical Theology 39, 58–63, 104, 109–60
  Tight Corners in Pastoral Counselling 39–40, 65, 67, 73, 138–54
  With Respect 71, 73, 104, 154–60
  Mutual Caring (unpublished) 73
Lake, John (father) 35–41
Lake, Marguerite (daughter) 53–6
Lake, Mary (mother) 35–41
Lake, Monica (daughter) 51–3, 74–5
Lake, Ralph (brother) 35, 42
Lake, Sylvia (wife) 36–41, 44–9, 57–8
Lambourne, Bob 60–61
Lawson, Ronald 19
Lysergic acid (LSD-25) 125–32

MacNutt, Francis 147–50
Marteau, Louis 85–6
Maslen, Mary 87–8
Maternal–foetal distress syndrome 138–54
Melinsky, Hugh 171, 206
Montefiore, Hugh 1–2
Moss, Roger C. 82–4, 138, 203

Object relations theory 124–5

Primal integration therapy 175–86, 203–4

Reeve, Dick 95
Roberts, John 1, 6
Robinson, John 5

Sanford, Agnes 146, 149
Seminar experience 28–32
Smail, Tom 84–5, 178
Swaby, J. E. 91–2

Tutorials and tutors 24–7

Urquhart, Colin 150

Valentine, James 49

Warren, Max 49
Weston, Judith 92–3
Wilkinson, Alan 5–6
Wimber, John 150